Women and Microcredit in Rural Bangladesh

Women and Microcredit in Rural Bangladesh

Anthropological Study of the Rhetoric and Realities of Grameen Bank Lending

Aminur Rahman, Ph.D.

Westview Press
A Member of the Perseus Books Group

Copyright © 1999 by Westview Press, A Member of the Perseus Books Group

First published in 1999 in the United States of America by Westview Press, 5500 Central Avenue, Boulder, Colorado 80301–2877, and in the United Kingdom by Westview Press, 12 Hid's Copse Road, Cumnor Hill, Oxford OX2 9JJ

Published in paperback 2001.

Find us on the World Wide Web at www.westviewpress.com

Cataloging-in-Publication Data on file with the Library of Congress.
ISBN 0-8133-3930-8 (pbk)

The paper used in this publication meets the requirements of the American National Standard for Permanence of Paper for Printed Library Materials Z39.48–1984.

PERSEUS
POD
ON DEMAND   10   9   8   7   6   5   4

Contents

Figures

Preface

Microcredit—small amounts of collateral-free institutional loans extended to jointly liable group members for self-employment—was first introduced by the Grameen Bank of Bangladesh in the mid–1970s. The programmatic success of the bank—recruitment of clients, investment of loans, recovery rates on invested loans, and profit margin—has internationalized microcredit. There is a growing sense that micro-lending projects for women have the potential to achieve the goal of equitable (women's entitlement to resources) and sustainable (independent stability and continuity) development. My study, however, which is based on thirteen months of ethnographic field research on Grameen lending to women in a rural community of Bangladesh, challenges the conventional understanding of small-scale lending and the orthodox view of its success.

This study consists of an anthropological analysis of women borrowers' involvement with the credit program and implications of the lending structure for women borrowers, their household members, and bank workers. In theoretical terms women's involvement with microcredit has been examined in the context of the normative entitlements of patriarchy. The concepts of public and hidden transcripts (Scott 1990) and practice theory (Bourdieu 1977) are used to present the discrepancies between the ideology and practices of the lending institution and the informants. Cultural hegemony (Gramsci 1971) helps to analyze the reproduction of an ideology of dominance and violence toward women in society, both unintended and organizational.

The research findings suggest that women become the primary target of the microcredit program because of their sociocultural vulnerability, that is, the requirements of regular attendance by borrowers in weekly meetings at the loan center and the rigid repayment schedule of loans. The program extends credit to women, but in the household women often pass on their loans to men, men take control over women's loans, or loans are used to meet the emergency consumption needs of the household. In this system, women borrowers often lose control over their loans but bear the consequences of the debt burden in their households and loan centers.

The research indicates a strong link between the programmatic success of the bank and current practices of credit extension to women. Debt cycling among borrowers is a consequence, that is, the need to pay off previous loans with new ones. Bank workers are expected to increase the disbursement of loans among their clients and press for high recovery rates to earn the profit necessary for institutional economic viability. The bank workers and borrowing peer loan group members in centers press on clients for timely repayment rather than working to raise collective consciousness and borrower empowerment as envisaged in the bank's public transcript. Institutional debt burdens on individual households increases tension and anxiety among household members, which in turn produces new forms of social and institutional dominance over many women borrowers of the project.

Acknowledgments

In preparing this work, I have incurred debts to a number of persons and institutions in Canada and abroad. First, my deepest gratitude is extended to my advisor, Professor Raymond Wiest, without whom I could never have completed this work. He has stimulated my interest in the Grameen Bank and helped and guided me every step of the way. His unhesitating support of my work; his careful reading of the manuscript; his comments, advice, and critique have enabled me to clarify my data, sharpen my ideas, and develop the organization of this book. I am indebted to Professor Ellen Judd for opening my eyes to contemporary theories that have become central for analyzing my field data. Her timely comments on some key issues of the research have also helped me to address and substantiate those issues. I owe thanks also to Dr. Emdad Haque, whose expertise on Bangladesh has been an asset to my research. His constructive suggestions about my work have enabled me to enrich my own understanding of rural Bangladesh society.

In Bangladesh, Professor Nurul Alam of the Anthropology Department at Jahangirnagar University acted as a local supervisor. Dr. Shanpan Adnan of the Shamabash Research and Advisory Council in Dhaka gave me the requisite feedback on my field research and encouraged me to challenge the orthodox views of the success of microcredit programs for women. I extend my sincere thanks to them. I would like to express my appreciation and thanks to Professor John Loxley in the Economics Department, University of Manitoba; Dr. Nancy Horn of Opportunity International in Chicago; Dr. Florence McCarthy at Columbia University; Professor Joan Mencher at Lehman College, CUNY, New York; Dr. Jonathan Morduch in the Economics Department at Harvard University; Dr. Jim Freedman in the Anthropology Department at Western Ontario University; Dr. Eva Friedlander in New York; and Dr. Anne Marie Goetz and Dr. Martin Greeley in IDS at Sussex University for their moral support and constructive criticism.

I owe a very special thanks to my colleague and good friend Deborah Woodman for reading, commenting on, and editing most of my early drafts; to Dr. Ansari Khan for helping me organize my field data and generate figures; to Michael Bridgeford-Read for computerizing the study village map; and to Mr. Maksudul Alam for providing the contact at the Grameen Bank in Bangladesh. I give thanks to Dr. John Matthiasson and Dr. David Stymeist for their support and encouragement, and to Lynne Dalman and Roxie Wide for their administrative assistance.

My most profound debt of gratitude is to my informants in the village and in the study branch of the Grameen Bank for accepting me as their "brother," providing me with required information, and sharing their experiences. I am grateful to Mr. Dipal Barua (General Manager, Administration, at the Grameen Bank Head Office in Dhaka) for his sincere cooperation. Despite his very busy schedule during office hours, Mr. Barua always gave his time to meet me whenever I visited the Grameen Bank Head Office in Dhaka, Bangladesh.

I would like to acknowledge various institutions for recognizing the potential of this research and for fellowships and grants. I conducted my field research with a doctoral research fellowship from the Bangladesh Studies Program of the Joint Committee on South Asia of the Social Science Research Council (SSRC), New York, and the American Council of Learned Societies; with the 1994 Richard F. Salisbury Award; and with a special grant from the Faculty of Graduate Studies at the University of Manitoba. The Harry Frank Guggenheim Foundation, New York (1996), supported the writing of my research findings. The Young Canadian Researchers Award (YCRA), International Development Research Center (IDRC), Ottawa, Canada, supported the follow-up research and my five-week visit to the Institute of Development Studies (IDS), Sussex University, as a Visiting Research Scholar for archival research in 1997. I acknowledge the Bangladesh Institute of Development Studies (BIDS) for giving me institutional affiliation during my fieldwork in Bangladesh. Special thanks goes to Ms. Gisele Morin-Labatut of IDRC, Ottawa, for providing a Corporate Research Grant during a period of dire need. Although all of the above individuals and institutions have helped and assisted in this study, they bear no responsibility for the interpretation presented or for any errors or inadequacies that remain.

My family has always been a source of strength and encouragement, often drawn from-to-face difficulties in life. I am grateful to my parents, especially to my father, who did everything to educate me. Nazma, my wife, and Prinon, my daughter, shared my life in the field. Prinon and my one-and-a-half-year-old son, Saad, have blessed our lives with love; they have endured long hours of loneliness during my write-up phase, but have always given me their smiles and hopes, even in times of duress.

I dedicate this book to Dilip Ghose, my first contact in the study village. He, a low-caste Hindu, despite our religious, social, and educational differences, has become a "ritual brother" (*dada*). During my fieldwork period, *dada* did everything he could to make my research successful.

1

Introduction

Microcredit—the extension of small amounts of collateral-free institutional loans to jointly liable poor group members for their self-employment and income generation—is a Grameen Bank innovation. Since 1976, the Grameen Bank has pioneered a credit delivery system in rural Bangladesh, bringing banking to poor villagers with a focus primarily on women. This bank is now the largest microlending institution in Bangladesh. It operates in fifty-six of the sixty-four districts in Bangladesh, with 1,100 rural branches covering 37,678 villages, more than half of all the villages in the country (see Figure 1.1). The cumulative investment of the Grameen Bank in rural Bangladesh is more than one billion U.S. dollars, disbursed among 2.3 million members, 95 percent of whom are women (Grameen Bank 1998).

In the 1980s the programmatic success[1] of the microcredit scheme of Grameen Bank among poor women in rural Bangladesh became a demonstration of a successful equitable (with women as equal partners) and sustainable (in regard to financial viability for service-providing institutions) development initiative. The programmatic success and the endorsement of this success by a large number of impact and academic studies (R. I. Rahman 1986; Hossain 1988; Shehabuddin 1992; Fuglesang and Chandler 1993; Mizan 1994) have contributed to spreading the microcredit concept worldwide. In recent years the Grameen Bank's approach of lending to poor women has attracted international interest, making microcredit "a new paradigm for thinking about economic development" (Morduch 1997:1). Now there is almost a global consensus that microlending to the poor is the key element for the twenty-first century's economic and social development (Microcredit Summit 1998a). Currently, most bilateral and multilateral development agencies incorporate microcredit in their development projects and are keen to push other multisectoral social development–oriented nongovernmental organizations (NGOs) and private voluntary organizations (PVOs) into the function of credit delivery (Wood and Sharif 1997).

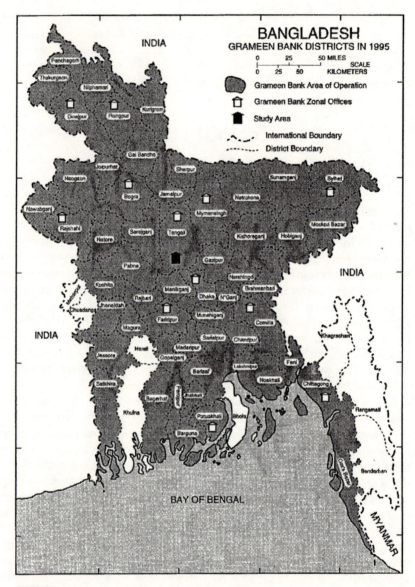

FIGURE 1.1   Grameen Bank Districts in 1995

Statement of the Problem

In this work, I examine the Grameen Bank lending structure of small loans among poor women in a rural community in Bangladesh and illustrate the implications of this lending for women borrowers, bank workers, and societal members. The study is a processual analysis of the credit program that enables a qualitative understanding of the impact of micro-credit on poor people, with special attention to the involvement of rural women in the process. The main questions of this study are why are only women now recruited for the program? What are the social and economic impacts of such recruitment? How does the lending structure of the bank maintain the high investment and recovery rates in the study village, and what are the consequences of the investment and loan recovery on borrowers of the program and societal members in the village? The primary focus of the study is on women borrowers of the Grameen Bank, their interaction with peer group members and bank workers at the loan center and with the members of their household, the use of loans in the household economy, and the specific role of bank workers.

Despite the success of the Grameen Bank in delivering loans to poor women and bringing socioeconomic changes to many of these women's households, my findings suggest that there are still many borrowers who become vulnerable and trapped by the system; they are unable to succeed. At the level of grassroots credit operation, bank workers encounter institutional pressure to increase loan investment and maintain high recovery rates on their invested loans. The bank workers and peer group borrowers inflict an intense pressure on borrowers for timely repayment, rather than working to raise collective responsibility and borrower empowerment as originally envisaged by the bank (Yunus 1994a:18). Many borrowers maintain their regular repayment schedules through a process of loan recycling (paying off previous loans by acquiring new ones) that considerably increases the borrowers' debt liability. The burden of debt on individual households in turn increases anxiety and tension among household members and produces new forms of social and institutional dominance over many women clients in the program. The entrapment of the borrowers in debts and the long working hours for bank workers to keep up with their installment collection in loan centers and paperwork in the bank lead informants in this study to question the vision of the lending institution. Consequently, the informants (borrowers and bank workers) generate their own critical assessment—treated as a "hidden transcript" (Scott 1990) in the analysis—about the impact of the project. The incorporation of the hidden transcripts of informants in the analysis is central to this study.

The Grameen Bank

The word *grameen* in Bengali literally means "rural" or "village." The Grameen Bank is a bank established with the objective of extending credit to poor people in rural Bangladesh who have no physical collateral. The story of the Grameen Bank is almost a legend. The founder, Muhammad Yunus, is a former economics professor who returned from the United States to Bangladesh in 1972 with his doctorate from Vanderbilt University. He joined Chittagong University, which is located in a rural area among many villages. During his tenure at the university, Yunus was confronted by the poverty that overwhelms many poor people in rural Bangladesh, who live in a world of debt alongside the rich people; the poor are kept in an omnipresent poverty circle (Yunus 1997). Through his direct encounter with rural people, Yunus was inspired to consider microcredit as a means of alleviating rural poverty.

Before institutional credit for poor people was introduced, there were primarily two credit sources available in rural Bangladesh—commercial banks and moneylenders. The commercial banks do not give loans to the poor because the poor are unable to provide collateral, whereas moneylenders will lend money but with very high interest rates.[2] Both of these arrangements are incompatible with the return in small business. Yunus realized the implications of microcredit for the first time in 1976 through his interaction with a poor woman in the village of Jobra who made bamboo stools for a living. The woman could not afford to buy bamboo herself and borrowed money from a trader on the condition that she must sell her product to the trader at a price he decided. Because the woman could not sell her finished product to anybody else, the trader took advantage of the situation and paid a price that barely covered the cost of the raw material. The socioeconomic circumstances of this woman led Yunus to think that if the woman had a small amount of working capital then she could work for herself, retaining the surplus now appropriated by others. All she needed was the "small credit" necessary for working capital.

In 1976, Yunus first experimented with the microcredit concept in the form of an action research project—Grameen Bank Project (GBP)—in the village of Jobra (Counts 1990).[3] This project was financially supported by a national commercial bank and supervised by students of the Economics Department of Chittagong University (Yunus was then department head). From 1976 to 1978, in collaboration with various commercial banks in the country, the microcredit action project was introduced in different villages in the same region. The experiment helped Yunus develop the appropriate supervisory and timely recovery measures of his microlending project. In 1979, with the financial assistance of the Bangladesh Central Bank, the project was introduced to the Tangail district (where I conducted my fieldwork). During 1979 to 1982, with financial support from the International Fund for Agricultural Development (IFAD), the Grameen project was further extended to three more regions of Bangladesh and became a national project. On October 2, 1983, a government ordinance transformed the Grameen project into the Grameen Bank, a specialized credit institution with the mandate of providing credit services to poor people in rural Bangladesh.

The Lending Structure of the Grameen Bank

The Grameen Bank lends to groups of borrowers, rather than to individuals, through a hierarchical structure. In this lending structure, more than 90 percent of Grameen Bank field staff—bank workers, managers, program officers, and area managers—are men, but 95 percent of borrowers are women. The borrowers in the project must address men bank workers as "sir"; the real power of bank workers (men) over borrowers (women) may therefore be reinforced by cultural norms of male status (Montgomery 1995:10). Figure 1.2 reflects the bank worker and borrower hierarchy.

At the bottom of the lending structure are individual borrowers and the peer loan groups. The bank workers organize interested persons in

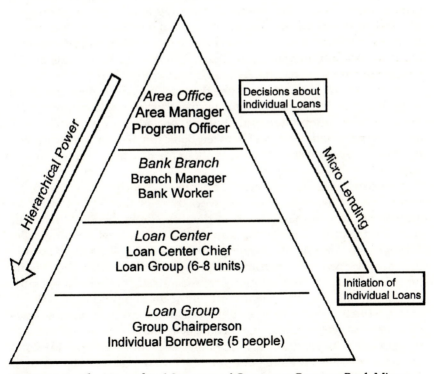

FIGURE 1.2   The Hierarchical Structure of Grassroots Grameen Bank Micro-Lending

groups of five borrowers of the same sex and with similar socioeconomic background. The explicit criterion for borrowers to be included in Grameen loan groups is "landlessness," which is also considered the main cause of rural poverty in Bangladesh (Siddiqui 1982; Jansen 1987; North-South Institute 1990; Rahman and Hossain 1996). The borrowers are supposed to be from households "owning less than 0.5 acre of cultivable land" or from households in which "total assets do not exceed the value of one acre of medium quality, single-cropped land in that area" (*Bidhimala* [Grameen Bank Constitution], 3.1; see Appendix C; Bernasek 1992:11). Formation of loan groups is followed by the selection or election of a group chair to be responsible for maintaining group discipline in the weekly meetings, conducting weekly transactions with the bank worker in the loan center, and proposing loans for other group members.

The loan center is the second-lowest position in the hierarchy of the grassroots loan operation. Six to eight loan groups in a village are federated into a loan center; they find a space or build a center hut in their vicinity for the weekly meetings and select or elect a center chief. The center chief is responsible for maintaining the overall discipline of the center, conducting center meetings, ensuring borrower attendance and installment payments, supervising individual borrower loan use, and reporting to the bank worker. At the center level, the center chief also holds the final authority to approve or disapprove the loan proposals of individual borrowers, which are initiated by the group chair.

The third level in the hierarchy is the local branch. Its workers are directly involved in executing the loan operation in the loan center. Bank workers form loan groups in the village, provide group members with adequate information on the Grameen Bank's operation, and work with borrowers to establish their conformity to the discipline of the Grameen Bank.

After forming a loan group and teaching the borrowers the rules and regulations of the bank, the bank workers refer the group to the local branch manager for his or her consideration. From the local branch the proposal for group recognition goes to the fourth level, the area office. The area office is where the group gets final recognition as a Grameen group and borrowers become eligible for initiation of the lending process. In addition to these four grassroots strata, the lending operation is also influenced by the superior officers of the zone and head office.

In 1994 and 1995 the Grameen Bank offered four main types of loans: (1) general loans for year-round income generation, (2) seasonal loans for investment in agriculture activities and seasonal business, (3) house loans for building a tin-roof house, and (4) group fund loans based on the 5 percent deducted as the group tax by the bank on every loan approved to an individual borrower and deposited to a group fund account

(GFA).The borrowers pay this deducted amount along with their capital. Until 1996, borrowers had no personal claim or right to their deposited amount in the GFA; they were allowed to borrow from the GFA only with the consent of the other members of the group (see *Bidhimala*, Section 4.6, Appendix C).

The borrowers reported that during its operation in the village the bank also has experimented with a few other types of loans, such as collective, family, tube well, and capital recovery loans. The bank introduced these different loans for its borrowers but gradually eliminated them because of the failure of their rates of recovery. In May 1997, at the time of my follow-up research, I found that the bank had introduced two more types of loans—animal sharecropping and leasing loans (macroloans of 100,000 to 200,000 taka)—for its borrowers to offset the declining investment trend in the study area.

The microlending of the Grameen Bank operates in a fifty-two week cycle. The weekly installment is 2 percent of the principal amount. Borrowers must repay the entire principal amount in fifty equal installments. In 1994–1995 the annual rate of interest for microloans was 20 percent and the emergency fund was 25 percent of the calculated interest on a particular loan. The interest and emergency fund payments add up to 12.5 percent more than regular weekly installments; borrowers must pay them in the remaining two weeks of the year to become eligible for their next new loan.[4]

Each loan proposal from individual borrowers in a center receives three successive and separate formal reviews before it can be finally approved by the area manager. The loan amount requested by an individual borrower needs to be agreed on by all members of the group. The group chairperson then approaches the center chief with the proposed loan. The center chief initiates the formal loan proposal, signs it, and gives it to a bank worker. The bank worker approves it and gives it to the branch manager. The branch manager approves the loan proposal and sends it to the area office. In the area office it is first approved by the responsible program officer and then finally countersigned by the area manager.

Once a group is recognized and approved by the Grameen Bank, loans to individual group borrowers are granted sequentially—by establishing a time cycle—rather than simultaneously. Two borrowers in a group receive their loans in the initial allocation and their loan repayment behavior is observed for a month or two. Their successful repayment entitles the next two borrowers in the group to apply for loans. The satisfactory repayment of four borrowers in two different time cycles entitles the last member of the group to a loan. By establishing such sequences in loan disbursement, the Grameen Bank creates peer pressure whereby each group member becomes responsible for other borrowers' loans. In this microlending program the group is to function as an institution to ensure mutual accountability. The individual in the system is kept in line by a considerable amount of pressure from other borrowers of the group. The pressure of the group acts as the collateral for the bank.

Loans are approved for individual borrowers for specific projects for immediate investment in a cash income venture. According to explicit bank guidelines, the group chairperson and the center chief are obliged to supervise loan utilization immediately after the loan is disbursed. Upon their satisfactory investigation, they both are to report to the bank worker in a written form. The bank worker is obliged to verify the claim of the group chairperson and center chief and prepare a written description of the investment. Additionally, the investment of the borrower is supposed to be further supervised by the responsible branch manager and the program officer from the area office.

The objective of the organization of borrowers in groups and centers for the lending operation is not only to provide them economic opportunities but also to create an environment in which borrowers are able to exchange socially needed information, encouragement, and motivation for confidence building. The stated goal is to build unity, solidarity, and leadership among borrowers and ultimately to improve their social development and empowerment. The bank workers, policymakers, and even academics in Bangladesh usually generalize about Grameen microlending through quantitative representation. Representatives of public institutions appear to have played a commanding role in sustaining the international prominence of the bank and the pride of the country as an innovator of the microcredit concept.

Studies of the Grameen Bank

A substantial number of studies have been conducted, primarily by economists, on the microcredit program of the Grameen Bank since its beginning in 1983. Most of these studies are evaluative in nature,[5] with the researchers examining the kind of impact the Grameen Bank microcredit programs have had on its borrowers (Ghai 1984; Ahmed 1985; R. I. Rahman 1986; Atiur Rahman 1986a and 1986b; Hossain 1988). These studies provide both quantitative and descriptive information on gradual changes in the number of Grameen Bank memberships, the amount of loans taken out by borrowers, income earned from loan money, household income, areas of investment, and social development indicators such as the practice of the "Sixteen Decisions" by borrowers (see Appendix B). A few other studies have been conducted on the Grameen Bank program in the 1990s that try to investigate the impact of loans on the empowerment of women borrowers (Hashemi and Schuler 1993 and

1996; Wahid 1993; Schuler and Hashemi 1994 and 1995; Goetz and Sen Gupta 1996; Schuler, Hashemi, and Riley 1997a and 1997b; Todd 1997). I outline these studies briefly here.

One of the early evaluations of the Grameen Bank was conducted by Ghai (1984), who attributed bank success to recruiting women into the program. At the time of his evaluation female clients of the bank had risen from 31 percent in 1980 to 46 percent in 1983. Ghai also found a positive impact on the income of borrower households and on the status of women in these households. Mahabub Hossain (1988), who also conducted his study in 1984, focused on the impact of Grameen Bank credit on employment, income level, and economic productivity of poor rural women. His primary source of data came from a sample survey conducted by the Bangladesh Institute for Development Studies (BIDS) among 612 randomly selected Grameen borrowers. Hossain also used monthly statistical reports of the Grameen Bank and the bank's annual report to support his findings. Hossain (1988) found that loans enabled the women borrowers to add additional resources to their family budget. Whatever women borrowers earned by using their Grameen loans increased household per capita income and enhanced the overall status of women in the household.

R. I. Rahman (1986) and Atiur Rahman (1986a and 1986b) of BIDS conducted a series of surveys of the credit program of the Grameen Bank in different regions of Bangladesh. Both of them found a positive impact on women borrowers, specifically in regard to income-generating work—the major impact of women's borrowing from the bank. In his study, Atiur Rahman (1986a and 1986b) focused on the consciousness-raising efforts of the bank among women, institution building and empowerment among women, and the impact of microcredit programs on the rural power structure of Bangladesh. He maintained that women in the loan centers of the Grameen Bank are able to gain strength in collective solidarity, to challenge traditional norms and values, and to fight against social injustice.

Ahmed's (1985) study on Grameen women borrowers showed a positive economic impact of credit, but in terms of the Grameen Bank's efforts to raise women's consciousness, Ahmed found variation between the awareness of women borrowers about social issues and their real practices. His study revealed that even though the Grameen women borrowers in his sample (n=120) were aware of social issues such as the negative effects of dowry, repression, desertion, and violence against women, only 48 percent supported equal rights between men and women. Physical violence against women—wife beating—was justified by 19 percent of the women on the ground that it is a controlling mechanism for disobedience and slowness in household chores (Ahmed 1985:14).

Wahid's (1993) edited volume *The Grameen Bank: Poverty Relief in Bangladesh* is claimed to be "the first comprehensive study of Bangladesh's Grameen Bank" by its publisher. The editor includes sixteen papers presenting the performance of the bank and the potential of the bank's lending model for replication in other parts of the world. (I discussed some of the papers, e.g., Atiur Rahman 1986a and 1986b, and Mahbub Hossain 1988, earlier in this section,). The papers address three major areas of the Grameen Bank and its lending: (1) the historical background and origin of the bank and its objectives, lending structure, early success in incorporating borrowers, investing loans, and recovering invested loans from borrowers; (2) expansion and growth of the bank, impact of lending on the socioeconomic status of rural women, and the social and political status of the rural power elite; and (3) the group lending that enables the Grameen Bank to achieve remarkable rates of success in recovering loans, the institutional economic viability of the bank, and the replication of Grameen lending in other countries. Wahid's collection attempts to give readers a general view of the success and potential of the Grameen Bank. A number of papers in this volume are reproduced by their authors from Grameen Bank impact studies, however, and most of them are based entirely on survey methods that present quantitative indicators of the bank's performance but fail to uncover and address the on-the-ground processes of microlending.

Mizan (1994), in her study *In Quest of Empowerment: The Grameen Bank Impact on Women's Power and Status,* investigated the impacts of women's economic participation and earning on their marital decisionmaking power. Under the auspices of the Grameen Bank, Mizan conducted her study among women borrowers in two of the oldest program villages in two different regions (Chittagong and Patuakhali districts). The data were collected primarily through survey methods and were analyzed from the family sociology perspective of "cultural resource theory" (Rodman 1970). The study concluded that "women's participation over a long period of time had a stronger impact on household decision-making than the money women brought to fulfil family needs" (Mizan 1994:145). The bank has touted this study as evidence of its success in empowering women. But Mizan (1994:144) also argued that in rural society women's advancing age and life cycle, for example, changing roles in motherhood and in becoming mothers-in-law, influence their decisionmaking power in the household. The mean age of her informants was thirty-two years, suggesting that most borrowers in Mizan's study were in advanced life-cycle stages. Therefore, we must question specifically the extent to which decisionmaking power gains for women are a product of normative role expectation changes associated with advancing age or are a result of their involvement with the bank.

S. M. Hashemi, an economist, and S. R. Schuler, an anthropologist, have an ongoing Grameen research project, "Rural Credit, Empowerment of Women and Contraceptive Use in Bangladesh" (Grameen Trust 1997:12). They have produced a series of journal articles on the impact of credit programs on the contraceptive behavior and empowerment of women. The primary focus of their study is fertility and reproductive health, not the long-term economic and social implications of credit lending for women (Schuler and Hashemi 1994 and 1995). In some of their recent journal articles, however, they argue that the credit programs of various nongovernmental organizations, including the Grameen Bank, are helping poor rural women achieve socioeconomic empowerment in the society (Hashemi, Schuler, and Riley 1996; Schuler, Hashemi, and Riley 1997a). They have also developed a set of operationalizing indicators, such as women's mobility and visibility and their assertiveness and interaction in the public sphere (Hashemi and Schuler 1993:11–15) to measure the empowerment of the clients of credit programs.

Anne Marie Goetz, a political scientist, and Rina Sen Gupta, an economist, conducted their 1996 study of credit programs in a project titled "Women's Leadership in Rural Development in Bangladesh." They categorized the loan use patterns of three major microlending organizations in the country (Bangladesh Rural Advancement Committee [BRAC]; Grameen Bank; and Rural Development–12 [RD–12], a government-run microcredit poverty alleviation program funded by donors and coordinated by the Bangladesh Rural Development Board [BRDB]) and found male control over women's loans. On average, women in these programs retained full or significant control over loan use in only 37 percent of the cases, whereas 63 percent of the cases fell into the three categories of partial (17.8 percent), very limited (17 percent), or no control (21.7 percent). This indicates a significant pattern of women borrowers systematically losing control over their loans; they are even victimized by the process. Many women borrowers bear the risk and burden of institutional loans without directly benefiting from them.

Helen Todd (1997), a journalist and wife of a microcredit visionary from Malaysia, conducted a study of forty women borrowers in only two loan centers in two villages in the Tangail district. The study populations consisted of women borrowers who had been involved with the credit program for at least ten years. Sponsored by the Grameen Bank, Todd worked through local interpreters, which presents considerable limitations. With regard to the use of loans and installment payments by borrowers, she found many practices violating the principles of the bank. Todd (1997:24) found that in her study villages 49 percent of women's loans were used in "land transactions" (purchase or mortgage-in). She pointed out that bank policy does not allow borrowers to use their loans in this sector, but women in her study claimed that investment in land provided them with increased status in their households. Todd argued that the bank needs to change its policy in this matter. Todd also argued that the success of individual borrowers depends on many factors, such as the women's own personalities, their relations with their kin and household members, and the number of income earners in the family. Both in the credit program and in the long term some of the borrowers became successful and others did not. Goetz and Sen Gupta (1996) and Todd (1997) each suggest that a better understanding of the implications of credit programs for women borrowers and women's status in their households in rural Bangladesh would come through a commitment to long-term anthropological research.

Microcredit in Development Projects

The Grameen project started its microcredit program in a single village in Bangladesh twenty years ago; it has continued to grow and extend loans in rural Bangladesh, particularly to poor women. Since it became a bank in 1983, the Grameen Bank has grown remarkably in terms of its branches, centers, membership, and cumulative loan disbursements. The growth and expansion of the Grameen Bank is presented in Figure 1.3; from 1985 to 1994 the number of branches increased by 462 percent (226 to 1,045), the number of loan centers 831 percent (7,210 to 59,221), the borrowers 1,185 percent (171,622 to 2,015,131). The cumulative investment during the same period increased by 2,786 percent from 985 to 44,640 million taka.[6] Since the mid–1980s, the bank has emphasized recruitment of women borrowers. The proportion of male borrowers among all borrowers declined dramatically from 34.9 percent in 1985 to less than 6 percent in 1994, but the number of female borrowers increased by about 700 percent during the same period (Khandker, Khalily, and Khan 1994; Grameen Bank 1994).

The expansion of the bank, its incorporation of women as the principal borrowers, its investment portfolio of over one billion U.S. dollars, and its maintenance of 90 percent recovery rates on its investment has brought the bank into the international scene. Before 1990, the programmatic success of the Grameen Bank's microcredit, combined with Yunus's advocacy, attracted considerable international interest and encouraged some bilateral organizations to increase their funding for microcredit and microenterprise development initiatives in developing countries (Auwal 1994; Johnston 1995).

In the 1990s, the microcredit approach of the Grameen Bank has attracted even wider international interest and is being incorporated in mainstream development agendas. The popularity of microcredit in the

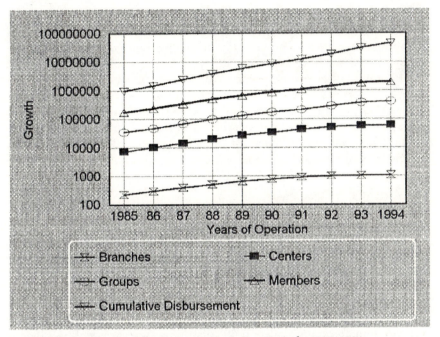

FIGURE 1.3   Growth of the Grameen Bank, Bangladesh, 1985–1994

SOURCE: Adapted from Khandker, Khalily and Khan 1994

West and its incorporation in mainstream development seem to have a political context. The President of the United States, Bill Clinton, and the First Lady, Hillary Rodham Clinton, "have publicly come out in support of Yunus and the concept" (Johnston 1995:1). In recent years, primarily because of the support of political personalities in North America, both microcredit and Yunus have received extraordinary press attention in the West (Auwal 1994; Johnston 1995).[7]

Currently, almost all national and international development organizations incorporate microcredit as one of the main components of their programs. Most bilateral and multilateral[8] development institutions have increased their funding for microlending programs in order to reach the poor—particularly women—to help them to achieve sustainable livelihoods through the creation of earning opportunities and the eradication of poverty. The Grameen Bank microlending model has now been replicated in fifty-six countries (Isa 1997), including many developed countries such as the United States and Canada. Through various development projects and financial institutions microlending services now reach about eight million borrowers on six continents (Balkin 1993; Gugliotta

1993; Microcredit Summit 1998a). In February 1997, the promoters of the microlending projects organized the Microcredit World Summit with a commitment to create a poverty-free planet by the year 2025 through microlending. They have launched a plan of action to provide microcredit for 100 million borrowers, particularly women, and to reach 500 million people (if family members are included) by the year 2005. Currently, microcredit is not only an antipoverty development tool but is also an emerging sector for financial markets and profit-making potential. Many private financial institutions from the rich capitalist countries are getting involved with microcredit initiatives (Microcredit Summit 1998b).

Women in Development and Incorporation of Microcredit

For more than four and a half decades rich capitalist countries from the West have initiated efforts to promote economic development in developing countries. These development initiatives in many cases have brought positive changes in economic growth (per capita income), increased literacy, and life expectancy at the macro (national) level, but they have failed to provide the benefits of such development to poor people at the micro level (Chambers 1986; Korten 1990). In addition, serious concern remains about the equitable distribution of the benefits of development along gender lines. A great deal of energy has been invested in documenting the distributional effects of development on various groups in society and very often this is expressed as a concern for women.

In the 1960s modernization theory (e.g., Rostow 1960; Lewis 1966), equating development with progress, predicted that development would benefit all segments of the population in society irrespective of gender, class, or race. In the modernization paradigm women were seldom considered separately; when they were, it was assumed that a modern secular society would automatically improve women's situation by freeing them from the constraints of traditional cultures. The assumptions of modernization theory were challenged by Boserup (1970) for the first time in her study *Women's Role in Economic Development*. Boserup used available data from Asia and Africa on women's work to show that the modernization approach of development had helped mainly men in society and had bypassed poor women. She argued for women's integration in the development process as equal partners with men (Bandarage 1984).

Boserup's work was criticized on the grounds that she did not question the viability of a "Western" model of development for the poor in non-Western countries (Madhuri 1992:15). But despite criticism, her work contributed to a comprehensive overview of women's roles in the development process and has successfully sensitized many international donor agencies to their inattention to women in their development programs. Inspired by Boserup's work, a new subfield of development—Women in Development (WID)—gradually emerged in the liberal tradition (Parpart and Marchand 1995). This subfield of development assumes that all women can be emancipated within capitalist development through their incorporation in the public sphere, specifically through women's access to an expanding cash economy.

The debate over women's development during the 1970s and 1980s has been influential in the policy and programming of many government and nongovernment organizations. Following the establishment of WID, many bilateral aid agencies; international development organizations such as the United Nations (UN), the United States Agency for International Development (USAID), the World Bank, the Canadian International Development Agency (CIDA), the Ford Foundation, and others; plus many national and local agencies started to change their philosophy toward women's incorporation (Jahan 1992). In the 1980s most development agencies added a WID division to bring women's issues into the mainstream of development. A few bilateral programs, such as USAID, CIDA, and the Norwegian Agency for Development (NORAD), even received special mandates to address women's needs and to give preference to programs and activities that tend to integrate women in the economic development of developing countries (Charlton 1984:102).

The Decade of Women in Development (1975–1985) and advocacy of women activists around the world encouraged international organizations to allocate funds for women in development projects. During this period a large number of projects were initiated for women in most developing countries. In some cases, for local agencies, incorporation of women in their projects became a way of getting funds from international organizations (Jahan 1992). The WID projects mostly focused on women's skill development, the integration of women into income-generating projects, and raising women's income. The broad objective of such projects was to enhance women's status in the household and society. In these projects women were involved in income-generating activities and educated about family planning and health, nutrition, sanitation, and child health.

In WID, women's development was seen as a logistical problem, rather than something requiring fundamental reassessment of gender relations and ideology (Rathgeber 1990; Tinker 1990). The WID approach of integrating women in development has been challenged by many feminist thinkers on the grounds that these projects do not address the question of gender inequality and relations of domination and subordination (Benería and Sen 1982; Mies 1986). Benería and Roldán (1987) asserted that the involvement of women with WID projects may increase their income but this increased income does not imply changing women's position in the household in terms of power and authority. They suggested that women in such projects most often find themselves working harder but having no control over their production or decisionmaking participation in the family or in the community (Mies 1986; Wilson-Moore 1989). In addition, Buvinić (1989) categorically showed that international organizations that funded development projects for women in developing countries had their own agenda; in most cases it was the control of population growth. To achieve the goal of reduced population women were targeted and incorporated in a comprehensive development approach in which income-generation projects became the central issue for women.

The income-generating initiatives for poor women evolved over several decades as a component of larger sectoral development programs. By the mid–1980s disillusionment with income-generating activities began to surface in many development agencies. There was increasing recognition that the income-generating projects were in many cases failing to raise income levels, and in some cases were additionally burdening poor women (Chen 1989; Albee 1994). By the end of the 1980s many development agencies were avoiding the use of the term "income generating," as it continued to conjure up images of women undertaking marginal economic activities far removed from the increasing thrust toward gender issues and women's empowerment.

Scattered evidence also revealed that an increasing number of poor women in poor Southern countries were creating their own jobs in small-scale agriculture, manufacturing, services, and petty trade (Berger 1989). Such evidence also reinforced the idea that the smaller the business the greater the chance of its being owned and operated by a woman (Accion International 1988); thus women's inaccessibility to finance was recognized as a constraint for poor women and credit became the "common missing piece" in WID (McKee 1989:995).

The gender-sensitive promoters of development saw credit as a source of acquiring capital so women could practice their livelihoods in more productive and profitable ways. It was postulated that making capital available through credit would unlock considerable potential for self-employment, allowing enterprises to start up and expand. Since the mid–1980s the focus of women's development projects in many development agencies has turned toward using credit as a development tool. Microcredit now has become a central part of many women-focused development projects, and numerous strategies have been developed to provide women with access to the missing piece of development, that is, credit.

Some Northern and Southern scholars began to call for a new approach to women's development in the late 1980s. Several studies on growing poverty in the South and on global patriarchy (e.g., Mies 1986;

Sen and Grown 1987; Agarwal 1988) have contributed to the emergence of a new discourse that uses the concept of Gender and Development (GAD) instead of Women in Development (WID). In GAD discourse the main focus is on gender rather than women, particularly the social construction of gender roles and relations. As Kabeer (1991b:11) explained, "Gender is seen as the process by which individuals who are born into biological categories of male or female become the social categories of men and women through the acquisition of locally-defined attributes of masculinity and femininity" (quoted in Parpart and Marchand 1995:14). Even though the GAD proponents also rarely challenge the goal of modernization, some scholars believe that GAD provides the possible discursive space to do so (Udayagiri 1995).

Women in Development: A Bangladesh Context

In response to the demands of the women's movement and the United Nation's mandate, in the 1980s and 1990s WID projects have emerged as a visible field of policy and action in most countries, especially those dependent on foreign assistance, such as Bangladesh (Jahan 1992). Since the independence of Bangladesh in 1971, women's issues have been a concern of official policies of the government. This concern is reflected in the promulgation of constitutional equal rights for women (Khan 1988) and, in the late 1970s, establishing a ministry of women's affairs—one of the few countries in the world to do so (Sobhan 1992). A brief sketch of the government's policies for incorporating women in the development process in Bangladesh is presented here.

Bangladesh started its journey of socioeconomic development with the First Five-Year Plan (FFYP; Government of Bangladesh 1973) of 1973–1978. The FFYP had neither an explicit focus on women nor any sectoral resource allocation for women's involvement (World Bank 1990); only a passing reference to women was made, associated with social welfare and the rehabilitation of liberation war victims.[9] During the interim Two-Year Plan (TYP, 1978–1980; Government of Bangladesh 1978) the government set up the Ministry for Women's Affairs. In the Second Five-Year Plan (SFYP 1980–1985; Government of Bangladesh 1980), an explicit allocation of resources was made to incorporate women in development by setting up projects focusing on population, health, education, and employment generation. Rehman Sobhan (1992) stated that the SFYP was implemented in the middle of the United Nation's Women's Decade of Development, which compelled planners to incorporate concerns specific to women in their plan objectives.

The Third Five-Year Plan (TFYP 1985–1990; Government of Bangladesh 1985) continued the effort of bringing women into development, and special emphasis was put on the concerns of rural women in Bangladesh. Poverty alleviation became one of the central themes (Khan 1988), and the focus was to extend credit to women for employment, income generation, and poverty alleviation. The dynamics of promoting women's concerns both in the SFYP and in the TFYP remained largely donor driven and was sustained by the expectation of readily available funds for women-oriented projects. In the TFYP, 57 percent of donor funds went to the health and family-planning sectors.

In Bangladesh, it is not only for the Bangladesh government that "women's issues" present a potential resource, but also for NGOs involved in women in development. There are at least 500 registered medium to large-size development NGOs working in Bangladesh. Jerry Buckland (1994) maintained that substantial efforts are made by many of these NGOs in rural Bangladesh to target women and currently "a large and growing share of NGO participants are women" (114). David Korten (1990) analyzed the development process of NGOs in Bangladesh and noted that there are similarities between the government and NGO initiatives in development. The first generation of development workers was involved in relief and rehabilitation; the second generation was in family planning, informal education, and sectoral programs under a comprehensive development approach (see Buckland 1994). Currently, the effort of both the NGOs and the government have shifted toward credit extension and development with a special focus on poor women.

Sarah White (1992:15) presented the perspectives of donors and NGO initiatives on women in development in rural Bangladesh. She wrote that before the 1980s many NGOs did not consider women's issues to be included specifically in development. The same NGOs later on realized that the inclusion of women's issues is the way to expand their activities and gain new sources of funding. Although these NGOs are working with women, their commitment toward gender issues remains only instrumental, and they have reproduced rather than challenged the established pattern of patriarchal ideology.

Group-based institutional lending to women is a recent addition to development initiatives in Bangladesh, although saving and borrowing have a long tradition among women in rural Bangladesh (Maloney and Ahmed 1988; Ebdon 1995). Traditionally, women in villages have organized themselves in small groups (*samity*), saved small amounts, and borrowed from their savings funds in times of need. The institutional credit extension program was first introduced in the country by the Bangladesh Rural Development Board (BRDB) in the early 1970s. BRDB extended credit to women through organizing them in cooperatives. In the period 1976–1989, it organized hundreds of women's cooperative societies (*Mahila Samabay Samity*) in different areas of Bangladesh and distributed more than 2 million U.S. dollars in small loans to 122,000 borrowers (World Bank 1990). Since 1985 the BRDB sought to target landless poor women to organize a special cooperative (*Mahila Bhumihin Samabay Samity*). This program distributed about 24 million U.S. dollars in rural Bangladesh among its 147,000 women members (Sobhan 1992). Another initiative of rural credit was implemented by the Swanirvar ("self-help") program initiated in 1976. By 1988 this project had distributed about 19 million U.S. dollars to its 464,000 borrowers in 9,070 villages. Among these, about 300,000 were women. In rural Bangladesh, in addition to the Grameen Bank and the Bangladesh government programs, at least 150 NGOs now extend credit to women and reach about 8.5 million borrowers in the country.

The Significance of This Study

Most studies of the Grameen Bank—both impact and academic—are conducted by economists and sociologists who rely heavily on survey research, generate quantitative data on the performance of the bank, and provide the "bird's-eye view" of the program. To my knowledge no in-depth anthropological research has been conducted on this internationally reputed lending program. My in-depth study presents a qualitative analysis of the program and contributes to an understanding of the lending process. It provides the "worm's-eye view" of the program.[10] My study focuses on both social and economic processes to understand how the bank maintains its success in microloan investment and recovery and to investigate the implications of the microlending structure for its borrowers and societal members and for the sustainability and growth of the microlending enterprise itself.

The insights from my anthropological study on the Grameen Bank address the international demand for new knowledge about microcredit and microenterprise development. Since the mid–1970s scholars and activists have shifted their attention from massive infrastructural development to small-scale participatory development. The transition in development thinking ensued from the failure of the modernization paradigm (Rogers 1976) to bring benefits to the poor (Chambers 1986; Yunus 1995). The critics of the modernization paradigm argue that poor people need mechanisms to organize themselves and establish microenterprises that require small amounts of capital and in which they can use their local knowledge and skill.

The qualitative analysis of this work not only complements the existing research on the Grameen Bank by adding yet another study but presents a different picture from other research findings on the bank. My study raises questions about the conventional understanding of small-scale lending by the Grameen Bank and about the orthodox views of its success and empowerment of women in society. The processual examination of microcredit in this study explicates the lending structure for borrowers and fills the gap between quantitative and qualitative studies. My study indicates increased violence and aggression toward women borrowers (which has not otherwise been reported to date) and provides some explanation for rising tension and violence in the society in response to the lending structure and practice. The significance of this study lies not only in its recommendation for procedural and structural changes in the lending operation but in theoretical terms the study also challenges the orthodox view of the success of microcredit and empowerment of women in society.

The Structure of the Book

This book comprises eight chapters. In the first chapter, I have described the problem and set up the background context of the study with a presentation of the Grameen Bank, its lending structure, and the incorporation of microcredit in international development projects. Women in development and the significance of my study are also discussed here. Chapter 2 covers my field research strategies and data collection. The main topics of this chapter are the rhetoric and realities of anthropological fieldwork, research ethics, advantages and disadvantages of being a "native" in the field, and limitations of being a male working among women informants. In Chapter 3, I present the theoretical framework of the study—the normative entitlements of patriarchy—together with an examination of selected concepts, that is, public and hidden transcripts, practice theory, and hegemony, used to analyze the field data. Chapter 4 presents an ethnographic overview of the study village—its location, social organization, population, and economy. In Chapter 5, the public and hidden transcripts of the recruitment of women borrowers, the creation of "social collateral" for lending, and the formal and informal networks of the borrowers and bank workers are discussed. The implications of social collateral and power hierarchies are also discussed in this chapter, with examples and case studies. Chapter 6 deals with the lending and recovery process of the bank. I discuss the use of loans in borrower households, loan supervision by bank workers, and increased violence and aggression toward women borrowers. Chapter 7 focuses on the concern of institutional financial sustainability. I discuss sustainability and capitalist finance to address the implications of institutional sustainability for borrowers, bank workers, and members of society generally. The conclusion—Chapter 8—contains a summary of the findings and an assessment of the theoretical constructs used. Policy suggestions for better planning and implementation of microcredit programs are offered.

Notes

1. I derive the expression *programmatic success* from my personal communication with Dr. Nancy Horn, a microenterprise specialist with Opportunity International, Chicago. Here, programmatic success refers to quantitative indicators, i.e., number of borrowers recruited for the program and amounts of loans invested among these borrowers and recovered from them.

2. A moneylender in the village often charges as high as 200 percent yearly interest on the capital amount. In rural Bangladesh culture, borrowing from traditional moneylenders is considered a more sinful act than borrowing from formal institutions because a person is not to personally benefit from lending assistance; assistance is a matter of reciprocity.

3. Jobra is located in the vicinity of Chittagong University, where Yunus was a professor and head of the Department of Economics. Other sources (Hossain 1988; Shehabuddin 1992) state that Yunus met this bamboo worker who inspired his thinking in 1975.

4. The borrowers paid 20 percent annual interest on their loans and an additional 25 percent of the interest on each of their loans into an emergency fund. The emergency fund was created as a kind of insurance against death, default, disasters, and accidents (see *Bidhimala*, Section 4.7, Appendix C, and Chapter 6 of the book).

5. There are also other publications produced and published routinely by the Grameen Bank. The *Annual Report* of the bank consists of quantitative data on bank activities. A quarterly newsletter and the *Grameen Dialogue*, a newsletter published by the Grameen Trust, give information on the bank's success and its replication in other parts of the world.

6. *Taka* is the name for Bangladesh currency. At the time of my fieldwork forty-two taka were equivalent to one U.S. dollar.

7. Clinton first met with Yunus in 1986 when Clinton was the governor of Arkansas. Clinton established the Good Faith Fund, a microcredit program in Pine Bluff, Arkansas, in 1988. In November 1993, then President Clinton honored Yunus when he came to Washington to receive an award from the Good Faith Fund. In this meeting Clinton described himself as the "No.1 publicist" and "No.1 activist" for the Grameen Bank (*India Abroad*, No. 19, p. 32, quoted in Auwal 1994:116).

8. Here bilateral refers to national government assistance programs to developing countries, such as the United States Agency for International Development (USAID) or the Canadian International Development Agency (CIDA). Multilateral refers to institutions such as the World Bank or the United Nations (see MacIsaac 1996).

9. The liberation war caused large numbers of women to be widowed, raped, and otherwise victimized in the social upheaval that characterized the emergence of Bangladesh.

10. Yunus, in his writing and lectures, has used the analogy of "bird's-eye view" and "worm's-eye view." When researchers use a survey questionnaire, they only gain a sketchy picture of the situation. Researchers need to look at a problem by staying in the field and collecting detailed information on the ground.

2

Field Research Methodology

The material for this work was collected during two anthropological field studies in a rural community in the district of Tangail in Bangladesh (see map in Figure 1.1). The first field study was conducted from November 1994 to September 1995. In the Summer of 1997, I returned to my research community for six weeks and conducted a follow-up on my research findings. This chapter introduces the pre-fieldwork research plan, the realities of the field, and the resulting shifts in research objectives. The discussion also covers the methods and procedures of data collection, advantages and disadvantages of being a "native" (Bangladeshi researcher) in the field, types of data, analysis of field data, research ethics, and the reliability of research findings.

Pre-Fieldwork Research Plan

During the 1980s and 1990s several studies in rural Bangladesh documented that persistent poverty in rural Bangladesh caused a breakdown in social norms and entitlement (Sen 1981), compelling many poor women to accept work outside the household for their survival (Kabeer 1991a; White 1992; Zaman 1996). According to these studies the acceptance of work by poor women in the "public domain" was a challenge to the dominant patriarchal ideology and male power structures of the Bangladesh rural society. Grassroots organizations such as the Grameen Bank organize and incorporate poor women in their credit programs with the objective of enhancing the women's earning capabilities, which eventually results in women's economic and social empowerment (Atiur Rahman 1986a and 1986b; Abecassis 1989; Agarwal 1990; Fuglesang and Chandler 1993).

Since 1976, the Grameen Bank has pioneered a credit delivery system bringing access to credit to rural poor people, particularly women. During the 1980s and 1990s several studies of the Grameen Bank's microcredit program suggested that women's access to credit encouraged their rise as independent producers and providers of valuable cash resources to their household economies. This access to credit also enhanced the self-confidence of women and increased their status in the family and was said to have led to their social and economic empowerment and challenged the generalized domination over and violence against women in rural Bangladesh society (R. I. Rahman 1986; Atiur Rahman 1986b; Shehabuddin 1992; Mizan 1994; Schuler and Hashemi 1995; Hashemi, Schuler, and Riley 1996; Schuler, Hashemi, and Riley 1997b).

I drew on these studies for my field research plan. The central topic of the research was to examine the changes in gender roles and relations in rural Bangladesh in the context of the Grameen Bank's work with poor women. The research plan was primarily based on the results of previous studies that emphasized the empowerment of women in rural society through their incorporation in the credit program of the Grameen Bank. The main objective of my research was to explore the prospects for the empowerment of women by investigating the involvement of women in a microcredit program in a traditional patriarchal society. The research was intended to investigate the prospects for women's empowerment primarily using two indicators. The first indicator was new roles emerging for women through their involvement with the microcredit programs in relation to the acceptance of these new roles for women by other societal members. The second was whether women themselves were willing and able to transfer the advantages of their achieved empowerment to the next generation, that is intergenerational ideological change (Aminur Rahman 1994).

We researchers often develop our research plans in academic settings far from the field. In many instances such plans do not fit the realities of our field situation. Such was the case with my original research plan despite widespread "evidence" in support of the plan. At the initial stage of my field research, I traveled to several branches of the Grameen Bank in different areas of the Dhaka and Tangail zones to select a suitable research site. During these visits, I noticed that whenever women borrowers came to a bank office to accept their loans or discuss problems with bank workers, they were often represented by men. I observed several cases where women borrowers, after receiving their loans from the bank manager, handed the money over to men. The apparent transfer of money from women to men sometimes took place in the bank office and in front of the bank workers.

During my field research it became clear that most women borrowers are not the direct benefactors of the credit extended to them. Instead, these women appeared to be mediators between their male household members and the bank. Thus the lending institution invests loans in the village to generate profit, but it uses the prevailing patriarchal norms of the village society and the positional vulnerability of women (immobile, shy, passive) for timely repayment and distribution of new loans. This unexpected but omnipresent reality of the field situation guided me to shift my research focus and make changes to my research plan. Originally, I planned a study of the dynamics of the empowerment of women. But it became necessary to examine women borrowers' lack of power; their limited involvement in the microcredit lending operation of the Grameen Bank; and the implications of this lending operation for societal members, particularly women.

Initiation of Field Research

Initiation of anthropological field research involves a lengthy and complicated process. This process in most cases starts with acquiring "formal consent" (permission) from the research community and proceeds with settling in a research site, building contact with informants, collecting information, and maintaining the ethical commitments of the research. Formal consent from the Grameen Bank is a prerequisite for conducting research in any of the bank program areas in Bangladesh. My request for research permission was made to Muhammad Yunus, the managing director, chief executive officer, and founder of the Grameen Bank. Six months prior to my departure for Bangladesh, I had received no response. After my arrival in Bangladesh, I contacted the Research and Evaluation Division of the Grameen Bank in Dhaka immediately. The division is headed by a senior officer—deputy general manager—who listened to my explanation of the purpose of my visit and showed interest in my research but expressed his inability to give me permission. Research permission would have to be obtained from Yunus, who was then on sick leave and would not be returning to the office for at least two more weeks.

My encounter with the Research and Evaluation Division of the Grameen Bank was frustrating. The division is run by a divisional head who appeared to have no decisionmaking power regarding academic research on the Grameen Bank. I submitted a new request and waited for Yunus to return. On the scheduled day of his return, I attempted to meet Yunus directly, but I was stopped at the front desk by his personal secretary. The secretary sought Yunus's permission for my visit and returned to inform me of Yunus's consent for my research. The formal permission letter was issued by the Research and Evaluation Division of the Grameen Bank. Although Yunus's prompt decision regarding my research impressed me, I became concerned about the centralization of decisionmaking power in the Grameen Bank. Over the course of my fieldwork in Bangladesh and my work with the Grameen Bank, I came to realize that not only is permission for research on the Grameen Bank left to Yunus, but most decisions are left to the founder of the bank.

centralization of power

Finding the Site

My success in getting consent for the research was a morale boost for me. The Grameen Bank gave me the freedom to choose my research site from any of its program areas in Bangladesh. The letter of consent included Yunus's instruction to his bank workers at the grassroots. They were to help me find a research site to conduct my research. I left for the field feeling confident about the prospects for my research in Bangladesh.

The Grameen Bank has microcredit extension programs among women in half of all the villages in Bangladesh. Selecting one village out of more than 37,000 as my research site seemed at the time to be the most difficult part of the fieldwork. To select the site, I set out specific criteria consistent with the main objectives of the research—changes in gender roles and relations in the context of women's involvement with the credit program and intergenerational transmission of gender ideology in society. To document such changes, I was looking for a research site in an area where the bank had been working for at least ten years. The duration of the program in the area was important so that I could examine and comprehend the long-term socioeconomic and cultural implications of microcredit for its women borrowers. The next criterion was to find a village with no more than 250 to 300 households, a manageable group considering my research time and resources.

At that time, there were only four out of a total of twelve Grameen Bank zones where the bank had existed for more than ten years. Of these four, I decided to select my research site from the Tangail or Dhaka zones (see Figure 1.1). The other two zones—Chittagong and Rangpur—were excluded because Chittagong is considered one of the most conservative areas in the country (Mizan 1994) and Rangpur had the largest number of defaulting borrowers (personal communication, Dipal Barua, General Manager, Administration). Neither one of these is sufficiently typical of the general features to further understanding of the general impact of the credit program on women. During the first one and a half months of my fieldwork, I traveled extensively to eight different local branches in the Dhaka and Tangail zones to find and select a specific research site. In that quest, I used both formal (institutional) and informal (friends and relatives) networks. The justification for using these networks is discussed briefly.

Formal Networks. During the first month of my research, I tried to use institutional networks to find the site. I traveled to eight local branches carrying the consent letter from the Grameen Bank head office with an expectation of getting strong cooperation from local bank workers. But at the local branches the bank workers are overburdened with their job obligations and had little time for my academic research. At local branches the managers received me cordially but other bank workers often expressed candidly that my stay in the branch would ultimately add an extra load to their already-overloaded regular job responsibilities.

I traveled to different branches at least three or four times a week. During such visits, I would usually sit with the manager in the bank office for the whole day and observe the daily activities in the bank. Neither the branch managers nor the bank workers showed any interest in my search to find a research site. On some occasions my persistence compelled managers to arrange field visits with bank workers, although they were uninterested in the arrangements required by the research or my accommodation in the village. Three of eight branch managers I visited had already experienced having researchers (local and foreign) in their branches. These researchers either commuted from Dhaka or stayed in the bank building for one or two weeks. They could not grasp why I, an anthropologist, was looking for accommodation in a village and wanted to live there for ten months.

After traveling extensively for almost a month in the Dhaka and Tangail zones, I realized that my efforts to look for a research site through the institutional network would not be successful. I also realized that although I might find the site through formal networks, I would not get any assistance regarding accommodation in a village or other necessary assistance for setting up my anthropological research. I decided to try informal networks in searching for a suitable research site.

Informal Networks. Informal networks in many instances are more effective than formal networks in finding anthropological field research sites and building contacts with a study population (White 1992; Kotalova 1993). As a native of the country (I was born, raised, and pursued my education through the university level in Bangladesh), I was in an advantageous situation to explore the option of informal networks. The news of my return to Bangladesh with the agenda of doing research on the Grameen Bank had already spread among friends and relatives. To take advantage of my networks, I went to the alumni association of Dhaka University (where I graduated in sociology) and collected a list of fellow graduates. Of 250 graduates, I discovered three who came from the areas where I was looking for a potential research site. Their cooperation enabled me to visit these areas, but none of the sites fulfilled my criteria for the research site.

Finally, after months of angst, one of my university friends asked me to visit his father-in-law's village, which was in the Tangail zone. My friend knew that the Grameen Bank had been working in that village for the past fifteen years. This friend also assured me that there would be accommodation in his father-in-law's homestead and cooperation in setting up my research project in the village.

Settling in the Field

The study village in the Tangail zone is one of the oldest program areas of the Grameen Bank. The bank started its credit program in this village in the 1980s. The village had appropriate numbers for my study population—295 households, 154 Grameen Bank members (120 women and 34 men), and 12 bank workers (nine male, three female). The next step of the research process was to get settled in the field and then conduct the investigation. For me to use the anthropological field techniques of participant observation and in-depth unstructured interviews with informants, living in the community among the study population was necessary. Three options were available to me for accommodation:

1. I declined accommodation with my friend's in-law's household. The household is economically and socially the richest in the entire village. In Bangladeshi village social stratification, the lineage that enjoys the highest strata and members of this lineage usually do not mix with poor people in the village. Since my potential informants in the village were likely to belong to the poorest households, I felt that my stay with the richest household would jeopardize my interaction with my chosen primary informants for the research.

2. The Grameen Bank has a two-floor building in the study area. The first floor of the building is used for the branch office of the bank; the second floor has three bedrooms for bank workers and visitors or outside researchers. I declined accommodation with bank workers in this building, concerned that my staying with bank workers would identify me as one of the Grameen workers and jeopardize my research.[1]

3. I therefore decided to rent a house in the study village. This option was not immediately available and I had to wait for two more weeks for a house to be vacant for rent. During these two weeks, I commuted to the field from Dhaka (sixty kilometers) three days a week. At the end of December 1994, I moved into a rented house and maintained my own independent household

in the village with my wife and daughter until the last day of my fieldwork in Bangladesh.

The Native as Researcher, and Rapport Building

There remains a powerful debate in the anthropological literature on the issue of the "native" as researcher (e.g., Jones 1970; Hastrup 1990; Palsson 1993; Rappaport 1993). In anthropological fieldwork an "outsider" comes into the community and typically goes through "rites of passage," eventually becoming somewhat of an "insider." Anthropological knowledge is concerned with an understanding of other cultures from the native's point of view (Malinowski 1922/1972); thus anthropologists' "close association with the natives" (Hastrup 1990:78) becomes a precondition for acquiring anthropological knowledge. Margaret Mead (1977) wrote, "As the inclusion of the observer within the observed scene becomes more intense, the observation becomes unique" (6).

In anthropological fieldwork, "trained natives" with their intimate knowledge of the society, their familiarities with the informants' language, and their better understanding of cultural codes face less difficulty in becoming engaged with the study population. The materials collected by trained native anthropologists may have "immeasurable advantage of trustworthiness, authentically revealing precisely the elusive intimate thoughts and sentiments of the native, who spontaneously reveals himself [or herself] in these outpourings" (Lowie 1937:133). Franz Boas often emphasized the training of native anthropologists on the assumption that in describing the total way of life of a group of people from the point of view of the people themselves, it was the trained native who could best interpret native life from within (Jones 1970).

But it is important to emphasize that fieldwork in anthropology is not only an act of participation and observation in informants' lives and in their society and collecting information on informants' behaviors and actions, as implied by Malinowski and Mead. It is also a confrontation and dialogue between two different actors—informants and anthropologists—who are involved in the joint creation of "otherness and selfness" (Dwyer 1977:119). In any fieldwork situation, what the informants tell anthropologists may not be the "cultural truth" but the circumstantial responses to the anthropologist's presence and questioning (Clifford 1986:107). Hastrup (1990) argued, "There are implicated truths behind the explicit statements of informants to whom no 'native' has immediate access. That is where anthropological training and knowledge of the discipline are important to sensitize researchers to see inside from the perceptions of an outsider" (8; see also Appadurai 1988; Das 1994).

The local language of the village—*Bangla* (Bengali)—is my mother tongue, and familiarity with the language enabled me "to read meaning into the way a person says something as well as to record what is said" (Jones 1970:254). The familiarity with the language and the rural culture also enabled me to grasp other modes of communication, such as "kinesics—body language" (Birdwhistell 1960) and "proxemics—geometry of interaction" (Hall 1966). A researcher's insight into these modes of communication is imperative to uncover implicit meanings of informants' actions and expressions (Holy and Stuchlik 1983), and it also minimizes the risk of misunderstanding (Palsson 1993). The advantages of being native in building rapport with informants are worthy of some discussion and exemplification.

The main issue for my research was to study and document women's involvement with the microcredit program of the Grameen Bank to understand the implications for their households and societal members. I planned to gather information on women borrowers' interactions with each other in the loan centers, in their households, and in the community; information on loan use in the household; and information on household economies. The information required for the study was located in the social processes and relations of individuals (Berger and Luckmann 1987); it could be collected only through building rapport with and gaining the confidence of informants, both borrowers of the program and workers of the bank. In general, the anthropological literature does not provide any specific guidelines or strategies to be followed in the field to build rapport with informants. The strategies for developing contact with informants are different according to the issues in the research and the field situation. For my field research the following three strategies were important:

1. Observing informants' interaction with each other, understanding the logic behind these interactions, and acting accordingly was a helpful strategy in building good rapport with informants.
2. Finding common issues to discuss with informants and placing myself in fictive kin networks—brother, maternal uncle, or nephew—with informants was very useful and effective.
3. Putting informants "first" was another strategy employed in the field to build rapport.

In any field research situation the informants are the most resourceful consultants on the research topic, but it is the researcher who is dominant in power relations (Fluehr-Lobban 1994) and who determines the topics to be discussed. I would argue that the researcher's interest and ability to listen and learn from informants can bridge the gap between researchers and informants. To elaborate my argument, I present here a few examples from my field experience.

Introduction as a New (Natun) *Sir from Canada*

The Grameen Bank maintains a rigid structure of hierarchical and authoritative relationships between bank workers and borrowers in its credit program (Fuglesang and Chandler 1993; Auwal 1994). When any borrower of the program encounters a male bank worker, the borrower must address this person as "sir"[2] and must salute to show respect. This form of address and salutation is strictly practiced between borrowers and bank workers in the village and among bank workers in the bank according to rank. During my initial visits to the women's loan centers in the village, I was accompanied by bank workers. These bank workers invariably introduced me to the women borrowers in the center as a *"natun sir* from Canada sent by Dr. Yunus to observe Grameen activities in the village." I politely protested such an introduction, but the bank workers felt that my failure to keep a distance would result in the borrowers' disrespect toward me.

Becoming a Brother in the Village

In the early stages of my fieldwork, when I visited informants in their own households, they addressed me as "sir" and saluted spontaneously, consistent with the norms of the Grameen Bank. I disclosed my identity to informants again and again to make them realize that I was not a Grameen Bank worker. I persuaded them to call me their *bhai* ("brother," a fictive kin relation commonly used in Bangladesh rural society) instead of "sir." My effort to become a "brother" with informants was one of the strategies I employed in my fieldwork to separate myself from bank workers. It took more than a month and persistent persuasion to change my status from "sir" to "brother" among my informants in the village. Later on during the field research the informants often stated that it was difficult for them to call me "brother" because they were not used to it and they had no experience of addressing a person like me (a researcher) as their brother. My informants had encountered other male researchers, but they always called them "sir."

The Grameen Bank policy strictly prohibits close ties between its workers and borrowers; workers are not allowed to accept either food or drinks from members of the credit program. Hence, accepting food from the borrowers appeared to be a most effective way to distinguish myself from bank workers and a way to establish trust. In the early stages of the research many informants tested my identity by offering me food or drink (date juice or homemade punch). My first experience was to accept a homemade cake from one informant. The very next day the news of my accepting food from the informant had quickly spread throughout the village. The informant with whom I had the cake told others that she was convinced I was not a Grameen worker but a "real brother" because I had eaten food with her. Thereafter, whenever opportunities arose I accepted the offer of food or drink from informants. I also invited my informants to my house on occasion and eventually the exchange of food became a reciprocal practice between my informants and me.

The successful transformation of relationship between the researcher and the informants—from sir to brother for the researcher and to *bon* or *chachi* ("sister" or "aunt") for the informants—made it easier for us to interact with each other comfortably and freely. This transformation of my relationship with women borrowers in household units enabled me to develop "respected" ritual kin terms—brother *(bhai)* or nephew/niece *(beta)*—with men of their household. As the fieldwork progressed the relationships between my informants and myself became stronger. Later on, if any of my informants addressed me as sir others would correct them instantly by saying that "he is a brother, not a sir." Because of this relationship my informants not only shared many of their personal experiences with me as "sisters" but also rationalized to others—household members or villagers—the sharing of such information with me by telling them that they shared such information with a brother and not with a stranger.

Data Collection

The main method of gathering information was by participant observation and unstructured interviews. The strategy of participant observation allowed me to observe and document interactions of informants in different local settings (in loan centers, in households, and in the bank). Data from unstructured interviews were collected by me mainly from "primary informants"—120 women borrowers in the study village and 12 bank workers in the local bank branch. I conducted unstructured interviews with "secondary informants"—male borrowers; male relatives to female borrowers; and societal members, for example, village leaders—particularly if they were related to case studies of primary informants.

A significant portion of my information came from the weekly loan center meetings and from the meetings at the local branch. My attendance at these meetings provided me with the opportunity to observe and document interactions between peer group members and between borrowers and bank workers. The arena of these meetings was also an appropriate place for conducting unstructured interviews with primary informants. Direct participation at these meetings also gave me an opportunity to construct appropriate questions for generating information needed for the study. In the meeting center, I was able to ask direct questions about specific issues by using concrete examples raised during informants' interaction with each other in the meetings.

Data on household economy, loan utilization, loan repayment strategies of the household, and interaction among household members were mainly collected through unstructured interviews with both the primary and secondary informants in their own households. I was able to visit borrower households in the village either during the daytime or at night, at the convenience of the informants. Visiting households and interviewing informants there provided opportunities to observe and document both verbally stated information and actual behavior (Holy and Stuchlik 1983) in the household domain. Most case studies used in the analysis were based on these interviews.

Unstructured interviews, in most instances, do not have any specific agenda. These interviews often start with "open-ended" questions (van Mannen 1988; Nelson 1989; Patton 1990) on the research topic. This approach is strategic for the researcher in directing the focus of inquiry but providing flexibility for informants. By reviewing the initial interviews, an outline of topics for generating information from the fieldwork was developed. Topics covered in the informal and unstructured interviews with the informants were

A. Borrower experiences with Grameen Bank
B. Borrower interactions with bank workers (in centers and in the bank)
C. Bank workers' experience with the bank and with borrowers in the field
D. Interactions between peers in the loan center
E. Intrahousehold gender relations
F. Borrower interactions with household and community members
G. Household economies—income, expenditure, assets, and liabilities
H. Loan utilization histories, loan supervision, and repayment strategies
I. Activities of other nongovernmental organizations in the village
J. Social development programs of the Grameen Bank

Data were also generated from a household survey of the study village. A survey questionnaire was used to elicit information on village demography, landholding patterns, occupational and educational structures, and involvement of community members with various development organizations in the village. The household survey was conducted during the last one and a half months of the field research, after I had gained the confidence of the informants. I developed and pretested the survey questionnaire under a local supervisor, a professor of anthropology. The survey of 295 households was conducted by me with assistance from four locally hired research assistants.

Archival documents from the Grameen Bank and from other local research institutes were gathered. In the Summer of 1997, I spent one month at the Institute of Development Studies (IDS) at Sussex University, England, as Visiting Research Scholar. While I was there, I collected a broad range of research information on microfinance from various parts of the world. I used archival documents selectively in my work—either to compare my findings or to make cross-references.

Research Assistants

Two research assistants—one female and one male—were hired locally at the beginning of my field research period to assist me. Both these individuals have bachelor of arts degrees and work experience with local NGOs. To further enhance their competence in the field, they were given practical training by me in the study village for two weeks. This training covered the objectives and the issues of the research, an outline of topics to be explored in the field, and strategies of taking field notes.

After four months of fieldwork the male research assistant resigned from his position for a higher-paying job in Dhaka. I did not replace this assistant because at that stage my rapport with the villagers was strong and I was satisfied with the progress of my data collection and confident of completing the research without the male research assistant. Prior to the completion of the field research (two months before leaving the village), however, I hired four local workers (males; no qualified females were available at that time), trained them, and sent them to the village to help me complete the household survey. The female research assistant assisted me for the whole period of my field research.

Reliability of the Research

The information from the field research was cross-checked on a regular basis to improve the reliability of the research findings. Information collected by myself as principal researcher was frequently cross-checked with key informants and other informants in the village before it was recorded in the journal. The research assistants met me twice a day—before and after their day's fieldwork—and submitted their field notes once a week. I read their field notes and commented on issues to recheck with informants. In many instances, I personally went back to informants to cross-check information.

Because of my rapport with my informants, I was able to gain substantial knowledge about the informants' livelihoods. It was difficult for my informants to report "untrue" information. The assistants who helped me conduct the household survey filled out ten to fifteen questionnaires every day and returned them to me in the evening. As I went through the completed questionnaires, I often found that some of the information was inconsistent with things already reported to me by informants. Because this information did not match data collected from the unstructured interviews, I usually returned to these informants at their convenience and asked them to explain the discrepancy. The common response would be that I was their brother and they could not lie to me. But my field workers (who were from the same village) came with pen and paper, writing about the Grameen Bank loans and their family circumstances. Telling them the truth about bank loans may have jeopardized their future loans (see Johnson and Rogaly 1997). Discussing intrahousehold gender relations and household matters could be an embarrassment to the household, lineage, and homestead. This cross-checking of the information not only gave me the opportunity to verify the data but also demonstrated the difficulty and serious limitations of relying on survey research in a rural community.

Research Ethics

In this section, I describe how research ethics were addressed in the field, including the problems of using an "informed consent" form in the rural Bangladesh culture. Following the guidelines for ethics review of research submitted to the Department of Anthropology, University of Manitoba, I disclosed the purpose of my research to the informants. I informed them that I wanted to study Grameen Bank activities in the village and its impact on borrowers and their households. I also made it clear to my informants that I had no authority to approve loans or any influence in the operating structure of Grameen Bank. At the first meeting with each informant my assistants and I always sought the informant's consent to this research by stating clearly that participation in the research was voluntary. All but one borrower in the village consented to participate. This one borrower talked with us at the loan center but was unwilling to talk with me or my research assistants in her own homestead.[3]

It was virtually impossible to maintain complete privacy in the study village during informal or formal interviews with informants. Most often we talked with informants in the presence of numerous people. In the loan center it was generally in front of their peers, and in the household it was in front of other household members. In Bangladesh rural culture the concept of privacy as it is used in the West is almost unknown (Kotalova 1993). In rural areas and in the organizational culture of the Grameen Bank it is unlikely that any researcher could interview a person "privately." The presence of others and their side talk in most cases was advantageous to information gathering through reminding the informant about certain significant events or experiences (Auwal 1994).

Use of an informed consent form has become an integral part of social science research dealing with human subjects. The importance of this informed consent form is in obtaining personal and informed permission for doing research among informants, providing protection to informants through a commitment to confidentiality and anonymity, and assuring them of their right to withdraw from participation in the research without negative consequences. Obtaining such consent through a signature or fingerprints on a form is a Western concept (Fluehr-Lobban 1994) that is difficult to use meaningfully in many other cultural contexts.

In rural Bangladesh society most people do not know how to read or write. Those who know how to read and write are traditionally the rich and influential in society. Rural illiteracy has been exploited by the rich in Bangladesh for centuries for the purpose of land grabbing. Ample Bengali literature describes how for centuries the rich in society have deceived the poor by using their fingerprints in legal battles in court for the appropriation of land. There is a historically built fear among people in rural Bangladesh of signing or putting fingerprints on any paper. In the study village, it was thus inappropriate to ask informants to sign or put fingerprints on the consent form.

The real issue here is informed consent, not the consent form itself. Because some informants consider it culturally inappropriate to sign the forms does not mean they withhold their consent to the research. The issue of obtaining consent and becoming an insider has been discussed in some detail in the section on rapport building. Here, I argue that during my ten-month field research I lived in the community, encountered informants face to face, discussed the research on a continuous basis, and received important and scarce information. Furthermore, I was received well when I returned to the study village in 1997 for follow-up research. These facts reflect the intent and the spirit of informed consent. I further my argument as to the intent and spirit of informed consent by examples from the field that illustrate the relationship between a researcher and his or her informants and explain the informants' understanding of consent to this research.

Anthropological fieldwork usually occurs over extended periods of time and in the context of face-to-face relationships with informants. The nature of the research provides the anthropologist with negotiated entry to the community, which lends a dynamic character to informed consent to research. In many instances the reciprocal relations between the researcher and informants crosses the boundary of information taker and information giver and produces an emotional involvement—an empathy with and commitment to one another. They may become concerned about each other's welfare and may start to share each other's happiness and sorrow. This was indeed the case in my fieldwork, explained here with examples from my field research.

During the course of my fieldwork my wife and my daughter were away from the village on occasion to visit our natal families in Khulna, a district town located about 600 kilometers from the study village. During these periods, I generally did not cook for myself but had my meals in a household in the neighboring village. On such occasions many of my informants became concerned about my health and expressed it openly as *bhai moga hoye geche*, literally meaning "brother has become skinny." At this stage my informants were concerned not only about giving information to me but also with my health and my well-being.

In the rural society of Bangladesh children typically relate a nonkin male outsider to their elder male kinsmen and address the outsider male as *chacha*. As women borrowers were my primary informants, I became a *mama* ("maternal uncle") to children in a "patriarchal" village instead of *chacha* ("paternal uncle"). On one occasion, I was returning to my study village from a trip to Dhaka; I reached Tangail—the district town—at sundown. I was waiting for the next *tempo*—a three-wheeled motorized car that carries eleven passengers, who share the fare—to return to my study village. I was walking unmindfully at the taxi stop and heard a little girl shouting to her mother and referring to me as her *mama*. She was the daughter of Achia, one of my primary informants from the village. The girl was only five years old but certain about my relationship to her mother—"a brother"—and her own relation to me—"a maternal uncle."[4] In the process of my anthropological fieldwork my informants and I developed trust and affection for each other. This "mutual trust and, sometimes, affection" enabled me to conduct the "finest fieldwork" in the village (Wax 1971:373).

The protection of my informants from any potential harm emanating from this research is given high priority in my research. The anonymity of the informants and the community is strictly maintained in the analysis of research findings. The identity of informants is codified numerically and fictitious names (pseudonyms) are used in place of the informants' real names in the analysis.

Limitations of the Research

The gender of the researcher plays a significant role in the collection of information. A substantial number of studies suggest that male researchers face limitations in collecting information especially about women in patriarchal and sex-segregated societies. The common belief is that where women are segregated and secluded, only female researchers can hope to be able to get the "true" perspective of women (Papanek 1964:161–162). But James Gregory (1984) argues that this traditionally accepted view concerning the inaccessibility of the women's world to male researchers "is largely a myth" (316). He divides the informants' world into three scales of accessibility—the upper, middle, and lower. Information from the upper end of the scale can be collected from female or from male informants and the gender of the researcher plays an insignificant role in information collection at that level. In my research, information about loans to women or the use of loans in household economies would be at this level. The lower end of the scale is located in the female and male domains of the society, and the gender of the researcher plays a significant role in collecting information at that level. Information about women's sexuality is a good example of an area to which only female researchers may have access. Other kinds of information are scattered between the two ends of this range. These kinds of information can be obtained from both women and men. Men and women may, however, have different interpretations about the information in the middle of the scale, such as gender relations in the household or the interactions of household members of interest in my research. Information from the middle of the scale requires special solicitation and verification to ensure its reliability because of these varying interpretations.

The data collected for my study (see the preceding section) were primarily at the upper level of the scale. In addition, the primary informants—women borrowers of the Grameen Bank—have been involved with the program for several years; they interact every week not only with peers but also with male bank workers. These interactions made them more vocal and less hesitant to speak openly with me in comparison to other women in the village (also see Schuler, Hashemi, and Riley 1997b). Working as a male researcher on women's involvement with the bank in a patriarchal rural community—specifically data collection from the middle of the scale—was unquestionably a problematic issue, however. I was able to compensate at least to some extent for the limitations of my gender on information gathering for the following reasons: (a) topics such as women's sexuality, fertility, or family-planning practices were not the primary issues of the research; (2) I had a full-time local female research assistant during the whole period of my fieldwork who collected necessary information on topics at the lower end of the scale from women in the village; (3) as a Bangladesh national, I was able to use the native language and my own cultural knowledge to build a strong rapport with my informants; and (4) my previous research experiences of working with rural women in Bangladesh on contraception and the indigenous meaning of children (Aminur Rahman 1992) were helpful for this study.

Notes

1. During my fieldwork, a doctoral research fellow from the Institute of Development Studies (IDS), University of Sussex, England, was working in another region. She later told me that she encountered the same problems and finally had to move out of the bank office building and live elsewhere in the village.

2. The word "sir" has a colonial legacy and implies a relationship of superior and subordinate between two persons. These are forceful implications given that more than 95 percent of Grameen Bank borrowers are female and more than 90 percent of bank workers in the field are male.

3. At the loan center this particular borrower listened to me and responded to my queries. But when my research assistants and I visited her household she was unwilling to talk. The manager of the study branch heard about the matter and told me that he would instruct the concerned borrower to cooperate with me. I declined the manager's offer on grounds that it would be inappropriate to compel her to talk.

4. A finance professor from Dhaka University who has conducted research on the Grameen Bank once came to visit my study area. I shared my research findings with him and he was surprised to see the depth of the anthropological study. The professor wondered how anthropologists are able to gather information in such detail. My response to him was that in the field we do our research as "maternal uncle," i.e., through building rapport with informants.

3

Theoretical Framework

The theoretical framework of the study is presented in this chapter, together with an examination of selected concepts used to analyze the field data. In theoretical terms the patriarchal ideology, resource control in rural households, and male dominance in society are significant for an understanding of the Grameen Bank microlending scheme for women in Bangladesh. The patriarchal ideology of the society and its sociocultural institutions give entitlement primarily to men and deny women control of economic resources in the household. The authority of men in the rural household has a material base; men are expected to provide normative—family- and conjugal-based—entitlements for the survival of "dependent" household members (women and children). The normative entitlements to women in patriarchal societies in general are the primary source for women's social survival and economic security in the household and the community (Cain, Khanam, and Nahar 1979; Agarwal 1990; Kabeer 1991a and 1997).

Entitlement, Enfranchisement, and Empowerment

In the context of South Asia, studies of gender relations, economic resource control in rural households, and persistent male dominance invoke several concepts: entitlement (Sen 1981), sociocultural-based entitlement (Kabeer 1991a), enfranchisement (Appadurai 1984), and empowerment (Agarwal 1990). Sen (1981), in his study of the Bengal famine, first used the concept of entitlement to explain individual members' legal and legitimate (entitled) rights in society. Kabeer (1991a:245) underscored the sociocultural and normative aspects of entitlement and extended the concept beyond Sen's original emphasis on legal domains. "One of the significant features of gender relations in rural Bangladesh is the highly differentiated and asymmetrical basis of resource entitlements. . . . There is therefore a fundamental asymmetry in the *distribution* of material and normative entitlements within the household" (Kabeer 1991a:255–256; italics added).

Appadurai (1984) introduced the concept of enfranchisement for the enforcement of entitlements in a given society. Enfranchisement is "the degree to which an individual or group can legitimately participate in decisions of a given society about entitlement" (quoted in Agarwal 1990:395). Agarwal (1990:394) argued that the approach of entitlement does not guarantee its enforcement in society but entitlements are usually mediated through the socioeconomic and political customs of the society. In patriarchal societies, customary practices such as marriage, female seclusion, intimidation, and violence obstruct women's enfranchisement and their claim to legal shares in decisionmaking about entitlement (Agarwal 1990:393 and 1994).

Sen (1981) originally conceived entitlements as "the legal means available in a society, including the use of productive possibilities, trade opportunities, entitlements *vis-a-vis* the state, and other means of acquiring food" (53). Since the formulation of the entitlement concept, Sen has widely adopted this concept in his studies (Sen 1977, 1981, and 1983). Sen's entitlement concept, however, received criticism for its "legalistic view of social relations" and for ignoring the societal bindings and culturally based moral entitlement claims of individuals in society (Appadurai 1984:403; see also Beck 1991; Kabeer 1991a; Agarwal 1994).

Sen in part responded to his critics by adding an additional category of "extended entitlement" (Indra and Buchignani 1997:29). The concept of extended entitlements recognizes the socially sanctioned rights of individuals and the accepted legitimacy of these rights in society rather than legal rights enforceable in a court (Dréze and Sen 1989:10). In the development of the "cooperative conflict model" Sen (1990) modified his entitlement concept and presented it as "what a society sees different members are entitled to and what is normal for them to expect" (140). I argue that the "normal" expectations of individual members in the society may encourage the vulnerable groups, for example, women, to become "disentitled" from material resources in the household; they often give their consent to men's control of economic resources. For example, women borrowers in the study community "pass on" their loans to men; they become disentitled from resources in the household but expect to get "normative entitlements" from men for their security and survival. The interrelationships of "disentitlement" of individual women and "normative commitments" of men in the household is a self-generating (involving mutual consent) process through which male dominance is reproduced and perpetuated in the household and in the society (Cloud 1994:80)

The modification of Sen's entitlement and different basis of claim on resources—sociocultural and economic—that prevail in the society is useful for expanding the analysis to microloans to women. As Kabeer (1997) wrote, "Entitlements can be seen as generated through the rules, norms, and practices which characterize different institutional arenas— market-based exchange; state provision; and the 'moral economy' of community and kinship—and which determine who gets what and on what terms" (4). The sociocultural-based entitlement provides a framework for analyzing gender relations beyond the economic focus. The gender relations and activities in rural society are primarily based on socially constructed definitions of who is entitled to what and on what basis.

Formulation of a "disentitlement" concept and its incorporation in the analysis of "entitlements and normative entitlements" expands the theoretical discourse on microlending to women in patriarchal societies such as rural Bangladesh. The Grameen Bank extends its credit to women to entitle women to new economic resources. In the household women often pass on their loan use to men (disentitlement) or men may take control over loans to women (disenfranchisement), thereby transforming women's entitlement to new economic resources into a disentitlement in the household. Women's disentitlement from their loans in the household unit in turn reinforces their dependency in the form of normative entitlements for their survival that are considered to derive from men. In other words, this disentitlement is a way of reinforcing the concept of women's rightful place in the patriarchal system. As Kabeer (1991a) wrote, "Even when women have independent entitlements [credit] . . . they may prefer to realize them in ways which do not disrupt kin-ascribed [normative] entitlements" (245). This is often so because the gender-specific constraint on loan investment and risks attached to women in taking control over their loans, without any alternatives provided either by the lending institution or by the village social organization, hinders women in any individual or organized efforts to depart from the social norms of gender ideologies in rural Bangladesh.

I analyze my field data on women in the microcredit program and the grassroots microlending structure in the village with the conceptual framework of three main theories: (1) James Scott's (1990) "public and hidden transcripts," (2) Pierre Bourdieu's (1977) "theory of practice," and (3) Antonio Gramsci's (1971) "concept of hegemony." The theoretical frameworks of Scott and Bourdieu are significant in illustrating the disparity between the social, cultural, and institutional ideologies and the actual practices of individuals living and working in a particular cultural setting. Gramsci's concept of hegemony provides a framework for analyzing the production of cultural ideology and social relations in the society.

Public and Hidden Transcripts

Scott introduced the concepts of public and hidden transcripts in his work *Weapons of the Weak: Everyday Forms of Peasant Resistance* (1985) to illustrate the "passive resistance" of subordinate groups in the society. The public and hidden transcripts present two faces of culture: (1) the official views—societal or institutional representation; and (2) individuals' views—constructed in the sociocultural and economic relations with the "other" (dominators versus dominated[1]) and through their interaction with the other and the institutions. The public transcript conveys the notions of expected roles of institutions and roles, behaviors, and practices of individuals of a particular sociocultural and economic setting. In examining the roles of an institution and the relationships between its members, one often finds that the members "as a whole" consent to the public transcript. This consent is not only expected by the society or the institution but may also be strategic for individuals themselves, thus making the public transcript as if it is acknowledged and accepted by both the power holders and the weak.

The public transcript is not the "real story," for offstage in their own "social sites" individuals—specifically those who are considered weak—construct their own hidden transcript. The hidden transcript in most cases "represents a critique of power spoken behind the back of the dominant" (Scott 1990:xii); it contains powerful insights and directions for understanding the interaction between different groups of societal members and their power relations in the society.

Scott's central argument is that people who are weak and deprived in society find ways to resist the oppression or exploitation through constructing and expressing their own hidden transcript. The formation of the hidden transcript occurs in a wide range of autonomous social sites situated outside the surveillance and interference of the power holders. The hidden transcript is often expressed and discussed in safe contexts such as in a group or a friendship "beyond the direct observation of the power holder" (Scott 1990:4).

In my work, I expand the definition of public transcript to include the official view of the microcredit program of the Grameen Bank and the expected roles of borrowers in the program and workers of the bank. The hidden transcript is the covert discourse of the borrowers and the bank workers developed offstage in the course of the credit operation and discussed in their own group circles. I also use the hidden transcript to demonstrate the micropowers of the weak and dominated—bank workers and women borrowers in the study village.

The borrowers of the Grameen Bank consent to the public transcript of the bank by obeying the rules of timely installment payments. But the pressure (social and institutional) for timely repayment of loans and the payment of higher interest rates force borrowers to accept bigger loans to pay off their previous loans with new ones. This lending practice considerably increases borrower debt liability and creates the context for hidden transcripts of borrowers and their household members. The pressures on bank workers for installment collection at loan centers and the long working hours in the study branch also stimulate them to create their own hidden transcript.

Discovery and exposure of the public and the hidden transcripts in the study of Grameen Bank lending, informants' involvement, and their interactions present the power dynamics of dominators and dominated and the dynamics of dominance and resistance in the system. In any system, however, the weak are often obliged to adopt "a strategic pose" in the presence of powerful people in their own interest (Scott 1990:xii). For example, during visits by higher officers of the Grameen Bank or outsiders to loan centers, the public transcript of the bank is maintained by both workers and borrowers. The bank workers follow the rules of the bank in conducting center meetings. The women borrowers invariably act and speak according to the instruction of bank workers—the public transcript—instead of complaining about the loan operation—a hidden transcript—as the borrowers normally do in their loan center meetings. Bank workers calculate their job prospects and borrowers calculate the prospects for future loans. Here, following the public transcript is strategic for both the borrowers and the bank workers, but it is not an adequate portrayal of their real actions.

In the same way, the power holders (bank officers and workers) may have interests in overdramatizing the reputation of the institution not only to influence borrowers but also to impress outside observers. In the village I studied, I often heard stories from some of the bank workers in the study branch about the economic success of borrowers through Grameen loans and about their solidarity, but I found little evidence to support such stories in the village. Todd (1997) described one such "charming tale" of a bank worker regarding mutual support in the 1988 disastrous flood. The bank worker gave this account to her:

> In one of my villages many houses were washed away and children were drowned. One GB member was very worried about another member of her group. So she made a raft of banana stems lashed together and paddled to

her group member's house to see if she was O.K. There was no one there. Even more worried, she paddled back to her own *bari*. There, to her relief, she found her friend, also on a banana raft. "I wasn't at home, because I had to come and see if *you* were all right," her group member said. (162)

Stories like this illustrate and reinforce the public transcript regarding the social development policy of the bank and solidarity of members; for example, "We shall not inflict injustice on anyone, neither shall we allow anyone to do so," and "We shall always be ready to help each other. If anyone is in difficulty, we shall all help him" (the "Sixteen Decisions"; see Appendix B). During her research in two loan centers, Todd found that most of these stories narrated to her were untrue and she "grew increasingly sceptical of how much they represented reality"(1997:162).

The public transcript of the Grameen Bank is often used by academics and researchers to represent the operation structure of the bank, but this gives only a partial view of the process. It is also used by development workers to describe the harmony and success of development initiatives in Bangladesh, but this use also obscures part of the reality. The incorporation of the public and hidden transcripts to address the lending structure of the Grameen Bank enables me to present a more complete picture of the loan operation processes and the implications for borrowers and bank workers in the study community. At the theoretical level, the contradiction between the hidden transcript of the weak and the public transcript of the lending institution and wider society also exposes the dynamics of resistance and domination. The discursive practice—a hidden transcript—of the borrowers and the bank workers represents a form of protest against the system. It is a demonstration of power relations and power use by the weak (whatever little power they have and can exercise). The discursive practice of the weak on occasion constitutes a formal protest against power holders or the system, as demonstrated in this study (see "Spiraling Debt Cycle" in Chapter 7).

Practice Theory

The "theory of practice" with its three-tiered hierarchical notion of social structure—habitus,[2] field, and capital—presents a resolution to the subjectivist and objectivist problem (Bourdieu 1996:148). The theory of practice addresses the realities of social interactions and the implicit potentialities as these are unfolded in time and in response to the particulars of a situation (Schatzki 1987). The human experience is an avenue through which aspects of the social world are internalized by individuals, what Bourdieu calls "habitus." Habitus is an imbued disposition of "social agents"—in this research, the borrowers, bank workers, and community members[3]—embodied in the shared existence and social processes of the actors, and it influences individual actors' actions and behaviors.

> The notion of *Habitus* is central to Bourdieu's theory of practice, which seeks to transcend the opposition between theories that grasp practice solely as constitut*ing*, as expressed in methodological and ontological individualism (phenomenology), and those that view practice solely as constitut*ed*, as exemplified by Levi-Strauss's structuralism and the structural functionalism of the descendants of Durkheim. To this end, Bourdieu treats social life as mutually constituting interaction of structures, disposition, and actions whereby social structures and embodied (therefore situated) knowledge of those structures produce enduring orientations to action which, in turn, are constitutive of social structure. Hence, these orientations are at once "structuring structures" and "structured structure"; they shape and are shaped by social practice. (Postone, LiPuma, and Calhoun 1993:4; original italics).

Individuals' actions are neither predictable in advance as the product of conscious intent nor simply a "realization" of structure that already exists in the unconscious. The actions are the product of interaction between habitus and the "objective structure," which is played out by actors themselves with their practical engagement in the local cultural "fields" (Kleinman 1996:203). Habitus invariably produces actions in response to the particular features of the current settings, and in the face of changing circumstances the habitus also allows for continuous improvisation. Bourdieu (1977) explained, "Through the habitus, the structure which has produced it [habitus] governs practice, not by the processes of mechanical determinism, but through the mediation of the orientations and limits it assigns to the habitus's operations of inventions" (95).

not as mechanical as economics

The structuring principles of the society—explicit statements and instructions about what to do and how to act—are produced by the society or the institution. These structuring principles are made available to social actors, who internalize them to construct their habitus. The individuals, however, act within various forms of bounded rationality; they can hardly be perfect as rational actors according to the principles of the society or the institutions. Therefore, understanding social practice requires consideration of the socially produced means of generating strategies and the organization of the fields in which social actors behave and act (Calhoun 1993:81). The Grameen Bank workers become conversant about the "objectives and principles" of the bank through their extensive training with the bank (at least six months). Nonetheless, in their grassroots microlending they hardly rely on their theoretically informed habitus; instead, they often use their practical knowledge and experience for lending and recovery of loans and for conducting a "successful operation."

In the case of Grameen Bank workers, the habitus is an intersubjective concept, the site of the constitution of the person-in-action. It is a dynamic intersection of structure and action in socially defined space, which, in this research context, is analyzed as taking place between bank workers and borrowers. The actions of the informants in this study are objectively coordinated without being solely the product of structured principles, on the one hand, or conscious rationality, on the other.

The "field"—the other fundamental concept of the theory of practice—has its own history. "The purpose of Bourdieu's concept of *field* is to provide the frame for a 'relational analysis', by which he means an account of the multidimensional space of positions and the position taking of agents" (Postone, LiPuma, and Calhoun 1993:4; original italics). The actions of a particular social actor are an outcome of interplay between that person's habitus and her or his position in the field (Brow 1990). The field is semiautonomous, characterized by its own determinate agents—borrowers, household members, and bank workers—who have their own logic of action. The social fields are located in a "field of power" defined with respect to the internal dynamics of a class, based on differential access to power—sociocultural and economic: "The classes are located within the general field of class relations. Analysis of any specific field must, in Bourdieu's view, take account of its social and structural hierarchy. This view of social structure tries to link class and status, relate both to action and practice through the habitus, and provide an account of the reproduction of hierarchy" (LiPuma 1993:16).

The other key notion of practice theory is that of "capital," which is neither Marxian nor formal economic capital (immediately convertible into money), but cultural and social capital. Cultural capital is the credential of individuals—good bank workers or good borrowers, good wives or good husbands—and social capital is the social connections of the social actors (Calhoun 1993:70). The cultural and social capital entail the capacity of individuals to exercise control over their own future, and theoretically it serves to mediate between the individuals and the society. At the societal level, it is structured by the differential distribution of capital—males/females and bank workers/borrowers. The actors at the individual level are, however, capable of increasing their capital in the field of social actions.

Three elements (situations) in practice guide individuals for their moment-to-moment actions: (1) "forthcoming reality," that is, what is actually occurring in the actors' own setting; (2) "objective potentialities," which are things to do or not to do; and (3) ongoing action of the habitus itself. The individual action is the product of habitus in response "to objective potentialities immediately inscribed in the present" and the "forthcoming reality characterizing the current setting" (Bourdieu 1977:76). In the Grameen Bank program both borrowers and bank workers internalize the "objective potentialities," that is, the ideology of the program, and they are aware of program ideology. Nonetheless, the actors in the program act differently to meet the reality of situations and their anticipated consequences. For bank workers, the forthcoming reality of leaving their defaulting installments in the loan centers and returning to the bank office is to encounter the angry manager at the branch, to prepare to provide the manager an explanation of their actions in the loan centers, and to face the possible consequences in relation to job promotion. The bank's rules do not allow the bank workers to create pressure on borrowers or coerce them to pay installments but only to motivate them for regular payments. But the bank workers in loan centers do not practice these strategies for installment collections, and they rationalize their actions on the grounds of the forthcoming reality of the situation.

The practice theory of Bourdieu is based on the model of the "practical intelligibility" of individuals developed in the context of their specific social, economic, and cultural situations. Practical intelligibility "is what it makes sense to someone to do. It governs actions because people more or less always do what it makes sense to them to do" (Schatzki 1987:120). The women borrowers hand over their loans to men and often use the loans for purposes other than originally approved by the bank, sometimes for meeting household consumption needs, by making use of their practical intelligibility. They rationalize their actions, which differ from the ideologies, on the grounds of such intelligibility.

Furthermore, a number of factors determine the actions of actors. According to Schatzki (1987) these factors include

> the states of existence for the sake of which the actor is willing to act (e.g. goals), his or her ideas and thoughts, the rules, paradigms, customs, and states of affairs with which he or she is familiar, the events, objects, people, and actions that he or she encounters in settings, the tasks and projects he or she is are already engaged [in], and most importantly, how things matter to him or her. (120–121)

Social actors acquire familiarity with practices through encountering entities in settings that present, embody, and represent them, for example, stories, discussions, and group activities. The logic of practice comes to the actors mostly from the worlds through which they live. The bank workers in the village invest their best efforts to collect installments or approve loans to borrowers, but they commonly avoid the obligatory supervision of loan investment. Such actions of the bank workers are driven by their experience of working with the bank and by their everyday discourse in the bank. The bank workers learn from their experience

that one's reputation of being a "good worker" lies in collecting installments, not in supervising loans, so putting all one's effort into collecting
installments is a practical decision for the worker.

Practical logic describes the principles of the practical mastery responsible for ongoing action. The habitus plays a dual, sequential role in ongoing action. First, it composes a "definition" of the current situation and
of the function of action in that situation and then "generates an action to
fulfil these functions given the means available" (Bourdieu 1977:142).
The bank workers never deny their obligations—habitus—nevertheless,
they always put forward and define the "practicability of the situation"
to rationalize their actions that go against their habitus.

In the study village, many practices of both the borrowers in the lending program and workers of the bank are different from the official ideology of the lending institutions. The theory of practice enables me to analyze the gulf between the Grameen Bank's stated goals (the public
transcript) and its practices in the study village. Through practical needs
informants often rationalize such practices. The theory of practice not
only assists in explaining the distinction between the ideal and the implementation (praxis or action) in the lending operation of the microcredit program but also provides a framework to analyze the habitus of the
informants acting according to their personal trajectories. These trajectories stem from informants' interrelations with other members in different
local settings, such as in the household domain, the loan centers, and the
bank, and from the experience of their interaction. The informants learn
the way to accumulate social capital through their interrelations and interactions with others in the socioeconomic and cultural settings of the
society and the institution.

The Concept of Hegemony

Gramsci's concept of hegemony is used to explain the dominant ideology—patriarchy—and its use in lending to women borrowers and for
loan activities in the study village. The main focus here is to examine
how hegemony is produced and maintained through the consent of societal members. The idea of hegemony is central in Gramscian thought, but
his translated writings contain no precise definition of "cultural hegemony"; it lies "fragmented and dispersed" throughout his voluminous
works (Bates 1975:351). For more than thirty years scholars in the West
have tried to elaborate Gramsci's social thought and his political philosophy (e.g., Salamani 1974; Adamson 1980; Femia 1975; Anderson 1975;
Mouffe 1979). They have not, however, agreed on the meaning or meanings of hegemony. Kiros (1985) noted, "The concept of hegemony has
prompted a variety of interpretations; each interpretation has served as a

convenient tool with which scholars and activists alike have managed to produce their own Gramsci" (245).

The basic premise (with which very few would disagree) of Gramsci's concept of hegemony that I use for the analysis of my work is that human beings are ruled not only by material conditions, as the "mainstream Marxist" tradition suggests (Femia 1975:29), but also by ideas. The notion of idea embodied in the concept of hegemony is widely accepted as the basic theoretical point of departure and the central nucleus of the Gramscian conceptual system. The dominant groups in society establish social, moral, and cultural values as conventional norms and practical behavior of individuals; "Hegemony is therefore *the predominance obtained by consent* rather than force of one class or group over other classes" (Femia 1975:31; italics added).

At the theoretical level, the notion of hegemony—the cultural and ideological dimensions of subordination—provides a basis for a critical understanding of subaltern classes. Since the early 1980s the "Subaltern school" (a group of scholars, e.g., Spivak 1985; Chatterjee 1989; Guha 1996) has applied the Gramscian concept of hegemony to studying the dialectical nature of elite-subaltern relations in the social and cultural settings of colonial South Asian societies. The insight of Gramsci's work also has influenced the "post-Marxist approach" in anthropology and contributed to the development of new theoretical perspectives where "the core of the 'cultural' lies in publicly developed symbolic productions" (Keesing 1994:308). The clarification of the functions of these cultural symbols helps in understanding how ideas reinforce or undermine existing social structure (Scheper-Hughes 1992) and "who *creates* and who *defines* cultural meanings, and to what ends" (Keesing 1987:161–162; original italics).

Gramsci stressed the importance of "ideas and thoughts" in shaping individuals' actions in the society. The "social world" of individuals is determined by their relationships with others living in the same social and cultural settings (Counihan 1986:5). Individuals cannot act entirely on their own, a point made by Gramsci (1959):

> It is essential to conceive of man as a series of active relationships (a process) in which individuality, while of the greatest importance, is not the sole element to be considered. The individual does not enter into relations with other men in opposition to them but through an organic unity with them, because he becomes part of social organisms of all kinds from the simplest to the most complex. (77)

Although the dominant in society develop and propagate hegemony, the members of society give consent and also make it their own "culture." Williams (1977) wrote: "It [hegemony] is a whole body of practices and expectations, over the whole of our living: our senses and assignments of energy, our shaping perceptions of ourselves and our world. It is a lived system of meanings and values—constitutive and constituting—which as they are experienced as practices appear as reciprocally confirming" (110).

Gramsci relates hegemony in general to force and consent, but "cultural hegemony" is primarily obtained by consent rather than force exerted by one group over another. The cultural hegemony "is attained [and perpetuated] through the myriad ways in which the institutions of civil society operate to shape, directly and indirectly, the cognitive and affective structures whereby men perceive and evaluate problematic social reality" (Femia 1975:31).

In the paradigm "consent-consensus-hegemony," Femia (1981:37–38) argued that by consent Gramsci referred to the "psychological state" of human beings. This psychological state involves an implicit acceptance, hence conformity. Conformity is a consequence of fear, a consequence of habit, or simply the conscious attachment to or agreement with certain values of society with which individuals live. The given consent may also be "pragmatic" for individuals receiving benefit from the system. Cultural hegemony is also an "ideological consensus" in which individuals become convinced that their consent to the hegemony and their behavior and actions in accordance with the hegemony are also the demands of the society at large (Williams 1977; Godelier 1978).

For example, the bank workers in the study village conform with "patriarchal hegemony" because they want to facilitate their loan transactions and loan recovery from women in a rural sociocultural setting. Many women borrowers hand over their loans to men because for them "handling money is men's job." This notion is a part of rural women's cultural reality; it illustrates how hegemony operates on the ground (Scheper-Hughes 1992:200). The transfer to men by the women themselves of the loans allocated to the women may also be a strategy for the women to secure the future prospects of family marriages. The borrowers in the study village consent to the hegemony of the Grameen Bank to ensure future loans from the bank. In the same way, the academics, researchers, and bureaucrats in Bangladesh also produce and maintain the hegemonic discourse of the Grameen Bank to establish it as a development "icon" and to enhance their own reputations.

The grassroots local institutions in rural Bangladesh reproduce and perpetuate the cultural hegemony in rural society; the public institutions produce and propagate the hegemonic discourse on microcredit initiatives.[4] The grassroots social institutions are household, homestead, neighborhood, village, *shamaj*, and *shalish* (the village court) (see Chapter

4). The public institutions are governmental and nongovernmental agencies, academic institutions, bureaucrats, and research scholars in the society. The local institutions are responsible for the formation of the "common sense"—a general conception of the world—that informs the practical everyday consciousness of ordinary people in a particular society (Gramsci 1971:323–331). Through these local institutions individuals learn certain ways of viewing the world based on the dominant ideology (Counihan 1986); thus common sense becomes natural, practical, and transparent in the society (Geertz 1983:73)

Through its training and workshops for borrowers, the Grameen Bank—a prominent institution in the country—plays its role as a cultural educator in the village. The bank develops its hegemonic discourse from its grassroots lending and endeavors to develop a "Grameen culture" through its "Sixteen Decisions" and through disciplining borrowers (see Chapter 5). But the Grameen culture exists in the larger structure of "patriarchy" that consequently retrenches patriarchal hegemony and reproduces new forms of domination over women in society (Aminur Rahman 1996; also see Chapters 5 and 6 of this book).

The representatives of public institutions—bank workers, policymakers, and even some academics—produce and reproduce the hegemonic discourse of microcredit. They play important roles in sustaining the international prominence of the credit programs for poor women in Bangladesh. During the period of my fieldwork in Bangladesh, I interviewed several representatives of the public institutions. My analysis reveals that they obscure the realities of the microlending situation through quantitative representation of programs for local and international popularization.

The concept of hegemony is important for analyzing and understanding the production and reproduction of cultural ideology in society. In the study community, cultural hegemony—the patriarchal ideology—is constructed in sociocultural processes and maintained through the consent of both male (dominator) and female (dominated) groups. Analysis of this hegemony facilitates an examination of the roles of different members of the society and the roles of civil and political institutions in reaffirming the patriarchal hegemony in society.

The theories of Scott, Bourdieu, and Gramsci provide complementary theoretical frameworks for understanding and analyzing the ongoing contradictions of "ideology" and "practice" in the society. These theories also offer perspectives for examining the nature and relationship of dominant and dominated. The broad premise of these three theoretical frameworks is social class, however; none has specifically considered gender in the analysis. I argue that in these theoretical approaches gender analysis can and must be integrated and addressed.

The hidden transcript of women borrowers and its development in the village show that women are not passive recipients but are fully aware of their self-interest and their own situations (Agarwal 1994); they become active agents in the process. Bourdieu's practice theory demonstrates that the habitus of women acts in the field—households, loan centers, and the bank—according to women's expected roles or normative relationships with others and with the objective of gaining social capital. The actions of women may conflict with rules and ideology, but women act according to their "practical intelligibility" and become "philosophers" in the Gramscian sense.[5] In his theory Bourdieu also provides a boundary between the "field of opinion" (practice) and the "field of ideology" (doxa) that is crucial for a hegemonic struggle. According to Bourdieu (1977:169), the dominated have an interest in pushing back the limits of doxa and exposing the arbitrariness of the taken-for-granted. In the Gramscian framework, the struggle for hegemony is always a process of contestation and incorporation and of negotiation and resistance as much as accommodation. None of these processes, however, is either uniform or unassailable. The contradictions and distortions in the hegemonic discourse, as well as the discrepancies between it and the popular understanding of common sense, leave it ever vulnerable to penetration, criticism, and refusal.

Notes

1. James Scott (1985 and 1990) used "dominated," "weak," and "powerless" synonymously throughout his works. My use of these terms, however, implies that weak and dominated groups also hold power (perhaps less in comparison with the dominator, but they are not powerless).

2. Scheper-Hughes (1992:184–185) mentioned that Bourdieu appropriated the term "habitus" from Marcel Mauss's (1950) term "habituated."

3. The borrowers, bank workers, and community members have their own "social world" in which they interact and share their common existence and thus develop their habitus.

4. Gramsci divides societies into two components—civil and political. These two concepts have been used widely in Western social and political thought in various contexts generating different meanings. Therefore, instead of using the concept of "civil and political" societies, I have used "local and public institutions."

5. Gramsci (1971) maintained that "all men are philosophers," "every man, inasmuch as he is active, . . . tends to establish 'norms,' rules of living and of behaviour" (265).

4

The Study Village and
Its Socioeconomic Organization

This chapter presents an ethnographic overview of the study village—geographical location, demography, social organization, economic organization, literacy, and education level—with special attention to women in the village society and economy. The purpose of this chapter is to provide the background against which the microlending structure and women's involvement in the credit program are viewed.

The Location

The study village, Pas Elashin, is located in the Tangail zone of the Grameen Bank and in the district of Tangail (see Figure 1.1). Bangladesh is known as a land of villages. In Bangladesh the village is the lowest unit in the hierarchy of national administrative units (Figure 4.1), and it is often defined by its physical boundary. According to the census of 1991, there are 59,990 villages in Bangladesh, containing 79.9 percent of the country's total population (Statistical Yearbook of Bangladesh [SYB] 1994). Local variation notwithstanding, the basic pattern of the society is quite similar in all these villages.

The study village is located about 106 kilometers northwest of Dhaka, the capital of Bangladesh, and sixteen kilometers from the district town, Tangail. A concrete road *(paka rasta)* connects Tangail, the main center of trade and commerce for the region, with the study village. The residents of the study area can reach Tangail in twenty minutes by *tempo* (a three-wheeled motorized car) or by bus, which runs between the study area and the capital city, Dhaka, twice a day. It takes about two and a half hours by bus to reach Dhaka from the study village.

The largest local market *(bazar)* in the area (Elashin Bazar—traditionally known as a jute-exporting center[1]) and the *union parishad* (the local

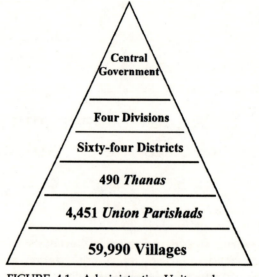

FIGURE 4.1   Administrative Units and
Villages in Bangladesh

SOURCE: Statistical Yearbook of Bangladesh, 1994

administrative unit covering twenty to thirty villages and run by elected
representatives) are located next to the study village (see the map of the
study village in Figure 4.2). The main social services in the Elashin Bazar
to which the villagers have access include the Grameen Bank, the health
post, one nationalized commercial bank, the post office, boys' and girls'
high schools, and one cinema hall (established at the time of my fieldwork). There are more than a hundred small businesses (retail stores,
tea shops, clothing stores, pharmacies, tailoring shops, furniture stores,
and sawmills) in the *bazar*. The daily *bazar* runs from 8 A.M. to noon, and
the *hat* (weekly market) is on every Tuesday afternoon from 2 P.M. to
9 P.M.

The Elashin Bazar is the center of socioeconomic life for the people
from the study village and surrounding villages. In the evening, many
villagers, particularly village leaders *(matubbars)* and the elected chairman and members of the *union parishad*, gather in tea shops in the market
and exchange their views about local issues and problems and also about
national politics. Women from the study village seldom go to the Elashin
Bazar, with the exception of the headmistress of the local girls' high
school and two of her daughters who are studying in Dhaka. They go to
the *bazar* to browse in different stores. The headmistress is a local woman

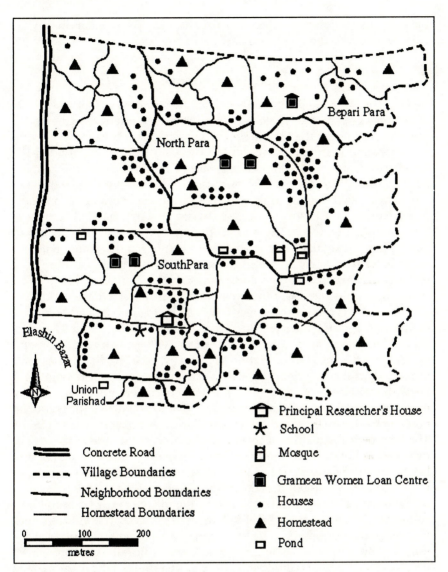

FIGURE 4.2   Map of Pas Elashin (The Study Village)

whose natal home is in the neighboring village. She is married into the study village and is known to local people for her outgoing behavior. Men in the *bazar* often talked about these three women behind their backs and stigmatized them as *ashalin* ("immodest"). Poor women who are Grameen borrowers pass through the Elashin Bazar on their way to the bank to receive new loans, but usually they cover themselves with veils or sit under the hoods of rickshaws.

Social Organization

In most parts of rural Bangladesh, houses are scattered so that one village often fades imperceptibly into the next. The British rulers were the first to impose an order on the seemingly chaotic settlement pattern of the rural areas to facilitate their collection of taxes and tolls. They divided the countryside into village units called *mauza* ("locality" or "ward"), which have continued to serve official purposes to the present day (Hartmann and James 1983:17). For people who live within the boundary of a village *(geram)*, the village is not only a space where they live, but it also conveys a meaning for their identity and affiliations. When a person speaks of "my village" it signifies the person's own identity and becomes a matter of pride for that person (Aminur Rahman 1992).

Social organization in the village is based on a distinctive hierarchical structure. In this hierarchy the *geram* and its *shamaj* ("village" and "village council") is placed at the top, followed by the *para* ("neighborhood" or "hamlet"), *gusti* ("lineage") and *bari* ("homestead"), and finally *ghar* or *khana* ("household"). The inhabitants of the village also categorize and understand the social organization in this way. To them, first comes their village, then the neighborhood, then the homestead and lineage, and lastly the household or family. Each level of social organization is led by one or more designated male leaders who are responsible for enforcing moral behavior by those within its boundaries (Arnes and Buerden 1977). The hierarchical structure of social organization in the study village is illustrated in Figure 4.3. I present a brief description of the structure and functions of the different levels of social organization (from lower to upper) to give a sense of the social arrangement of the village.

The most basic organizational unit in the village is the household, "a co-residential and commensal unit" (Wiest 1991:247). The villagers conceptualize the household as a *ghar*, or coresidential unit, but for local administration purposes the household is defined officially as a commensal unit—a *chula* ("cooking unit") or *khana* ("eating unit"). Like other parts of Bangladesh, the common form of the household in the study village is a "nuclear household unit" consisting of a conjugal couple and their children. As a commensal unit the household also may include married sons of the conjugal couple and their wives—"multiple nuclei household"—or unmarried and widowed persons who are either agnatic or affinal kin to the household head—"extended household" (Wiest 1991, 1998).[2] Data from 1994–1995 show the average household size in the study village is

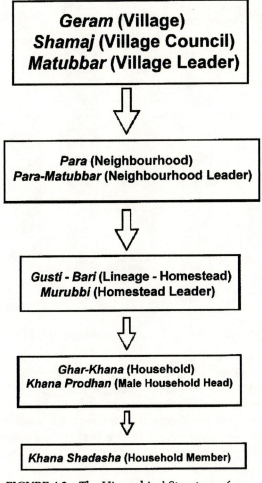

FIGURE 4.3   The Hierarchical Structure of
Village Social Organization

4.82 persons (Figure 4.4), lower than the national average household size
of 5.6 persons (SYB 1994).

Although the members of a household unit maintain several sets of
"dyadic relationships" (Wolf 1966:61), the household unit, following the
patrilineal descent ideology, functions under the authority of a *khana prodhan*—a male household head (Cain 1978). Through the *khana prodhan* the
household is agnatically related to other coresident units in the homestead.

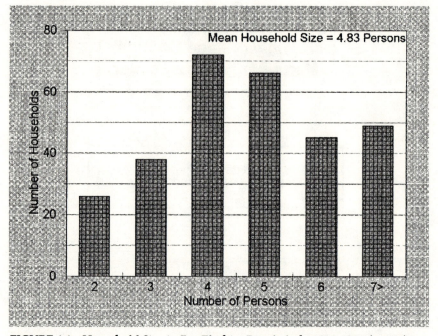

FIGURE 4.4   Household Size in Pas Elashin, Bangladesh, 1994–1995 (n=296)

Individual members are born and brought up in the household and it is therefore an area of close interpersonal relations. The social relations of individual members with other members of the homestead, neighborhood, and village are also determined through the household unit. In the village, the primary residential practice is patrivirilocal residence (wife moves into husband's father's homestead), but 5 of 296 households practice uxorilocal postmarital residence (husband moves into wife's father's homestead).

The practice of uxorilocal residence in rural Bangladesh goes against the norm of the patriarchal ideology. This residential practice gives the man low status in social matters in the village, and the status of the man is further reduced because of his dependency (socially and materially) on in-laws. In the rural culture of Bangladesh a man's dependency on his in-laws is seen as a matter of shame *(lajjar bepar)*. The absence of a man's agnatic kin in his own village or severe hardships and the absence of alternatives may drive a man to set up residence in his wife's father's homestead (Wiest 1991:251; Aminur Rahman 1992:37; Indra and Buchignani 1997:27).

In the hierarchy of the social organization, the *gusti* corresponds to the anthropological notion of patrilineage, that is, a group of people from different households whose males are agnatically related to each other. The *bari* ("homestead") refers to a space often surrounded by a physical boundary where a group of people with their distinct agnatic kin establish their residential homes. The link of a common male ancestor and coresidence provides the physical, social, and emotional basis of the *bari*. The *bari* is further embodied in the office of the *murubbi* (eldest male in the lineage), entrusted with the responsibility of maintaining dignity and the good image of the *bari*. The *murubbi* is also the spokesperson for members of the homestead and the lineage; he represents his *gusti* and *bari* in the community and in the *shamaj* regarding social, moral, and legal matters. The existence of a *gusti* is frequently revealed by its members in their daily language, and its honor *(ijjat)* must be defended by the members of the lineage.

The *para* ("neighborhood" or "hamlet") is a territorial-cum-moral boundary surrounding the community. For its population the *para* is a frame of reference for social and political activities such as exchanges of food in connection with life-cycle ceremonies and religious feasts. The study village is made up of three neighborhoods—Uttar Para ("North"), Dokhhin Para ("South"), and Bepari Para.[3] Physical boundaries between these neighborhoods in the village are not noticeable, but the moral dimension of each *para* boundary shows clearly in the manner in which villagers direct their allegations. For example, during the time of my fieldwork the Grameen borrowers from the North and the South neighborhoods often complained about the behavior of women in Bepari Para. Three borrowers from these two neighborhoods (North and South) withdrew their group membership from the loan center at Bepari Para. Their reason for withdrawing was the Bepari women's behavior; Bepari women were said to quarrel frequently with each other during loan center meetings (improper behavior for women in Bangladesh). In the study village, there exists a consensus among residents of different *para* about each *para's* place in the moral hierarchy (Kotalova 1993). The inter-*gusti* grouping within a *para* is achieved through the *shamaj*, which is rooted in the notion of "going together" (Bertocci 1984). One or more *para matubbars* (male leaders) lead the neighborhood *shamaj*, and through these leaders the members of the neighborhood are further linked to the wider society through the village (Jansen 1987).

The households in the study village are usually integrated in homesteads and neighborhoods. In turn, the lineages, homesteads, and neighborhoods are integrated in the *geram* ("village") and the *shamaj* ("village council"). The *shamaj* is "the largest intra- and inter-village social unit" (Zaman 1991:680); it is administered by a group of *matubbars* from different neighborhoods in the village. The *shamaj* in the study village consists of six *matubbars*. The primary responsibility of the *shamaj* is to conduct the village court to resolve disputes either by *bichar* ("trial") or by *shalish* ("compromise"). The following is an example of a *shalish* in which I participated.

During my fieldwork period, a dispute between two women borrowers (Rani and Yuri) in a loan center in the South neighborhood led to a fight among male members of two lineages in the *para* (this case is discussed in detail in Chapter 6). Two persons from the disputing lineages were physically injured in the fight. The manager of the study branch of the Grameen Bank went to the *para matubbars* in the neighborhood and asked them to arrange a *shalish* to resolve the matter. One of the two *matubbars* in the *para* belonged to one of the disputing lineages, so the other lineage refused to sit in a *shalish* with these *para matubbars*. The manager approached the chairperson of the *union parishad*—a prominent leader in the study area—to call a *shalish* of all *matubbars* in the village and resolve the dispute between the two lineages of the Grameen borrowers.

In addition to resolving and mediating disputes, fights, and quarrels among societal members, the *shamaj* in the village also holds the authority to decide matters relating to the moral code and conduct of individuals living in the village. The *matubbars* are responsible for maintaining and preserving the *ijjat* ("honor") of the village. In the study village, the *shamaj* is also responsible for slaughtering sacrificial animals and for religious and social feasts. On the occasion of *kurbanir eid* (Muslim religious festival), the rich households sacrifice animals (cow or goats). The male members of the households that sacrifice animals on this occasion must bring their animals to the *shamaj* in front of the mosque. The *matubbars* supervise the slaughtering and distribute one third of the sacrificed animals among poor households that are unable to make sacrifices.[4] Upon the death of a *matubbar*, the office is usually passed on to the eldest male member of the lineage.

Several studies indicate that rural elites, particularly *matubbars* and *mullahs* ("rural religious leaders"), act against the activities of NGOs and hinder their development efforts in rural Bangladesh (see Atiur Rahman 1986b; Ray 1987; Kramsjo and Wood 1992; Fuglesang and Chandler 1993). Todd (1997) referred to these studies and noted, "There are many stories of landlords and *mullahs* opposing the creation of new Grameen centres" (21). In my study village, I did not find this to be an accurate portrayal. Four of six *matubbars* in the *shamaj* in my village are from rich households (in terms of the ownership of agricultural land), and so are most other village leaders in the study area. The *matubbars* from whom I collected my information claimed to be supportive (with one exception) of the bank work when it first came. In fact, one *matubbar* in the study area gave one of his houses to the Grameen Bank for an office from which it could conduct its business. Sofia (whose case is discussed in detail in Chapters 5 and 7), the organizer and initiator of four loan centers for women in the study village, is a cousin of Zamir, a *matubbar* from the neighboring village and an elected member of the *union parishad*. I found that the only *matubbar* who withdrew his support from the activities of the bank in the village did so because of his rivalry with Zamir, who was a serious supporter of the bank. It is important to note that some of the *matubbars* now acknowledge that they are withdrawing their moral support from the bank because it is failing to bring real economic changes to the villagers. None has ever directly opposed the bank's work in the area, however.

The Village Population and Its Literacy and Education Level

The total area of my study village is about 0.85 square kilometer. According to my village census, conducted in August 1995, the total population is 1,428, of which 737 are males (51.6 percent) and 691 are females (48.4 percent). The population density of the village (1,680 persons per square kilometer) is more than double the national average of 755 persons (SYB 1994). The age structure (Figure 4.5) of the study population shows that the number of children in the 1–5 age group is 152 (10 percent), which is about 5 percent lower than the next age group of 6–10. This shows a decreasing birth rate in the village for the previous five years and is consistent with prevalence of contraceptives among both Grameen and non-Grameen borrowers in the village (see Schuler and Hashemi 1994 and 1995).

Figure 4.6 depicts the literacy and education level of the study population that is above five years of age. Three hundred and four persons in the sample (25 percent) have no literacy. One hundred and eighty-one persons (15.6 percent), of whom 105 persons (58 percent) are women, can only sign their name. The higher percentage of women in this group is related to the necessity for women borrowers to learn how to sign their name to receive loans from the bank. Almost equal numbers of women (118) and men (119) have completed Grade 1 to Grade 4, which supports other findings of the importance of education for girls to improve the prospects of marriage (Khan 1988). But only 98 (33 percent) of 609 women in the sample completed Grade 11 or higher, compared to 67 percent of village men. The lower numbers of girls at the postsecondary education level in the study village is consistent with national enrollment; in 1992–1993 the ratio of boys and girls in the postsecondary level was exactly the same: 67 percent and 33 percent (SYB 1994:482). Studies suggest stigma is attached to girls who remain unmarried beyond their puberty (Schuler, Hashemi, Riley, and Akhter 1996), which may add a

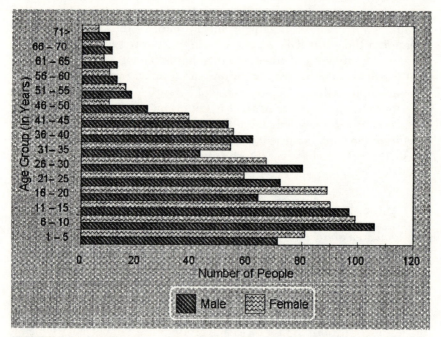

FIGURE 4.5   Age Structure of Population in Pas Elashin, Bangladesh,
1994–1995 (n=1428)

constraint on girls' education (Subrahmanian 1997). When girls finish
primary education, their parents tend to take them out of school (Khan
1988).

Economic Organization

The economic subsistence base in the study village is agriculture and
small business. Agricultural land is scarce in the study village, as in other
parts of rural Bangladesh, and primarily occupied by a few households.
Figure 4.7 shows the agricultural land ownership of the households. In
the study village, 189 households (64 percent) are landless or own less
than 0.5 acre of agricultural land. Thirty-eight households (13 percent)
own less than one acre of land. Only thirteen households (5 percent) in
the village own more than two acres of agricultural land.

The occupations of the villagers are diverse. The landless and func-
tionally landless households pursue various economic activities other
than agriculture. Male household members sell their labor in different activities in the Elashin Bazar, such as working as porters *(kulee)*, carrying
and unloading goods for different stores; working as wage laborers in

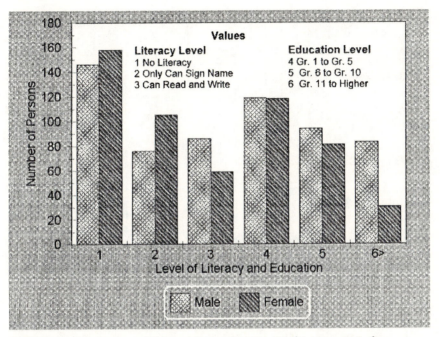

FIGURE 4.6   Literacy and Education Level in Pas Elashin, Bangladesh, 1994–1995 (n=1155)

sawmills; and pulling rickshaws or driving horse carts in the area. A few households also engage in small business enterprises.

Traditionally, small business as a primary means of livelihood was not typical for people in Bangladesh villages, and it was associated with low status for the household (Chowdhry 1982; Ahmed 1983). Increasing landlessness and persistent rural poverty in Bangladesh have contributed to increased emphasis on small business, which is now becoming common in rural Bangladesh (White 1992). Currently, the growth of small retail business enterprises is striking in the study area; a general trend toward a culture of business is visible. Even landowning households (households owning more than two acres of agriculture land) that are primarily engaged in agriculture also may pursue some kind of business. During my fieldwork I found three households engaged in *malrakha* businesses (buying seasonal crops during harvest time and storing them for off-season sale).

The geographical location of the area plays an important role in the development of business for its people. The study area was one of the first areas to receive the benefits of rural electrification in the country; more

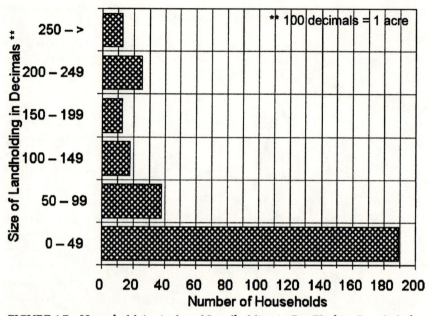

FIGURE 4.7   Household Agricultural Landholding in Pas Elashin, Bangladesh, 1994–1995 (n=296)

than half of the 296 households in the study village have access to electricity. The Elashin Bazar is located on the border of my study village. This market not only is the largest in the area (residents of other *union parishad* and *thana* come to the Elashin Bazar for shopping and trading) but has been known historically for its tradition of trade and commerce. During the colonial period the northwestern districts of the country were famous for the production of jute fiber, an important raw material for industries in England. In the nineteenth century the Elashin Bazar flourished as a jute-trading center, with eight British companies opening purchasing centers. These companies were run by Englishmen *(belati shahib)*, who were responsible for purchasing and shipping raw jute directly from Elashin to England to be processed for the world market.

In the mid–1940s, near the end of the colonial era, the British companies at Elashin were closed, causing a major decline in the importance of the Elashin Bazar. Since the 1960s plastic and other synthetic materials have replaced jute products, and jute consequently has lost its place in the international commodity market. Farmers in the region no longer produce jute for the commercial market and the Elashin Bazar declined in its prominence in the 1960s and 1970s.

Grameen Households in the Local Economy

After the independence of Bangladesh in 1971, the government built a road to connect the area of the study village with the district town. Since the new road was built, the area has become connected with Tangail and Dhaka, two big city centers, which has helped the Elashin Bazar to flourish again as a business center. The new road has made it easy for people in the area to take their salable commodities to cities for higher prices. The study area has also become a supplier of raw goods and commodities needed in city centers. For example, recently the Elashin Bazar has become known in the cities for its timber business. Three sawmills in the *bazar* process timber and supply products for construction industries in Dhaka.

The sawmills create employment for the villagers. In these sawmills eight persons from the study village work as wage laborers and three of them are from Grameen borrower households. Three Grameen borrower households are engaged in the business of timber cutting (*gas katar bebsa*). Male members of these households use Grameen loans to women in their business. They travel to different rural villages to find trees for sale and buy them from the owners, then cut these trees and supply timber to the sawmills.

Three households of Grameen borrowers in the study village run small businesses selling fruits and *sari* (women's dress in Bangladesh) and homemade pickles. The male members of these households buy their commodities from rural markets and commute at least two or three times a week to Dhaka or to Tangail to sell their goods. Six stores at the *bazar* are owned by members of six households in the village (none of them are Grameen borrowers). But of eleven households in Pas Elashin (the study village) that set up their shops every day in the open space of the *bazar*, five are owned by male relatives of Grameen borrowers. They sell commodities such as rice, vegetables, fruits, spices, onions, and oil.

Two male relatives of Grameen borrowers are engaged in door-to-door sale of cooking utensils. Ten households in Bepari Para are involved in oilseed pressing and sales. Four of these ten are Grameen borrowers who buy oilseeds from local markets for pressing in the mill at the *bazar*. The males from these households sell oil in the daily market and also in different villages in the area in exchange for more oilseeds, unhusked rice (*dhan*), or other commodities.[5]

Migration in the Village Economy

Labor migration—workers moving temporarily to other countries to obtain a higher return on their labor (Kearney 1986:331)—is a contemporary trend in Bangladesh. Since the early 1980s, the growth in the labor-ex-porting sector in Bangladesh (i.e., exporting skilled, semiskilled, and un-skilled labor, both men and women) to international markets has added a new dimension to the economy of many rural areas. To find work in for-eign countries, candidates not only pay large amounts of money, for in-stance, to private employment agencies based in Dhaka, but must also fre-quently visit and keep close contact with agency offices to find out about available opportunities. Rural people residing in areas close to Dhaka or in areas with good communication, such as the study village, can easily make their trips to Dhaka to explore overseas job opportunities.

In the Tangail district there are villages where one would find that at least one person from every homestead has migrated to a foreign country and is working there (for example, to Middle Eastern oil-producing countries or newly industrialized countries such as South Korea, Singa-pore, and Malaysia). One informant in the study village recalled that a few years ago going abroad *(bidesh jaoya)* was unknown to villagers. In a neighboring village the first person went to Saudi Arabia in 1980, and until 1985 very few people from the area went abroad to work. In 1988, however, an in-law of one household in the village[6] and a person from a neighboring village each established his own labor-exporting agency in Dhaka. Currently, these two agencies appoint at least ten local subagents in the area who recruit candidates from different villages and enroll them with these agencies in Dhaka. Two subagents are residents of the study village; one works in a nationalized commercial bank in Dhaka, and the other owns a furniture shop in the Elashin Bazar (he is also my key con-tact person in the village). These labor-exporting businesses are sec-ondary occupations for both of them.

Labor migration from rural Bangladesh to foreign countries and remit-tances to rural households are particularly significant. Research on the implications of rural labor migration is barely beginning in Bangladesh, but substantial literature is available from other countries. The studies by Wiest (1973 and 1984) of a Mexican town provide useful comparative analysis of the implications of the migration of male household members for household composition and household economics. Wiest's (1984:116) findings on Mexican labor migrants, regarding financing their trips and increasing their household income, are similar to what I find in the study village. In my study area, temporary migration to foreign countries and work there for a few years is viewed by the people as a way for house-holds to achieve upward economic mobility. During the period of my fieldwork, eight members of Grameen borrower households lived and worked abroad as unskilled laborers. Three of the eight are women who themselves are currently members of the Grameen Bank. People in the village who work in foreign countries regularly remit most of their earn-ings to their household economy. In addition to this positive effect of successful migration of household members, the households in the study village may also experience negative consequences associated with migration to a foreign country. I discuss here two such implications relevant to my analysis.

The trend toward migration abroad increases the demand for borrowing in the village for cash payments to labor-exporting agencies. The household head who wants to send a member overseas usually borrows money from relatives or moneylenders in the village. In 1994–1995, 14 of 217 loans to women in the study village were applied to the cost of trips abroad for a household member (see Figure 6.2). A few Grameen households also lent their loan amounts to others (relatives and close friends) either without conditions or as a moneylender with repayment conditions. Since households often sell or mortgage-out their landed property or other assets to collect money in support of laborers going abroad, landed property in the village is coming to be controlled by a few households that are supplying this money. As the remittances of migrating workers start to pour into the village economy, the demand for land increases, and so does the price. The remittances from abroad have also created a new group of moneylenders in the village.

Another dimension is that household members deposit their money with labor-exporting agencies and often wait six months to a year or more before they depart (if they are successful in arranging employment through these agencies). During this transition period the household must pay interest on its borrowed money, thereby building a debt burden. There are also situations where the efforts to migrate fail. During my fieldwork, I encountered two such cases in the village. After depositing 20,000 taka, one person waited more than two years and then still could not go overseas for work. This person was unable to get back the deposit from the agency. In another case, after depositing 50,000 taka for her eldest son to work overseas, Sofia (a Grameen Bank borrower) waited more than a year and a half. Just before I arrived in the village, Sofia's son departed for Malaysia, but after his arrival there he discovered he had traveled under falsified documents. Consequently, he could find neither his designated employer nor any employment in Malaysia. For the first few months he went into hiding with the help of fellow villagers working in Malaysia. During my stay in the village Sofia reported that her son had taken a low-paying illegal job for survival but he was unable to send remittances to his family. The son's trip to Malaysia placed Sofia's household in debt not only to the Grameen Bank but also to moneylenders.

Women and the Village Economy

An increasing number of women in Bangladesh now seek employment outside their homesteads. From the standpoint of the traditional norm of *purdah* ("seclusion"), acceptance of work by women outside their home has had a negative connotation for the honor *(ijjat)* of the homestead and lineage. The relationship between women, *purdah,* and social status is now changing in both urban and rural areas of Bangladesh. In urban areas elite and middle-class educated women now commonly seek salaried employment in both service and manufacturing sectors. In rural areas a growing number of women are being forced by poverty to seek work outside their homesteads and villages (White 1992; Zaman 1996). A large number of young women from rural areas now migrate to city centers and accept employment in export industries, particularly the garment industry.

Women in this study are directly and indirectly engaged in the economic activities of their households. In the study village the ideology of *purdah,* that is, that women are to remain inside and occupied with domestic chores in their own homesteads, is not strictly adhered to any longer. In a village society notions of inside *(bhitor)* and outside *(bahir)* are figurative, open to complex manipulation (see White 1992). In poorer households the scarcity of resources and subsistence necessities compel women to accept work with richer households in the village and sometimes outside the village. Even in rich households in the study village, where seclusion of women was followed strictly, women now go out of the homestead to perform some of their household tasks, such as washing utensils and clothes, bathing, and meeting other women in the village.

Women usually control household livestock and poultry products. In addition to the eight women who bought cattle with their Grameen loans, women also share-tend cattle, specifically milk cows and goats. The typical arrangement is for a richer woman to give an animal to a poorer woman to tend. The owner thus provides the capital and the poor women the care. When the contract period is over, profits are divided equally (if the cattle under care die, the owner cannot ask for compensation). Many women in the village also send their children to market to sell homegrown vegetables and fruits, collecting and controlling the proceeds of the sales.

Of 120 Grameen women borrowers, two women worked casually in and outside the village. They were engaged in cutting earth under the World Food Program's rural road-building projects. One borrower worked as a household servant (cooking and cleaning) for three Proshika (a national NGO) field-workers who rented a house in the village and lived there. Three women borrowers have now migrated to Malaysia and are working there in factories. Three women borrowers, along with their husbands, are running domestic-level small businesses (pickle making, weaving, and oil pressing). These enterprises are carried out in their homes. Wives and husbands work together and produce commodities for sale. The wives exercise control over both the enterprise and its income, and the husbands are responsible for marketing the products. Two women borrowers have become traditional moneylenders, relending their loans to other villagers. There are also a few women borrowers who are not directly involved with the household economic enterprise but nonetheless control the economic activities of their husband. For example, a woman borrower who bought two rickshaws with Grameen loans rents these rickshaws to her homestead members and collects the rent for herself. This borrower's husband uses her earnings to run his fish business in the *bazar*. He arranges and pays weekly installments to his wife and buys household necessities.

Most households in the study community are related to each other in social and economic terms. The majority of the borrowers in loan groups and loan centers come from the same village, usually from the same neighborhood. The socioeconomic and moral closeness of women borrowers in the study village, the control of the hierarchical village social organization, for example, the honor *(ijjat)* of the homestead; and regulation by the *shamaj* ("village council") all constitute powerful devices that ensure high repayment rates at the bank. The ethnography of the village, particularly the nature of its socioeconomic organization, provides a background against which the Grameen Bank lending structure and women's involvement with the credit project in the study community are analyzed in the following chapters of the book.

Notes

1. Jute, a natural fiber known as the "golden fiber" of Bangladesh, is used in making carpets, ropes, bags, and sacks. Jute was the main export commodity in the country until it was replaced in manufacturing by plastic and synthetic material in recent years.

2. Wiest (1991 and 1998), following the cross-cultural study of households of Hammel and Laslett (1974) and Hammel and Deuel (1977), has differentiated rural households in Bangladesh on the basis of the number of "nuclei." His study is based on analysis of 5,000 households studied in the 1980s (see also Haque 1988; Matiur Rahman 1992).

3. *Bepari* is an occupational group whose members work as oilseed pressers. The members of this occupational group are Muslim, but in the village stratification they belong at the bottom of the strata; members from other lineages usually do not interact socially with them.

4. It was the first time I observed sacrificial slaughter carried out under the supervision of a *shamaj*. I had lived and worked in rural areas in different regions of Bangladesh but had never seen a *shamaj* associated with this particular ritual.

5. This is a barter system—exchanging one commodity for another instead of paying in currency. Unhusked rice *(dhan)* is commonly used by women in the study area to exchange with vendors for goods such as spices, soap, and glass bangles.

6. He is also my classmate from Dhaka University who sent me to this village and gave me the name of a contact person (see Chapter 2).

5

Microlending and
Equitable Development

Since the 1970s, academics and gender-sensitive development workers from the North and the South have raised concerns about "equitable development," that is, bringing women into development as equal partners. In the 1970s and 1980s most studies on women's involvement in development programs revealed a negative impact on women and called for women's integration in the social and economic development process as equal partners with men (Boserup 1970; Charlton 1984; Afsar 1985; Mies 1986; Buvinić 1986; Agarwal 1988; Kabeer 1991b).

In the mid–1980s the programmatic success of the Grameen Bank microcredit scheme among poor women in rural Bangladesh became a demonstration of a successful equitable development initiative, establishing microcredit as the "common missing piece" in Women in Development projects (WID). The gender-sensitive promoters of economic development viewed women's lack of access to credit as a significant obstacle to equitable development. Their central argument was that credit gives women "entitlement to resources," so the more credit women receive, the more resources they can command and the more power they can achieve in society (Berger 1989; Bhatt 1989; McKee 1989; Yunus 1994b; Mayoux 1995).

The Grameen Bank extends credit in rural Bangladesh primarily to women through recruiting and organizing them in loan groups and centers. In this chapter, I present the process through which bank workers recruit and organize women borrowers in the study village. The recruitment process illustrates both the public transcript—philosophy and objectives of the Grameen Bank—and the hidden transcripts—covert discourse of members and bank workers. The illumination of hidden transcripts suggests the reinforcement of "ideological" domination over women in society and addresses the patriarchal hegemony as both "civil" and "political" societies are using it to lend credit to women (Gramsci 1971; Williams 1977; Scheper-Hughes 1992:171). I also discuss the social collateral, the importance of formal and informal networks of borrowers and bank workers in the loan operation itself, and the "social development" programs of the bank.

The Public and Hidden Transcripts for Recruiting Women

From the beginning of its microcredit extension project in Bangladesh, the Grameen Bank has maintained a mandate of poverty alleviation. The economy of rural Bangladesh is based on farming land and agricultural production. The livelihood of the rural population directly or indirectly depends on agriculture. Since the 1970s, the pressure of population growth has caused increasing landlessness in rural Bangladesh, which is a fundamental factor in rural poverty in the country (see Figure 4.7 for an example of land ownership patterns of rural households). The Grameen Bank started its microcredit program to alleviate rural poverty through extending credit facilities to landless households. The primary objective of access to microcredit for landless households was to create opportunities for the household members to undertake self-employment activities other than cultivation and to generate employment in nonagricultural sectors. Self-employment is intended to open income opportunities to landless rural people throughout the year, mitigating the present limitations of seasonally available income (Bernasek 1992). In the mid–1980s, the Grameen Bank incorporated social development programs in its microcredit project.

At the beginning of its operation, the bank extended credit to both male and female borrowers, with the vision of recruiting at least 50 percent of its clients among women (Yunus 1997:16). Figure 5.1 presents the membership pattern of the Grameen Bank and shows that until 1984 the membership was almost equally distributed among women and men. In the mid–1980s, the bank shifted its recruitment policy to focus primarily on women. The proportion of male borrowers among all borrowers declined dramatically from 55 percent in 1983 to less than 6 percent in 1994; the number of female borrowers during the same period increased by more than 700 times. This shift in the bank's policy has resulted in women making up more than 95 percent of the membership, totaling 2.23 million borrowers in 1997 (Grameen Bank 1998).

The rationale of the bank for focusing primarily on women—a public transcript—is explained by Yunus (1994b): "Women experience hunger and poverty in much more intense ways than they are experienced by men. Women have to stay 'home' and manage the family with virtually nothing to manage with. Given the opportunity to fight against poverty

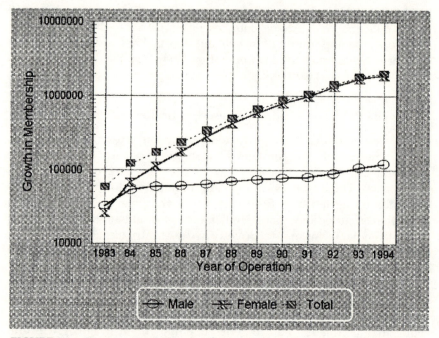

FIGURE 5.1   Grameen Bank Membership Patterns in Bangladesh (Women and Men), 1983–1994

SOURCES: Hossain 1988; Khandker, Khalily and Khan 1994

and hunger women turn out to be natural and better fighters than men" (40–41).

This statement by the founder of the bank explains the bank's ideology of lending to women. This ideology is based on the assumption that a woman's first priority is to invest her earnings on her children, followed by spending on other household necessities. Therefore, lending to women and increasing their earning potential brings more qualitative benefits to all members in the household than loans to men (Yunus 1994b:41). Lending to women empowers them to utilize their talents and skills and to increase their earning opportunities, and it also brings faster improvements in the socioeconomic conditions of the household.

Women in Bangladesh have always been excluded from institutional credit. By tradition rather than by law, women need the consent of their male guardian (husband, father, or son) to borrow money. This practice "limits the entitlement of the female half of the population" (Canadian Broadcasting Corporation 1991; Holcombe 1995:65). The Grameen Bank's vision of incorporating women in its microcredit program is claimed to have emerged in the context of the circumstances affecting rural women.

The public transcript of the bank for targeting women in the microcredit program is based on the following objectives: (1) to give women access to credit to increase their earning capabilities and bring faster improvements in the household socioeconomic conditions; (2) to organize women in groups to raise their collective consciousness, strengthen their group solidarity through weekly meetings, and assist them to attain a greater socioeconomic empowerment in society (for details see Ray 1988; Fuglesang and Chandler 1993; Yunus 1994b and 1997).

The hidden transcript for targeting women in the program gives a different picture than is maintained in the public transcript. In the study village, the Grameen Bank recruits only women members and excludes men from its microcredit extension program. Informants' explanations of why the bank now excludes men in the study village is an important aspect of the hidden transcript. In the study community, I found that in one male loan center there had been only four groups instead of the recommended eight for the past few years. Since this was an unusual case, I probed into the matter and discovered several male loan centers in the study branch with fewer than the recommended thirty to forty borrowers. Kazi, a male bank worker in the study branch, explained the reason for not replacing or forming new groups in these loan centers: "Our superior officers have asked us not to recruit any new male members and eventually to eliminate all male groups from the loan operation. The loan center previously had six groups and thirty male members, some of whom have either left the group or have been expelled by their peers, but we have not replaced them."

Kazi rationalized his statement in the context of "practical intelligibility" by explaining the "realities of the field situation" (Bourdieu 1977 and 1990): "In the field it is hard to work with male members. They do not come to meetings, they are arrogant, they argue with bank workers and sometimes they even threaten and scare the bank workers. It is good that our superior officers have decided not to recruit new male members, although we do not have any written instruction about it."[1] This statement by a bank worker—a hidden transcript—implies that targeting women for the program is strategic for the bank, that is, consistent with accomplishment of the goal of the investment and recovery of loans. Helen Todd (1997) noted this issue in her study, stating, "Mainly in response to increasing repayment problems within male centers, the Grameen Bank project began a shift toward recruiting women members" (159–160).

Patriarchal Hegemony in the Recruitment of Women Borrowers

The bank extends loans to women, but in the study community men predominantly use these loans and supply the installments to the women for their weekly payment in the loan centers (loan use is discussed in Chapter

6). This practice goes against the public transcript of the bank, yet all the actors involved with the loan operation (bank workers and borrowers) are aware of it. The borrowers and the bank workers have their own views on why women are exclusively targeted for the credit extension program. In the study village, both the Grameen Bank workers and the borrowers acknowledge that accepting women in the program is done because of the "positional vulnerability" of rural women in society. The positional vulnerability is understood and often explained by informants in relation to women's limited physical mobility and to their culturally patterned behavior (shy, passive, and submissive). The informants of this study rarely mentioned women's self-employment and empowerment as the objective of lending to poor women. Mafiz, a bank worker, said, "Women in the village are easily traceable. They regularly attend more group meetings than men. Women are more reliable and are more disciplined (passive/submissive) than men. Working with women is easier for us than working with men" (also see Goetz and Sen Gupta 1996).

In rural Bangladesh, patriarchal norms and values construct the gender ideology and perpetuate it with the consent of both men and women in the society. The literature on gender roles and ideology in rural Bangladesh suggests that women's status in society is intertwined with two concepts, namely, honor and shame (Arnes and Beurden 1977; Feldman and McCarthy 1983; Mandelbaum 1988; Kabeer 1988; Aminur Rahman 1992). As in other parts of Bangladesh in the study area, these concepts—honor and shame—are expressed in the two local terms *ijjat* and *lajja*. *Ijjat* has a deeper cultural meaning than its literal meaning of honor. In the South Asian context *ijjat* includes prestige and status, rank and esteem, respect and self-respect; "it expresses a salient theme and includes some of the most highly valued purposes of a person's life" (Mandelbaum 1988:20).

Most studies on women in rural Bangladesh (including my own previous research) argue that honor and shame and the status of women in South Asian Muslim society are linked with Koranic injunction (Jeffery 1979; Feldman and McCarthy 1983; Abecassis 1989; Aminur Rahman 1992). In the study village the concepts of honor and shame, although perhaps consistent with the Koran, have very little to do with Koranic injunction. They are most often used in terms of respectability and they mark culturally constructed norms. People's social values are focused on the status of women in society irrespective of religious beliefs. For example, a Bengali proverb, *lajja narir vushan* (literally, "shame is like clothes for women," but implying that woman's modesty is her nobility) is often expressed by both women and men and by both Muslim and Hindu in the study area.

In the study village there are extreme variations among women in practicing *purdah* (veiling or maintaining strong restrictions when meeting males; see Chapter 4), but women in the village in general bear more responsibility than men for family respectability, or *ijjat*. Women in society are expected to conform to "proper" behavior, such as shyness and passivity (indicators of women's *lajja*), which are dictated by certain norms, that is, proper levels of modesty bring *ijjat* to men and to the household.

The concept of *ijjat* is entrenched in the lives of the people and one is likely to encounter discussion about the *ijjat* of households and homesteads frequently during social interactions with people in the village. The *ijjat* of a household or homestead must be protected at any cost and increased whenever possible (Aminur Rahman 1992). Loss of women's *ijjat* in the household results in loss of public position for all the members in the homestead. Once the *ijjat* of the household or the homestead is diminished it hardly ever can be regained; "the loser, however, can live on the lost *ijjat* for quite a time before he and his family drop completely from a prestigious position" (Kotalova 1993:126).

In Bangladesh rural society gender ideology also commonly identifies women with modesty and purity (Aziz 1979; Blanchet 1984), which makes women's honor *(ijjat)* subject to closer scrutiny and more vulnerable in society than that of men. Vanu explained the issue of women's *ijjat* in this way:

> When a woman fails to make her installments on time, she experiences humiliation through verbal aggression from peers and bank workers in the loan center. Such humiliation of women in a public place gives males in the household and in the lineage a bad reputation *[durnam]*. In an extreme case peers may take the defaulter to the bank office. For a man, if he is locked inside the bank building for several days, it would mean almost nothing to other people in the village. But if this happens to a woman, then it will bring *durnam* to her household, lineage, and village. People in other villages will also gossip about it.

To make her point, Vanu spoke anecdotally of an occurrence in the neighboring Grameen Bank branch. Vanu heard that one woman in that branch failed to pay her loan installments for a few weeks and she was brought to the bank office by her loan group peers. The bank workers asked this woman to sit in a room in the bank and they locked the door from outside. Vanu reported that the woman felt so humiliated *(opoman-ito-hoy-se)* that she hanged herself from the ceiling fan with her own *sari*.

Such examples from informants, whether they are myth or fact, reinforce the significance of women's honor and its protection in the village culture. They also draw attention to the profound personal impact of shame. Therefore, to avoid any humiliation of the women in the loan center or in the bank, household members try their best to arrange women's loan installments on time. The safeguard of *ijjat* (women's honor) by men in the society—a public transcript—gives the lending institution an unwritten guarantee of getting back regular installments from its women borrowers. The bank workers in the study branch are well aware of the fact that in the household it is the men who often use the loans and who make the installment payments. Their explanation of the widespread awareness of this practice—their hidden transcript—is that the strategy of providing loans to women, instead of giving them directly to men, makes the field operation and loan transactions easier for bank workers.

In response to their initial involvement with the Grameen Bank program, 108 informants out of 120 women borrowers reported that male guardians in the household either sent them or influenced them to become members of the Grameen Bank loan group (see Figure 5.2). Male guardians of 8 female borrowers out of 108 reported that bank workers approached them directly and persuaded them to send women from their households to form loan groups. In exchange, the bank workers assured these men of loans for their own usage through the women's groups. In the study village there are several examples where women borrowers were not only asked or influenced by males but were forced to join the loan group and acquire funds for male usage. The experience of Bahar is an example of this.

Bahar was brought up in a conservative family and always observed *purdah*[2] until she joined the Grameen Bank loan group. Her household owns more arable land (two acres) than is permitted officially (0.5 acre) to qualify for Grameen loans. Bahar thus does not qualify. But within three to four years of bank operation in the village, a couple of women from neighboring households joined the bank and received loans even though their households owned more than 0.5 acre of arable land and did not qualify officially for a loan.[3] After that Bahar's husband insisted that she join the bank and get money for him. Bahar resisted and refused. Then her husband exerted pressure on her through verbal aggression. Bahar tolerated this aggression for some time and continued to refuse to join the bank. Finally, her husband warned her that if she did not try to join the Grameen loan group then he would send her back to her natal home and he would remarry. In 1989, Bahar joined the group and received her first loan. Until 1993, when her husband migrated to Libya as a manual laborer, the husband used her loans. He instructed Bahar to continue with the Grameen Bank. Now Bahar gives her loans to her brother in a distant village; he invests the money in his business and gives a share of

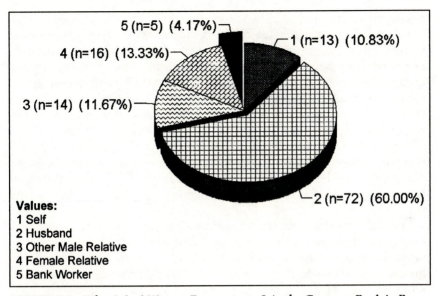

FIGURE 5.2   Who Asked Women Borrowers to Join the Grameen Bank in Pas Elashin, Bangladesh? (n=120)

the profit to Bahar at the end of each year. Bahar pays regular weekly installments from her husband's remittances.

The use of customary gender relations in targeting women for microcredit extension shows the importance of hegemonic ideology—patriarchy—in Bangladesh rural society. In the study village both workers of the bank and men in the household use this patriarchal ideology—women's positional vulnerability—in their own interests. The bank workers manipulate it to recruit and extend loans, and men in the household rely on patriarchal gender relations to use women's loans and to pay their installments. For the bank, reliance on traditional obligations in patriarchal gender relations offsets the cost of capital reproduction for the institution itself and thereby achieves a hidden transcript objective. The use of women's position to attain institutional interests and the interests of men reaffirms the hegemony in society (Scheper-Hughes 1992:199–200).

Organization of the Women and Social Collateral

The Grameen Bank is the first lending institution in Bangladesh to substitute social collateral (organized social pressure from group members) for material collateral (security, e.g., a pledge or guarantee) in its lending among rural poor people. The conventional model of institutional lending demands material collateral from borrowers. Poor people in rural Bangladesh in general and women in particular lack the required collateral to borrow; they are excluded from institutional lending services. The microcredit scheme of the Grameen Bank introduces the concept of "group lending" for the poor to overcome the limitation of the conventional model. In this scheme, the bank gives loans to an individual borrower through the group rather than giving to individuals directly. This creates a structure of joint liability. The group as a whole accepts accountability for repaying the individual loans of the group members. Thus, the group-lending scheme introduces "social" collateral, that is, organized social pressure from group members for its microcredit extension program.

The bank implements its microcredit program in rural Bangladesh through forming loan groups and organizing loan centers. The ideology of the bank in organizing loan groups is to make each borrower in the group responsible to the collective to enhance social solidarity. The women's loan center is intended to provide women with a space to meet with each other; pay installments; and discuss "social development programs," concerning, for example, health, education, the environment, and solidarity (Yunus 1997). The borrowers in the study village commonly stated that during the early years of bank operation in the village the workers used a good portion of their time in the center to discuss the social program with group members. In current practice, however, the organized group works primarily as a safeguard for investing money and for recovering loan installments from the borrowers (Bernasek 1992; Fuglesang and Chandler 1993; Goetz and Sen Gupta 1996).

The formation of Grameen loan groups is an "endogenous process" (Bernasek 1992:12) in which the bank leaves the responsibility to the borrowers to decide with whom they want to form groups (see "The Lending Structure of the Grameen Bank" in Chapter 1). The bank workers, however, give guidelines to borrowers for their loan group peer selection and hold the final authority over the group's recognition.[4] The public transcript of this endogenous group formation is to empower poor women through giving them the opportunity to decide on the recruitment of members. Nonetheless, the practice of "group recognition" by a superior officer of the bank (who is often a man) suggests that it is the bank officer who really holds the final authority to decide on the exclusion, inclusion, or replacement of borrowers, not the women themselves. The endogenous group formation by the borrowers allows the bank to transfer its cost of information collection about prospective borrowers' ability to repay. It transforms the individual liability of borrowers into joint liability and makes each member accountable for every loan extended through the loan center (Stiglits 1990; Varian 1990; Besley and Coate 1995).

A loan center consists of six to eight loan groups and thirty to forty borrowers. At the loan center the bank approves loans to individual borrowers in the loan group within the center by establishing a unique time cycle. In the first phase of the cycle only two members from a loan group receive loans. The bank worker observes their loan repayment behavior for at least two months; their satisfactory completion of the loan repayments entitles the next two in the same group to receive loans. In this credit scheme the individual client of the bank is kept in line by a considerable amount of pressure from her peers. The loan groups and the loan centers in this system function as institutions to ensure mutual accountability.

In all study village loan centers, I discovered the establishment of distinctive and independent cycles for every individual loan in the center. Each individual member in a loan center has her own time cycle in which she receives and repays her loans. Normally, not more than two borrowers in a particular loan center will belong to any single time cycle of the loan operation. These individual time cycles for members in the loan center create a conflict of interest that I illustrate here with a hypothetical example.

We assume that in one loan center there are forty borrowers. A, B, C, and D are four persons who belong to four different groups in the center. They have been involved with the microcredit program for five years. In January 1989, A received her first loan; B received her first loan in March, C in April, and D in December 1989. For five years they were able to maintain their schedule, repaying their loans and receiving a new annual loan. During the sixth year, in January 1995, D received her fifth loan of 5,000 taka. After receiving the loan D paid 500 taka to her moneylender, from whom she borrowed money to pay her interest and emergency payment, leaving 4,500 taka. At this point D loses nothing in quitting the group and not attending the center meetings. But the other three borrowers—A, B and C—will not allow D to quit the group, because they are almost at the end of their repayment schedules and expect their new loans in the coming months. In addition, they may have borrowed money (from kin or moneylenders) to maintain their installments with a promise to pay the money back after receiving new loans from the Grameen Bank. If D quits her group and leaves the center, then the prospects of new loans for A, B, and C will be in jeopardy. So the interests of loan group peers A, B, and C conflict with the interests of D. In this situation D will be kept in line by a considerable amount of social pressure from A, B, C, and other members of the center.

Tara, a center chief in the village, explained the social collateral from her own experience. As a center chief, every week she is not only responsible for paying her own *kisti* (installment), but she must also make sure that other members in the loan center pay their *kisti*. The bank gives loans to individual members but puts joint liability on all borrowers in the loan center. The bank worker "sir" comes to Tara's loan center every week. He sits on a nice mat on the floor of the center house and receives the *kisti* while the borrowers in the center quarrel and fight among themselves on the issue of installment collection. To make her point, Tara put forward a local proverb that the policy of the bank is to *bel diya bel bhanga*,[5] that is, "punish one person by using one's own people." In this case the borrowers take responsibility for recovering the bank's investment among poor women. The collection of installments in the center by using the borrowers creates feuds among peers. They become hostile to each other, but the bank loses nothing and gets back its invested loans.

In borrower training sessions before they join the loan center, the bank emphasizes to new applicants the importance of maintaining regular installments. Sofia, a bank borrower, explained that "even if someone dies in the household the borrower must come to the loan center, pay her installment, and then think about the funeral of the deceased." This happened in Banu's household, as explained by Begam, the center chief. Begam reported that Banu was a Grameen borrower for ten years and she built the loan center in her own courtyard. Banu's death one night in 1993 coincided with the weekly meeting of the loan center the following morning. The bank worker came to the center and asked everybody to submit their *kisti*, including Banu's *kisti*, even as her corpse *(lash)* was still lying inside her house unburied. The bank worker did not excuse Banu's installment that morning, and other members in the loan center paid it.

Following Banu's death the bank issued a condolence letter and approved 2,500 taka for the family from the emergency fund of the loan group. The bank worker gave the letter to the family and used the approved fund to adjust Banu's outstanding general loan from the bank.[6] The borrowers in this loan center considered the handling of Banu's case by the bank worker as an inhuman act *(amanabik)*. They brought the matter to superior officers of the bank during a one-day workshop at the study branch. The area manager responded that for "a Grameen borrower *kisti* comes first." During the period of my own fieldwork, I found that the deceased borrower's household is still paying weekly installments on Banu's house loan.

Ali described his experiences with the imposition of social collateral by peers in the loan center. During the early years of the bank's operation, if any borrowers of the loan center fled from the village without paying their dues, then other members would run after them to find them and bring them back to the center. He recalled one such incident in his own center, which occurred in the second year of the Grameen Bank's operation in the village.

During that time, Ali was the center chief and one member from his center (Male Loan Center 1) fled from the village just after receiving his second loan from the bank. He did not return to the village for a month. The other members in the center paid the weekly installments of the member who fled for two weeks but could not afford to continue any longer. The loan center came to a standstill for a while because the bank worker refused to accept any new loan proposals. The bank worker asked the borrowers in the center either to find the member who fled or to pay his weekly installments. To resolve the problem of the loan center, Ali and one of his peers traveled to Narsinghdi, in Dhaka district, which is 150 kilometers from the study village, to find the member who fled. They stayed in Narsinghdi for three days and brought the errant member back to the village. Ali explained,

> During those early days we accepted the Grameen Bank as our own bank. We did everything for the success of the bank. Now, after fifteen years we feel that the bank has made its profit and has become famous in the world but we are still as poor as before. The members of the bank have lost their hope and they are no more as concerned about the bank as they were during the early years.

Many borrowers of the bank in the village have expressed the same attitude about their concern with the bank. At the time of my fieldwork, however, I found that social collateral is still strictly practiced in investing loans and recovering installments from Grameen borrowers in the village. I encountered several instances where peer pressure was imposed not only on irregular borrowers but also on members of their households. When this peer pressure failed to convince the irregular borrower, then the institutional pressure (bank workers and bank officers) and wider social pressure (village *matubbars*—leaders) was imposed on the members of the borrower's household. Here is an example:

One morning I arrived at one of the women's loan centers in the village. Only four borrowers out of thirty-five and the bank worker were sitting in the center house. I inquired where the other members were. I was told that one borrower from one of the loan groups in the center, who came from the neighboring village, fled from the village with her new loan. This member was issued a new loan of 9,000 taka two weeks earlier. The member, along with her husband and child, fled on the night of her first scheduled installment payment. The news of her disappearance caused chaos in the center meeting. The female bank worker who runs the center refused to accept installments from other members unless they agreed to pay the installment of the missing member, but none in the center was either willing or able to pay the missing member's installment of 225 taka.

The bank worker was firm in her decision to not accept the installments. She made the point that since it was the members of the center who recruited the member who fled, and they who made the proposition for the new loan, it was therefore they who must be accountable for her installment. On the same day, this bank worker had to go to another loan center in a village two kilometers away for the weekly meeting and installment collection. She worried about being delayed in going to her second center of the day. Her delay in arriving there would allow many borrowers to depart from the center and create chaos. In the second center again it would take a few extra hours for the female bank worker to gather all the borrowers and collect installments from them.

The bank worker was also worried about the consequence for herself of not getting the escaped borrower's installment; she would be victimized in her encounter with the angry manager at the branch.[7] Therefore, she sent a message to the manager and informed him about the problem at the loan center. The manager, along with his senior assistant (the second officer of the study branch), came to the center and we all (the manager, bank workers, many borrowers from the loan center, and myself) went to the homestead of the member who fled. The manager called for the father-in-law of the borrower and inquired where his son and daughter-in-law went. The father-in-law, a man in his late seventies, told us that his son and daughter-in-law did not live in his household. They had their own household (nuclear family household), and neither the son or the daughter-in-law ever consulted anyone in the homestead about their matters. The borrower's father-in-law knew nothing about his son's destination. The manager then approached the borrower's husband's elder brother, who also was unable to help in locating his brother. As all these endeavors failed, the manager asked the bank worker to accept the other members' installments and to go to her next center.

The flight of one borrower with her new loan destroyed the credibility of the center and jeopardized the prospects of new loans for other eligible borrowers in the same loan center. The bank worker insisted that the other regular members in the loan center must find her or pay back her dues in order to get their new loans. Refusal to extend new loans to eligible borrowers in the center created hardship for the households of these borrowers. The male members of these households and the manager went to the chairperson of the *union parishad* and other *matubbars* and requested that they solve the problem through a *shalish* ("village court").

A *shalish* was called about one and a half months after the member fled. The father of the fleeing member's husband was asked to represent his son in the village court. After a lengthy discussion, the village court gave its verdict, explaining that the flight of the borrower's husband with a bank loan is not only an act of immorality, but it had brought shame to the village and also caused hardships for many other Grameen borrowers in two villages. The father was declared responsible for the act of his son and ordered to pay his son's dues to the bank within six months. The verdict of responsibility of the father of the fleeing borrower's husband reveals the framework of patriarchal ideology—the father as male head of the household or homestead must take the responsibility for his offspring irrespective of age and sex. It also reveals the effectiveness of the societal ideology as well as social sanctions in the operation of the credit programs in rural Bangladesh (Besley and Coate 1995:9). Juxtaposition of the public and hidden transcripts of the bank in this context exposes an ironic contradiction: The institution advocating individual responsibility and women's empowerment through a break from patriarchal hegemony is itself beholden to the continuity of patriarchal structures for its operation and realization of financial sustainability.

Networks of Borrowers and Bank Workers

An understanding of the formal networks (between borrowers and bank workers) and the informal networks (among borrowers in a loan center) is important for comprehending the loan operations in the village. The bank workers of the study branch, who run the loan centers, invariably maintain a strong clientele network with one or two influential members in each center in order to achieve smooth loan operations. These influential members are often favored by the bank worker and they are in a position to influence loan operation decisions in the center. In all five loan centers in the study village, I discovered an identifiable power hierarchy among borrowers. The influence of such power hierarchies on loan operation decisions also has implications for the aggression and violence escalation discussed in Chapter 6.

In addition to the formal networks between bank workers and influential members, the women borrowers in the center maintain informal social and economic networks among themselves. The informal networks, particularly those with influential members in the center, are strategic to the borrowers for receiving new loans in a timely manner and for getting loan group peer cooperation in times of crisis during weekly loan installment payments. In this section, I illustrate these networks and how they are produced and maintained in the study village.

It is possible to argue that the importance of building and maintaining networks by bank workers with one or two members in a center is obvious because of the current structure of the bank. The Grameen Bank extends credit predominantly to women in the rural areas of Bangladesh but through its male bank workers, who represent 91 percent of the total workers involved in the field-level operation of the bank (Todd 1995:187). Susan Holcombe (1995) concluded, "Grameen management has not had success in creating the conditions that encourage growing numbers of women to work with Grameen. . . . Senior management had not, by 1991, taken the strong measures, such as setting targets, for increasing women staff, as it did for attracting women clients" (93).

There is a common belief among male bank workers that female workers are not competent for the Grameen Bank work; women are seen as being unable to work as hard as men and unable to walk to distant villages for loan center meetings. At the time of my research none of the eight managers under the area office were women; the area manager and program officer were also men. In the study branch nine of the twelve bank workers were male. Female bank workers have often been accused by their male colleagues of being less effective in collecting installments. The manager of the branch stated, "Women bank workers cannot be as rigid as men workers when it comes to collection of installments." Goetz (1996) suggested that in village-level credit programs female field workers are more sympathetic to the constraints faced by women borrowers; due to their exclusion from most male networks they are less susceptible to co-optation by local male elites than their male colleagues.

Bank policy does not allow hiring of local male workers; therefore, all bank workers who work in a local branch are outsiders. The patriarchal norms of the rural society create obstacles for outsider male bank workers in contacting local women directly for organizing them in the credit program. These obstacles are resolved by utilizing the patriarchal hegemony—men as decisionmakers—through the mediation of household males. As bank workers at the study branch explained, "In establishing a new loan center in a new village the common practice of a male bank worker is to first approach a few men from the prospective borrowers' households and ask them to send their women to form loan groups. After the contact is made these women then organize other interested women in loan groups and set up their loan center."

There are at least two apparent consequences in establishing a loan center this way: (1) women who are first contacted through their men and given the responsibility of recruiting other members for the loan center accumulate some power in the process and they often become influential members in the center; and (2) the possibility arises for a bank worker to transfer his own responsibility for organizing loan groups to the women who are contacted first. This process indirectly contributes to the creation of a power hierarchy and uses this hierarchy to facilitate loan operations in the center. Even though female bank workers were able to contact women borrowers directly, in two village loan centers they maintained and used the power hierarchy of the borrowers for their loan operation. For these women, using the power hierarchy of borrowers in loan approval and installment collections is strategic to the development of a reputation for installment collection from borrowers; it increases bank workers' "cultural capital" and thereby enhances loan center operation.

I illustrate here the initiation and development of the loan centers for women in the village, which exemplifies the process through which borrower power hierarchies are built and maintained in the loan operation. There are five female loan centers in the study village. Ali's wife, Khatun, started the first women's loan center in Bepari Para in May 1980. Most borrowers in the first two loan groups were wives of male borrowers. In the study village the Bepari clan has the lowest social status, and not many women from other lineages in the village were interested in joining the loan center in the Bepari neighborhood. Sofia heard about the bank and became interested in joining the bank to borrow money for her husband's business. Her husband did not allow her to go to the loan center in Bepari Para, so she talked with a bank worker about her interest and asked his permission to organize loan groups and establish a loan center in Dhokkin Para.

Sofia, the most influential member of the study branch, thus started the second women's loan center in the village. She worked hard for more than a month to organize the first two loan groups to start this second center. Most women she approached were afraid and not interested in joining the bank. So she organized loan groups with her own relatives;[8] ritual kin; close friends from the neighborhood; and a few borrowers from her natal village, located near the study village. After forming two loan groups and establishing a loan center in a neighbor's homestead, Sofia started the center in June 1980. She became the first center chief and held the position for many years.

Sofia established three more loan centers for women in the village on her own initiative. She encouraged her own relatives to start all three centers but retained some power to recruit borrowers for these centers. At the time of my fieldwork, I found that Sofia maintained close contact with the starters of these loan centers and thus influenced decisionmaking. Sofia claimed that her leadership as a center chief and her hard work among other women in the village encouraged many borrowers to form loan groups to join her center. At the end of 1983, her loan center was full and unable to accept more borrowers.

In 1986, the bank worker asked Sofia to organize and start another new center (the third) in the village. After six years of bank lending operations in the village, most people knew about Grameen Bank activities. Many

women used to go to Sofia for her permission to start new loan groups
and open another loan center. Sofia gave the responsibility to start the
third loan center for women in the village to one of her *jaa* ("husband's
patrilateral parallel cousin's wife") but retained most of its member recruitment authority for herself. The third center, in which most borrowers are Sofia's relatives and quasi-kin, started its loan operation in April
1987. The *kendra ghar* ("loan center") of the third center is built on the
same homestead as Sofia's first one, and during my fieldwork the scheduled day of the weekly meetings of these two centers was the same day.
Such strategic settings for loan operations have enabled Sofia to retain
the loyalty of other borrowers toward her and to maintain her informal
network with her own people in the centers. The bank workers who
come to run these and other loan centers in the village always keep close
relations with Sofia, listen to her decisions about new loan approvals,
and use her influence in their centers to collect installments.

The last two centers in the village were established in 1989 and 1993.
The fourth center was organized and started by Rani, a niece (patrilateral
parallel cousin's daughter) to Sofia who is married into the study village.
Rani belongs to a landless household and Rani's husband casually works
in the Elashin Bazar sawmill. Even though Rani qualified to become a
Grameen borrower, her request for a membership in Sofia's loan center
was refused for many years by her aunt. Rani's husband and their son
are known in the village as big gamblers. Sofia was afraid that Rani's
husband may gamble with the loan money, which would cause problems
not only for Rani in paying her installments but also for Sofia's loan center. But Rani was persistent and eventually convinced her aunt *(fufu)* to
talk with the bank worker in favor of the new loan center. In 1989, Sofia
obtained verbal permission for her niece to start a new center on Rani's
own homestead.

Rani organized loan groups by recruiting women from her own homestead, from the neighborhood, and from her natal village. She built a
small hut as center house *(kendra ghar)* on her own homestead by collecting money from newly recruited members prior to the beginning of operations in April 1989. The fifth loan center in the village was also organized by Rani, who selected the first center chief; it has been operating in
Rani's *kendra ghar* since December 1993. In February 1994, two months
after the initiation of the fifth center in the village, Rani's eldest daughter,
Rubi, who is married but living in her natal home, joined this fifth center
loan group and became the center chief.

The Grameen Bank constitution *(Bidhimala)* states, "All the members of
the group must be inhabitants of the same village" (Section 3.3; see Appendix C). The constitution also discourages borrowers from forming
loan groups with close relatives (Sections 3.3, 3.5, and 3.6). The example

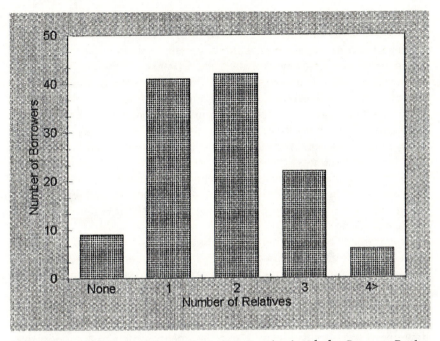

FIGURE 5.3   Relatives of Women Borrowers Involved with the Grameen Bank in Pas Elashin, Bangladesh, 1994–1995 (n=120)

shows, however, that Grameen borrowers in the village commonly establish and maintain their networks in the loan centers through relatives who are also Grameen members. Figure 5.3 shows that only 9 of the 120 women borrowers are without any relatives who are also Grameen Bank borrowers. Forty-one borrowers have at least one relative, 42 have two, 42 have three, and 6 have four or more relatives involved with the credit program of the Grameen Bank. There are also thirty-three households in which both husbands and wives have become Grameen borrowers.

The constitution sets forth regulations concerning election of group chairs and center chiefs, which should be done once in every year by the borrowers at the loan center. The group chairs and secretaries are to be elected by the group members in the month of Chaitra (the last month of the Bengali calendar year). Then the group chairs of each center elect a center chief every year in Asharh (third month of the Bengali calendar year: *Bidhimala*, Sections 3.7 and 10.2; see Appendix C). According to the Grameen *Bidhimala*, or Constitution, the elected officeholders in the loan center serve for one year and they cannot be reelected until all the other members have had their opportunity to serve in leadership positions (see also Bernasek 1992; Holcombe 1995).

The intent of setting up a structure of officeholders in the loan center is to facilitate a smooth loan operation by transferring accountability to the center leaders and ensuring regular payments of installments. The public transcript of electing new members each year to fill the positions in the center is to create leadership among poor women in rural Bangladesh and raise their self-confidence. According to my findings on loan centers in the study village, however, the original leadership of four centers was held by one member (Sofia). This one member then selected the leaders from among the borrowers in the center who are her kin, such as Rani and Rubi, but retained the authority to influence the decisions of these loan centers. Over the past ten to fifteen years the leadership in the loan centers in the study village was nominally handed to different persons, but in reality it was Sofia and Rani who retained control of loan operation decisionmaking.

I mentioned earlier in this section that the influential members in each loan center very commonly gain power as the organizers and the initiators of the center. By starting the loan center, they gain some authority to decide about the recruitment of peers. Through the loan operation activities in the center they develop a power position and status in the center. The organizers of the centers hold the position of center chief for the first few years and then typically hand the position over to someone from their own network but still in their sphere of influence. In 1994–1995, in two village loan centers out of five the initiators of the center were center chiefs; in the other three they are not center chiefs de jure but they hold de facto power, as they decide almost every issue in the center.

Perpetuation of such power relations in the loan centers is supposedly contradictory to Grameen Bank ideology, yet such power hierarchies have been noted in another study in Bangladesh (see Todd 1997). The bank workers in the local office not only recognize this power hierarchy in the loan centers but use the power structure to their own benefit. The bank workers report that influential members in the centers are helpful in conducting loan center operations. Influential members take the responsibility for installment collection from other members and ease the stress and burden of the bank workers.

The Social Development Initiatives of the Bank

In this section, I discuss the social development initiatives of the Grameen Bank. The interaction among borrowers and between borrowers and bank workers in the loan center illuminates the "rituals" of the bank—chanting slogans and performing physical exercise.

In 1984, after eight years of operation in rural Bangladesh, the bank introduced a comprehensive social development plan with various components for the borrowers. The Grameen "social development constitution" was said to be first formulated by women borrowers in a national workshop and then it was incorporated in the public transcript of the bank for propagation among members of the credit program (Fuglesang and Chandler 1993:120). The social development constitution of the bank, also known as the "Sixteen Decisions," concerns improved social practices to be implemented by all members of the Grameen Bank for their social, economic, and human development (see Appendix B). The prime objective of the Sixteen Decisions is to focus on fundamental social change among poor women in rural Bangladesh. Introduction of these decisions in the public transcript has brought recognition to the bank as an institution for the socioeconomic development and empowerment of women rather than a strictly economic development enterprise (Fuglesang and Chandler 1993).

The initiatives of social development start with the agreement of the members of the credit program to abide by the bank's four fundamental principles, that is, discipline, unity, courage, and hard work in every aspect of their lives. The members pledge to educate their children through center schools, ban dowries in their children's marriages, build better houses, and use pit latrines. In its public transcript the bank stresses that members of the credit program not only memorize the Sixteen Decisions but must practice them in their everyday lives. The process of indoctrination of the Sixteen Decisions in individual borrowers starts in the training sessions before they join the bank; members must continue their learning through regular participation in weekly center meetings in the village and through attending socioeconomic workshops occasionally organized by the bank (Khandker, Khalily, and Khan 1994; Yunus 1997).

In the study village, members who joined the bank during the early years of its operation recalled that they went through learning sessions provided by the bank workers and their loan group peers to become educated about the bank and learn how to write their names. Most women borrowers do not have any formal education (schooling) and do not know how to write or read. Borrowers must know how to write their name on loan applications before their loans can be approved, however (see Figure 4.6). Many women borrowers excitedly recounted to me their memories of learning how to sign their name. Sofia said, "We spent many hours before joining the bank to practice how to write the letters required to compose our names. We could not afford to buy paper and pen; we wrote on earth with bamboo sticks and did it not only during the formal training session but also when we cooked or sat and gossiped with other women in the homestead."

In the study village, I found five women borrowers who changed their given names, because they are long and complicated, and took new short

and easier-to-write names in order to join the bank and obtain loans.
Whether the names are given or arranged, the informants' ability to write
their name is a source of pride and encouragement for literacy for the
poor women in the village.

Both female and male borrowers in the village who joined the
Grameen Bank credit program in the 1980s remember that during the
early years of bank operation bank workers emphasized heavily the importance of the Sixteen Decisions. As Hafiza, who joined the bank in
1980, reported,

> Unlike now, every weekly meeting of the center had to start with slogans of
> four Grameen principles: "discipline, unity, courage, and hard work—we
> shall follow and advance these in all walks of our lives," and practice of reg-
> ular physical exercise. "Sir" [the bank worker] spent a good portion of his
> time in the center discussing the importance of practicing the *Sholo Shidhanto*
> [Sixteen Decisions]. Members were encouraged to adopt the components of
> the Sixteen Decisions in their daily lives.

Hafiza, however, emphasized that the Grameen Bank now has become a
kistir bank (having the main objective of collecting installments) and has
lost its agenda regarding the *Sholo Shidhanto*. Such shifts in program
agendas are also reported from other microlending institutions in
Bangladesh. Montgomery (1995) reported in his study on the Bangladesh
Rural Advancement Committee (BRAC), "Unlike in previous years,
when field staff were ideally 'facilitators' for strengthening solidarity
groups (VOs) [Village Organizations] into village level institutions, present day RDP [Rural Development Program] staff are more likely to perceive themselves (and be perceived by members) as 'policemen' and debt
collectors" (11).

During my stay in the village, I encountered a very different picture
from what Hafiza described to me for the early period and what I had
read concerning the function of bank loan centers. I participated almost
always in the weekly meetings of all five loan centers during my ten-
month stay in the village, but I am unable to recall a meeting that started
at its scheduled time. The normal scenario was that only a few members
came to the meeting on time or before the arrival of the bank worker, and
others showed up after receiving the news of the bank worker's arrival.
In two loan centers, the bank workers came after collecting their installments from other villages. They were invariably late in arriving at the
meeting. Their delay caused most members to leave the center to take
care of household chores.

After arriving in the loan center the bank worker insists that the group
chairpersons find their absent members prior to collection of install-

ments. Borrowers unable to manage their installments are always unwilling to come to the meetings, and they must then be forced by peers to turn up at the loan center. This causes delay in conducting the meetings; a good portion of the meeting time is spent in rounding up borrowers. After the majority of center members arrive in the center, the bank worker gets busy collecting installments, leaving hardly any time to concentrate on rituals or discussions of social development initiatives.

Meetings in loan centers usually start without the recitation of the fundamental principles of the bank, maintaining proper seating arrangements, chanting Grameen member mottos, or doing physical exercise (see Fuglesang and Chandler 1993). On a few occasions bank workers did ask the center chief to start the meeting formally, leading the ritual of the meeting (physical exercise and chanting slogans), but this is rarely followed attentively by most other members, who are busy counting or arranging their installments.

On the occasion of an outsider's visit (local or foreign guest) or the visit of the superior officers (zone, area, or branch managers), however, the discipline of the center is properly maintained and all rituals are practiced. Center visits by superior officers are infrequent, but whenever officers visit a loan center they discuss social development issues with center borrowers.[9] The higher officer for the area office always maintained that "every bank worker must spend part of his/her time in the center discussing the concerns of our members."

During my initial visits to the loan centers in the study village the borrowers were asked by the bank workers to maintain the discipline of the center. The bank workers also discussed the social development issues after their installment collection. As I stayed longer in the village, my informants (borrowers and bank workers) forgot that I was an "outsider" and did not bother to follow the discipline or the rituals.

Both bank workers and borrowers are aware of their obligation to practice the rituals in center meetings, but during the meetings both sets of people become busy with their own concerns and follow their "practical intelligibility" to meet the forthcoming realities of the situations (Bourdieu 1977). The bank worker is busy collecting installments, and the members are busy arranging their own installments. Shafiq, a bank worker, stated, "As a bank worker our first responsibility is to collect *kisti* from every member. We are not expected to return to the branch leaving behind any of our installments in the field. So we try our best to collect all due installments from the loan centers by all possible means."

This informant explained that in the loan center there really is no time to follow the discipline of the center or discuss issues of social development. Without exception, in every meeting some borrowers come to the center without their full installment in hand. They hope to either borrow the amount from peers or arrange their installment by recovering money they may have lent to other peer borrowers in the center. In the center meetings negotiations and disagreements between members on the issues of borrowing and recovering continue, often resulting in disputes and thereby creating a tense situation that requires bank worker intervention.

In addition to the rituals of the bank, the other important components of the social development initiatives are center schools for children, workshops for skill development, abolition of dowry, and sanitation for good health (Fuglesang and Chandler 1993:120). The Grameen Bank (1994) reported that by 1994 the bank had helped its borrowers to operate 14,084 schools enrolling 396,289 students (Khandker, Khalily, and Khan 1994:100). Such a school did not exist in my study village, nor did I hear about any Grameen loan center school in the study branch. In the study village there are two schools for children; one is a private elementary school, and the other is run by the Bangladesh Rural Advancement Committee (BRAC), a nongovernmental organization. The existence of these schools may be the reason there are no bank-sponsored schools associated with the loan centers in the village.

The bank organizes daylong and weeklong workshops for its borrowers to educate and train them in bank operation, nutrition, livestock and poultry care, and other social development issues. In 1994, the bank organized more than 11,000 seven-day workshops and over 26,000 one-day workshops for Grameen borrowers (Khandker, Khalily, and Khan 1994:100). During the period of my fieldwork, two one-day workshops (one for male members and another for female members) were held at the study branch, at which the discipline of the loan center and the importance of maintaining regular installments to keep the center in good shape were discussed. Prior to the beginning of my fieldwork, Rina (a Grameen Bank borrower) attended a weeklong workshop on nutrition, health care, pregnancy, and childbirth in the area office. Rina is a close friend of her center chief, Rani, and Rani selected Rina to attend this workshop. For Rina, the most rewarding part of this workshop was receiving a daily cash allowance and three free meals a day. Rina described her experience in this workshop this way:

> Sir and *apa* (male and female speakers) were from the city and they were very educated people. They talked and talked. Many times I could not understand what they were talking about. Other times they were talking about things which we already know, such as local practices during pregnancy and childbirth. Surely, I learned some good things from the workshops. I was asked to share my experience with other members in the loan center. But since my return from the workshop no one has asked me to discuss my experience with others in the center.

The Grameen social development constitution shuns the "curse" of wedding dowries, but the Grameen position is not adopted by the borrowers in the village. Dowry as a form of "premortem inheritance" has been practiced in India for centuries (particularly by Hindu families, in which women's inheritance is not recognized) as a way of transferring a woman's rights to property at her marriage (Goody and Tambiah 1973:1; Sharma 1993). The practice of dowry has now become widespread in every part of the subcontinent. With some variation, dowry is commonly practiced in all regions of Bangladesh (Ahmed and Naher 1987). In the study area, giving or accepting dowry in marriages is a decades-old tradition and is practiced regardless of socioeconomic class. Parents often discuss dowries openly and take pride in receiving high dowries for their sons.

The Grameen Bank reports that in 1994 there were more than 30,000 dowry-free marriages among Grameen borrowers (Khandker, Khalily, and Khan 1994:100). In my village, however, I could not find evidence of a dowry-free marriage. Moreover, all Grameen borrowers reported giving dowries for their daughters, accepting them for their sons, or planning to follow the practice in the future. I present here two examples from the study village.

Soon after the start of my fieldwork in the village, many informants (primary and secondary) told me that Ali, one of the first Grameen borrowers, had appropriated a large amount of money from a joint project loan fund of his center and used it to pay dowries for his daughters. Ali always denied the allegation and maintained that the joint project failed because of the dramatic drop of the market price of mustard seeds, which the project bought and stored for profit. As he is treasurer of the joint project, everyone blames him. Ali and his wife, both Grameen borrowers, reported their yearly household income as 10,000 taka but admitted paying about 60,000 taka in dowries for their daughters' marriages. Ali never regretted paying such a large amount because he has four sons and three of them are still to be married. He plans to bargain hard at the time of their marriages to get all the money back from the brides' families.

I also observed situations in the village where dowries are financed by Grameen loans. Here is an example. Milla, an elderly widow, has been a borrower of the bank since 1980. She lives with her youngest son and daughter. Her oldest son lives in Dhaka and works in the jute industry as a laborer. During the time of my fieldwork Milla's daughter got married, and the household members paid 20,000 taka as dowry to the groom's family; the groom had a low-ranking job in a paramilitary unit *(ansar)*. Half the amount (10,000 taka) was collected from Milla's eldest son's savings from his factory job and from the sales of household resources (one large tree was sold). The other half was arranged from a Grameen loan.

Before Milla's daughter's marriage was settled, this loan was negotiated by Sofia, who discussed the matter with the bank worker and then initiated the loan application. After receiving a 10,000 taka loan from the bank, Milla handed the total amount to the groom's father as her daughter's dowry. When the ceremony was over, I probed into the matter with Milla and indicated to her that giving dowry is against the social development component ("Sixteen Decisions") of the Grameen Bank. Milla's response was straightforward:

> If we do not give dowry no one would marry our daughters. If the bank asks us not to pay dowries then our sirs [bank workers] should marry our daughters. Sirs themselves demand and accept dowries in their marriages and ask us not to practice it!

The marriage of one of the bank workers at the study branch coincided with the marriage of Milla's daughter. I knew, and many borrowers in the village knew as well, that this bank worker had accepted dowry from the bride's family. Milla rationalized the use of her entire loan to pay dowry by situating it in the context of the marriage of the bank worker.

The examples of Milla and Ali illustrate informants' rationalization of why they do not abide by the rule banning wedding dowries. Milla is aware that in the present situation her daughter can only be married by giving dowry. The marriage of the daughters at an "appropriate age" brings *ijjat* ("honor")—social and symbolic capital—for the household. If girls stay longer in the natal home without marrying, then they not only bring *durnam* ("bad reputation") to the homestead and the lineage, but the parents must also pay higher dowries because of late marriages.[10] Ali and his wife, who gave dowries at their daughters' marriages, are unlikely to refuse dowries when the time comes for their sons to marry. The dowry their sons bring to the household will substitute for the dowries of their daughters. This cycle of giving and taking by the parents makes it hard to achieve an immediate removal of the practice from society. Moreover, the practice of dowry in the study area provides not only material transfers but also a way of gaining cultural capital, for parents take pride in securing high dowries for their sons (see Sharma 1993:353).

Another issue of social development is the encouragement of environmental sanitation through the use of pit latrines. The purchase of a pit latrine is a condition of receiving a house loan from the Grameen Bank. When a member is approved for a house loan she must buy one pit latrine from the Grameen Housing Project. At the time of my fieldwork, 49 of 120 women borrowers were approved for house loans in the village. In a few homesteads more than one homestead member received a house loan and therefore a requirement for more than one pit latrine for the household. The total area of the study village is 0.85 square kilometer, with a population of 1,428, which makes the village a very densely populated one. Because available space to set up pit latrines is scarce, many homesteads decide to build only one latrine. The other latrines required of loan recipients lie idle in the yard. In other cases where the space is scarce but each member decides to set up his or her own latrine, the latrines are often placed in improper sites, such as beside footpaths. In these homesteads there are more latrines in the homestead than are actually needed by homestead members. During my field research, a British development worker—now a resident in Bangladesh—visited my research site. As he was walking though the study village he commented that the "the pit latrine project of the bank is creating more pollution than it is contributing to public hygiene." I probed into this matter with members of borrower households and with the bank workers. The response of the bank workers was that the Housing Project is an independent project that has nothing to do with the bank's credit program. The policy of making latrines compulsory with the house loan is decided by senior management officers of the bank for the betterment of members. The bank workers admit that they are aware many latrines are never set up and are left unused on the ground for many years. They rationalized this fact by stating, "It is not possible for the bank to change its policy because a few members are not using their latrines."

Analysis of the social development initiatives of the Grameen Bank suggests that these initiatives are introduced to achieve improved social lives for members. Problems occur in implementing such initiatives, but with slight modification many of these problems can be addressed. With all the practical issues and problems, some informants feel that through their involvement with the group, they were able to bring some changes in attitudes and expressions. Achia, who has been involved with the Grameen Bank since 1989, expressed it this way:

> Before I joined the bank, I was very introverted and shy to speak in front of people. When I came to my husband's homestead ten years ago, people used to gossip about my quietness. After I joined the bank I have started to change my behavior. Within five years with the loan center I have become more vocal. In the center we meet different members, we talk with each other, we quarrel with each other, we fight for each other's *kisti*, which makes one more open and vocal. Now I am the center chief, and shouting and screaming at other members is my regular job at the center meetings. In fact, the survival needs in the center makes one more vocal and self-expressed.

Grameen borrowers in general are more vocal and articulate compared to other women in the village who are not Grameen members. Such openness and expressiveness in the borrowers is often presented as indicators of women's empowerment (Hashemi and Schuler 1993). Many borrowers in the study village, however, expressed feelings similar to Achia's; the survival needs of Grameen borrowers encourage them to be more vocal not only in the loan center but in many instances in their intrahousehold interactions.

In few instances, the organization of women in the study village has encouraged women borrowers to achieve some degree of self-esteem. Examples include Achia gaining power in intrahousehold decisionmaking and other borrowers learning how to write their names and taking pride in their accomplishment.

The organization of women within patriarchal hegemony also has helped the study branch to achieve its investment and repayment goals. But the social and institutional pressure for disciplining the credit behavior of the borrowers and the maintenance of a power hierarchy in a loan center produce unintended consequences for borrowers and their households. These dynamics are related to the escalation of aggression and violence, specifically against women, that is discussed in the next chapter.

Notes

1. The exclusion of males is also being reported in the 1993 and 1994 annual reports of the Grameen Bank. In 1994, there were 62,601 female members and "zero" male members in the Mymensingh Zone (the last zone the bank established in the 1990s).

2. The concept *purdah* usually means seclusion of women or their veiling. In this context, *purdah* also means that a woman must not see or talk to males who are not related to her by blood or marriage.

3. In my study village there are nine women borrowers whose households own more than two acres of land. Other studies indicate that landowning households are quite commonly included for Grameen loans; in fact, the Grameen Bank itself has taken up this issue in its internal discourse (see Grameen Bank 1995b; Matin 1997).

4. To get formal recognition as a Grameen group, all members must learn and memorize the rules of the bank and the "Sixteen Decisions." In the early years of bank operation in the study village, when a group was ready, it then participated in a seven-day training program arranged by the bank; all members were tested orally by a superior officer and had to pass the test to get formal recognition. During my fieldwork I could not find this practice in the study village.

5. *Bel* is a local fruit which has a very hard bark on it. If one tries to break this fruit by hitting it with another object, the other object may break instead of the *bel*. So wisest would be to break one *bel* with another one and whichever of the two breaks is good for eating.

6. A similar incidence is also documented by Todd (1997:27). She writes that when a male borrower died there was a ceremony in which the branch manager handed a letter of condolence and a 5,000 taka grant from the emergency fund to the widow. Immediately after the ceremony the bank worker took back 4,984 taka

that the deceased borrower still owed to the bank, leaving the widow only with the letter and 16 taka.

7. In general, female bank workers in the study branch carry a bad reputation of being ineffective in collecting installments. There were three female bank workers in the branch. The manager often complained to me about them on the grounds that they could not be as rigid as men workers when it comes to collection of installments. There is also a common belief among male bank workers that female workers are unable to walk to distant villages to collect installments.

8. Here, relatives are kinfolk from the borrowers' husbands' side and women's kinfolk from their natal villages.

9. During the ten months of my fieldwork, the area manager visited loan centers in my village once and the branch manager accompanied him. The manager of the branch came to loan centers in my study village three times to settle problems of installment payments by borrowers (see Todd 1997:181).

10. The informants believe that girls ought to be married soon after they reach their puberty as "the amount of dowry generally increases with the bride's age"(Schuler, Hashemi, Riley, and Akhter 1996:1733).

6

Disbursement and Recovery of Loans

Bases for Escalation of Violence?

In this chapter, I discuss the disbursement of loans by the Grameen Bank in women's centers, the uses of these loans in the household economy of the borrowers, and the structure of loan repayment in the study village. In the previous chapter, I discussed the gulf between the bank's vision of lending to women and the practices of informants (bank workers and borrowers) in the study village. I continue the discussion of this gulf in the practices of loan disbursement, loan use, and the loan recovery process. The current practices of loan disbursement, loan use, and loan recovery create unintended consequences in the form of escalating hostility and violence in the community in general. Why and in what way women borrowers are targets of this rising violence is analyzed in this chapter.

Loans in the Study Village

At the time of my fieldwork (1994–1995), the Grameen Bank extended three different types of loans—general, seasonal, and house—among its borrowers in the study village. The borrowers also mentioned a few other types, such as collective, family, tube well, and capital recovery loans, which had been approved previously but gradually eliminated because of the failure of their rates of recovery. In May 1997, at the time of my follow-up research, I found that the bank had introduced two more types of loans—animal sharecropping and leasing.

Microloans (General and Seasonal)

The general and seasonal loans of the Grameen Bank, which I term "microloans," are the mainstay of the bank. The bank approves general loans to borrowers for income-generating activities, for example, rice husking, cow fattening, and small businesses. The main objective in extending these loans is to provide Grameen borrowers with the opportunity to generate a regular flow of income throughout the year to supplement the seasonal income that is common in agricultural societies such as rural Bangladesh. In the study village, the size of general loans ranges between 3,000 and 10,000 taka.

The bank introduced seasonal loans in the study village in 1992. The main purpose of these loans is for borrowers to invest in seasonal culti-vation or seasonal businesses, such as irrigation of agricultural fields, purchase of fertilizer, or purchase of grains during the harvest season to sell during the off-season. In practice, however, the conditions for the use of seasonal loans are very flexible and "these loans tend to protect the general loan and to keep borrowers from reverting to the moneylender. They are also proving to be a factor in accelerating a branch's time to break-even financially" (Fuglesang and Chandler 1993:108–109).

At the end of 1994, the cumulative disbursement of the bank was about 45 billion taka (more than a billion U.S. dollars), over 85 percent of which was approved as microloans (Khandker, Khalily, and Khan 1994:94). At the end of May 1997, the cumulative disbursement of the study branch was over 1.5 million taka, 70 percent of which was disbursed in the cate-gory of microloans. Figure 6.1 shows the loan amounts in different cate-gories disbursed among women borrowers in the study village.

House Loans

House loans are approved for individual borrowers through the Housing Project (an independent project) and administrated by local branches of the Grameen Bank. The objective of house loans is to give the borrowers the opportunity to build better houses. The maximum amount for a house loan approved for individual borrowers is 25,000 taka. House loans include the condition that the borrower must buy eight concrete pillars to use in building the new house and a pit latrine to set up in the homestead. Both pillars and latrines are constructed and supplied by the Housing Project of the Grameen Bank. At the time of my fieldwork, I recorded 49 women borrowers out of 120 who received house loans from the bank.

The house loan appears to be a vehicle for keeping the loan centers and individual borrowers in regular standing. Nearly all women borrowers in the study village are attracted to house loans. Fourteen women of the 120 reported joining the bank just to obtain house loans; 5 of them had al-ready received their loan, a few others waited for their turn, and some had given up hope. For example, Hayat was sent by her husband to join

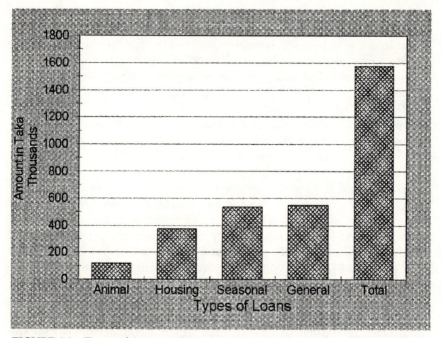

FIGURE 6.1   Types of Approved Loans to Women Borrowers in Pas Elashin,
Bangladesh, May 1997

the loan group in 1992 for a house loan. Hayat (a borrower in the study
village) accepted both general and seasonal loans for two consecutive
years and became eligible for a house loan in 1994.[1] Subsequently, she
tried to get her house loan but was unsuccessful because of her uncongenial relationship with Rani, the most influential member in her center.
Since Hayat failed to get a house loan, she was forced by her husband to
leave the loan group in early 1997 prior to my follow-up research. Ironi-
cally, the borrowers who received house loans in the study village frequently complained about the quality of the pillars supplied by the bank
and their cost, which was higher than the market price. Another complaint was that the cost of concrete pillars was deducted by bank workers from the loans before releasing the money to borrowers.

Cattle Sharecropping and Leasing Loans

Cattle sharecopping and leasing are two types of new loans introduced
in the study branch in 1996. The bank approved 6,000 taka to individual
borrowers to buy cows for sharecropping. The borrowers care for their
stock for six months and then sell them for profit. The borrowers must

pay the principal and interest—a total of 7,500 taka—to the bank in one installment after the six-month term of the loan is over. By the end of May 1997, the bank had disbursed over 100,000 taka among women borrowers in the village in the form of cattle sharecropping loans. The leasing loan is a larger amount (usually more than 100,000 taka) lent to the borrower for capital investment, for example, rice or flour mills. In this arrangement the bank holds the ownership of the project until the borrower repays the loan. The local branch has not yet disbursed this loan among women borrowers in the study village.

Group Fund Loan

The group fund is primarily an accumulation of the "group loan tax," the 5 percent deducted from the proceeds of every loan approved for individual borrowers and deposited in a joint group fund account (GFA) with the bank. Until 1996, the individual borrowers had no personal right or claim over their savings in the GFA and could only borrow a portion of it with the consent of other group members (*Bidhimala*, Section 4.6a; see Appendix C). The bank approves loans from the GFA for both household consumption and investment needs.

The Grameen Bank operates its microcredit scheme on a fifty-two–week (one year) fiscal cycle. The first fifty weeks cover 100 percent repayment of the principal amount, that is, the borrowers pay 2 percent on the capital amount every week. The remaining two weeks of the fiscal cycle is scheduled for payment of the interest and borrowers' contribution to the emergency fund.[2] In most investment loans the bank charges the rate of 20 percent interest; the emergency fund contribution of the borrower is 25 percent of the grossly calculated yearly interest on every repaid loan. The interest and emergency fund contribution together are twelve and half times greater than the borrower's weekly installment, but the borrower must pay it in the remaining two weeks of the year to become eligible for the next loan from the Grameen Bank.

Processing of Loan Applications

The hierarchical lending structure of the Grameen Bank, discussed in Chapters 1 and 5, is sketched briefly here to assist in the analysis of the approval and disbursement of loans. The lending structure of the bank involves the borrowers in processing requests for individual loans proposed by the group and formally initiated by the center chief. The public transcript, that is, the official policy, for involving borrowers in processing individual loan requests is to empower them by giving them the opportunity to take part in loan center decisions and to transfer an individual's loan liability to the collective. Each individual in the rural lending hierarchy holds the power to either reduce or refuse the loans stemming from the group (see Figure 1.2). In practice, the bank workers in this hierarchy hold the final authority over approval or refusal of new loans. This practice is a contradiction of the bank's basic philosophy of "empowerment" of women; it leads to their "disempowerment" by placing the actual decisionmaking in the hands of bank workers (United Nations Development Programme 1997:13).[3]

The normal practice in processing loan applications in all centers in the village deviates from the ideal of the bank. Loan proposals and loan disbursements in reality are accomplished by the cooperation between influential members of the center and the bank worker. At the center level, it is not the group chairs but influential members—often the center chiefs—who informally initiate the loan proposals. These influential members consult the bank worker prior to formal initiation of the loan proposal by the loan group.[4] The initiation of an individual borrower's loan application and receipt of her loan in a timely manner is influenced by the borrower's relationship with influential members in the center. If the borrower fails to maintain a congenial network (*bhalo shamparka*) then she may become a victim of personal malice. Dolly was one such victim.

Dolly was a casual wage worker. She mainly worked as a rural road construction worker in projects run by the nongovernment organizations (NGOs) in the study area. Her husband was an agricultural laborer. Dolly and her husband, Faju, decided that Dolly would join the bank and borrow capital for Faju to start a business in the weekly market as a secondary occupation for extra household income. Dolly joined a loan group and received her first general loan of 3,000 taka in February 1994. According to their plan, Faju started a business of selling fruit and vegetables in the open space of the weekly market. But he failed to earn enough to maintain the household's weekly installments from the profit. So they started to pay part of Dolly's weekly installment by using the capital borrowed from the Grameen Bank. At the end of forty weeks, the household had used the capital amount, and for the remaining ten weeks the installments were paid from the daily earnings of Dolly and Faju—selling fruits and eggs—and borrowing from other villagers. During her first loan year, Dolly missed one weekly center meeting because she went to her natal home to borrow money to pay her installment. She was unable to return on time to pay the installment in the center meeting.

In March 1995, Dolly paid off her capital amount, but in fifty-one weeks instead of fifty. Dolly was a week behind in her repayment cycle and she also failed to arrange funds to pay the "interest and emergency" portions in time to apply for the next new loan. Dolly's irregularities in repayment caused problems for other regular borrowers in receiving their new loans. Her group members and other borrowers of the center persuaded Dolly to arrange and pay the interest and emergency amounts while assuring her of the initiation of her next new loan proposal to the bank. Dolly discussed the matter with her husband and they decided to borrow Dolly's interest and emergency fund payments from Faju's patron (for whom he worked for daily wages) to clear all dues with the bank, apply for a new loan, and then repay the patron after receiving the loan.

Six weeks after the payment of Dolly's interest and emergency fund amounts her new loan proposal was not yet initiated at the loan center. The patron from whom she and her husband borrowed money had stopped paying Faju's daily wages and the household went through extreme hardship with only Dolly's wages. During one center meeting Dolly came to me in tears and explained her situation. I inquired into the matter at the center and the bank worker explained, "The loan proposal must come from the group and has to be initiated by the center chief." The group chair responded that she had proposed the loan to the center chief. The center chief explained to me that she tried to initiate Dolly's new loan, but it was stopped by one of the center members, Ripa, the daughter of the influential Grameen borrower Rani. Although not a member of Dolly's loan center, because of her relation with bank workers Rani was able to influence the decisions of other centers in the village. When I approached Ripa to probe into the matter, her response was simple. She said, "I have requested my mother to ask our "sir" not to accept any loan proposal for Dolly, because she is very arrogant and never listens to other members in our loan center. When she does not have funds for the installment payment she flees from the village and makes trouble for others. So I have expelled Dolly from our loan center."

Eventually, Dolly's case came to the branch manager's attention through my inquiries. The manager asked the bank worker to resolve the matter of disagreement between the loan group and the center chief, accept Dolly's loan proposal, and bring it to the manager for approval. Finally, Dolly was extended a second new loan of 4,000 taka.

Loan Disbursement

During my research the manager at the study branch was disbursing loans two days a week. On loan disbursement days, borrowers from different villages, some situated as far as five to seven kilometers away, came to the branch to receive their loans. The borrowers who come to the branch to get their new loans must bring two peers, including the center chief, who witnesses and countersigns the Loan Acceptance Form. The study branch is located only fifteen minutes walking distance from the study village. Nonetheless, the informants commonly complained about the loan disbursement arrangement. They found that their center chiefs and group chairpersons are not always willing to accompany them to the bank to receive their loans. This is especially true for borrowers who fail to maintain congenial relationships with their center chief and group chair. In the village, I encountered at least four occasions on which the recipients of new loans agreed to lend money to the center chiefs or group chairs as a favor for accompanying them to the branch to receive their new loans.

The bank worker responsible for the loan center completes the paperwork for disbursement and gives these papers and the loan money to the branch manager for transferal to the recipient. Each recipient must go through a ritualistic interview with the manager.[5]Recipients are expected to reply correctly to the manager's questions before receiving the loan. The manager calls them one by one, using the names written on their applications. The interview questions are always the same and asked in the same sequence:

What is your husband's name?
What is your loan group and who is your group chair and center chief?
What is your approved loan amount and how much is the weekly installment?
How much do you pay in "group loan tax" and what is the amount you receive after paying your group loan tax?
Will you get back your group loan tax from the bank?

The dominant Grameen discourse has often accused Bangladeshi banking institutions of being patriarchal by failing to recognize women's self-identities and women's independence in lending to female clients: "It [the bank] is anti-woman: banks do not want to lend money to women. If a woman wants to borrow from a bank, the manager will ask to bring her husband along, . . . this is a very biased way of doing business with one part of the society" (Canadian Broadcasting Corporation 1991:9). But the first interview question to women borrowers before handing over their loans implies women's subservience to their husbands—an issue that the Grameen Bank suggests it challenges in its dominant discourse. Women in Bangladesh rural society are often identified through their male guardians—fathers, brothers, and sons (Jahan 1975; Aziz and Maloney 1985; Aminur Rahman 1992). The construction and use of this question in lending to women indicate that Grameen's microcredit practice in rural Bangladesh does not deviate from the patriarchal ideology on an issue marked as fundamental by the bank; the question denies women their self-identity and reinforces their dependence on men.

I often participated in loan disbursement meetings and observed the interaction between bank workers and borrowers. During these interviews many borrowers failed to reply correctly to the manager's questions. The borrowers commonly failed to reply correctly as to the amount of a loan they would receive after the deduction of the group loan tax and the amount to be paid as weekly installments. I also encountered situations in which the borrowers forgot not only their group identification or the name of their group chair or center chief but also the name used on their loan application (the name on a loan application may be different from a woman's given name, as discussed in the last section in Chapter 5). When such situations occurred the manager first blamed the borrowers for not learning these answers properly and then blamed the bank workers for not teaching the borrowers the correct responses. As an outside observer of the Grameen Bank operation at the branch, I had difficulty comprehending the rationale for following the ritualistic interviews prior to the transferal of approved loans. The manager explained it to me this way:

> The disbursement of loans is a very special occasion for the Grameen Bank and for its borrowers. The nonliterate poor people come to the bank to accept their loans. The borrowers learn the rules and regulations of the Grameen Bank through intensive training and through their involvement with the credit program. They are proud to show they know how to write their names and express their knowledge on the Grameen Bank's system of operation. Interviewing borrowers before disbursing loans is obligatory and is also monitored by the area manager. I would not dispute that such practice is now becoming only a ritual and losing its spirit. The overburden of our work at the branch and in the loan centers is hindering proper orientation of borrowers. However, such practice in the long run will facilitate the learning process for the borrowers.

Loan Use and Loan Supervision

This section includes a discussion of the importance of loan use supervision by loan group peers, center chiefs, and bank workers; the use of loans for income-generating ventures; and the diversion of loans into household day-to-day economies. The central focus is to present the rationale of informants for diverting loans from specific loan projects to other productive ventures or household consumption and the practice of "passing on" loans for women to men.

The Grameen Bank approves microloans to individual borrowers in loan groups for their immediate investment in entrepreneurial activities for cash income generation. The borrowers must invest the loans themselves in their specific projects within seven days of acceptance of a loan. They start their installment payments—"the heartbeat of the Grameen Bank"—in the second week by using a part of the profit earned from the loan investment (Fuglesang and Chandler 1993:96).

Loan Projects and Actual Use of Loans

Poor households in rural Bangladesh live in poverty-stricken situations with limited alternatives for resource accumulation. These households commonly face a continuous resource scarcity in relation to fulfilling their basic needs of food, clothing, and health care. The scarcity of resources is an important dimension affecting the use of microloans in the household economy. The members of borrower households face multiple and conflicting needs, such as purchase of medicine, payment of dowry, or cost of travel for migrating household members, that set the context for household loan use. The bank approves microloans to women and women bring these loans into their household. In the household, the members "renegotiate" the loans made to the women according to the set priorities of the household and decide how the loans are actually used and by whom. In cases where the needs of household consumption come first, the members divert the entire amount or a part of the loan to meet these needs (see Chapter 5).

Figure 6.2 shows that in 1994–1995 the bank approved 217 microloans to women borrowers in the study village; 149 of these (70 percent) were actually used for purposes other than the approved loan projects. The diversion of loans is a deviation from the bank's microlending policy.[6] Figure 6.2 shows that the bank approved 84 loans (39 percent) to women for *dhekki*[7] (rice-husking) projects, but none of the women actually used her loan for this purpose. Eighty-one loans (32 percent) were switched from bank-approved income-generating projects to other entrepreneurial ventures, such as from rice husking to a small business or moneylending. The loans are also switched to building the household resource base, such as by mortgages in and purchase of land plots or travel for migrating household members.

Most borrowers switched their investment from one sector to another during their involvement with the bank over several years. The informants—borrowers and bank workers—admit that they are aware of the practice of loan diversion but justify such practice on the grounds of the "convenience of the loan operation." At the time of new loan applications the reported changes in investment projects must be justified by the borrowers. In a few cases, such as buying cattle, the investment must be supported with the evidence of purchase receipts. The reported changes in

Activities Based on Loans	Approved Loans		Actual Use	
	No.	%	No.	%
Cow	35	16%	8	4%
Rice Husking	84	39%		
Business	42	19%	71	33%
Rickshaw/Van	7	3%	11	5%
Agriculture	49	23%	6	3%
Moneylending			20	9%
Land Transaction			19	9%
Sponsoring HH Migrant Worker			13	6%
Medical Expenses			8	4%
Wedding Dowry			4	2%
Household Expenses			17	8%
Others			40	18%
Total	217	100%	217	*101%

FIGURE 6.2 Projected and Actual Use of Loans to Women Borrowers in Pas Elashin, Bangladesh, 1994–1995

General Loan (n=114) and Seasonal Loan (n=103)
*Rounding error

investment projects also increase the paperwork for the bank workers. Therefore, in the loan application it is convenient for both the borrowers and the bank workers to report the same project for each new loan application every year. Usually, the borrowers use the same project they used in first borrowing from the Grameen Bank. I illustrate this with the case of Dilu.

Dilu joined the bank in 1980 at the beginning of its operation in the village and received her first loan of 500 taka as a *dhekki* loan. For the first few years, Dilu was considered to be one of the best borrowers (*bhalo shadasha*).[8] In 1987, she was honored with the opportunity of becoming one of the two borrowers who laid the foundation stone of the local Grameen Bank building. The bank commemorated her by inscribing her name in the foundation stone of the bank building.

From 1980 to 1995, Dilu's general loans increased from 500 to 10,000 taka. These loans were used for various purposes, but all bank workers who came to run Dilu's center kept Dilu's general loan as a *dhekki* loan. Dilu reported that for the first couple of years she used a small portion of her loan in husking rice, but she never could generate enough profit to pay installments from that work. So she gave her loan proceeds to her husband, who used them in his vegetable business, making enough profit to pay regular installments (*kisti*) and saving a little to build the household resource base. In 1985–1986 the household used Dilu's general loans to buy two calves and paid the loan installments from her husband's income from the vegetable business. In 1987, the household failed to generate enough income to pay the installment for the first time. The loan amount increased during the years but the profit from the business dropped. The diminishing return from business investment encouraged the household to divert the funds and use part of three general loans (1990–1992) to mortgage-in agricultural land. During these years, Dilu paid the installments from her husband's business and sometimes by borrowing from moneylenders, whom she often repaid after harvesting from the leased land.

In 1993, Dilu lent 8,000 taka from her general loan to her mother-in-law—a Grameen member—to pay for the mother-in-law's trips to Malaysia as a migrant laborer (the total cost was 30,000 taka). Dilu explained that her mother-in-law had been a Grameen borrower since its inception. In 1989, Dilu's father-in-law became disabled because of an accident and quit his small business of timber cutting. Her mother-in-law invested her 1990 loan in *taka lagano*[9] and earned a good return in the first year. But in 1991–1992, the harvest was poor in the area and people who borrowed money from Dilu's mother-in-law could not repay the loan with the paddy. Her mother-in-law also failed to recover the capital and became heavily indebted not only to the bank but also to moneylenders in the village. To pay back her debt, the mother-in-law migrated to Malaysia in 1994 as a factory worker and has been sending remittances regularly.

In 1994, Dilu paid a 5,000 taka cash dowry for her daughter's marriage out of her general loan of 10,000 taka. Since 1993, Dilu's household paid weekly installments to the bank by borrowing from moneylenders; by mortgaging-out land they had mortgaged-in before with bank loans; and by selling household resources, for example, cows. In this process the household lost its resource base and Dilu herself lost the status she built up in the household domain during the years of her involvement with the bank.

In 1994–1995, Dilu's household experienced the same situation as that of her mother-in-law. Dilu decided to follow her mother-in-law's footsteps and travel to Malaysia as a migrant laborer. In 1995, her husband deposited 20,000 taka with a labor-exporting firm in Dhaka. This amount was arranged from the Grameen Bank loans of 1994–1995 and from Dilu's mother-in-law's remittances. The household also paid loan installments many times from the remittances sent by Dilu's mother-in-law. In early 1997, after waiting almost two years, Dilu was able to travel to Malaysia for a factory job.

When I returned to the village in the Summer of 1997, I found that during her three-month stay in Malaysia, Dilu remitted 50,000 taka to her husband, who used the money to pay household debts and to mortgage-in a plot of agricultural land. Dilu has started to regain her lost status in the household; her husband told me that he was proud of his wife. Dilu's husband also mentioned that Dilu has a two-year contract with the employer in Malaysia and in this two-year period the household hopes to be freed from debt, to build a good house, and to purchase some agricultural land. The couple also desire a better future for their only son.

Figure 6.2 shows that about 9 percent of loans are redirected and invested either to buy or lease-in land. Investing credit in land is not permitted by Grameen Bank policy, but for women borrowers in the village land is perceived as a good investment (see also Todd 1997). This is especially true in the context of rural Bangladesh society, where one's social and material value is virtually measured by land ownership (Chowdhry 1982).

Users of Loans to Women

The discussion shows that in rural Bangladesh the intrahousehold relations of members are fluid in nature, constantly negotiated, renegotiated, and manipulated by the members of the unit. Even though the household operates as a cooperative unit in rural Bangladesh, it is also a unit in which individual members bargain. Because of the nature of rural households it becomes difficult for the researcher to investigate and provide an exact account of the real users or beneficiaries of women's loans. Based on my 1994–1995 field data, I have attempted to approximate the "users"—the persons who control and use the major part of a loan and arrange installments—of loans to women in the household. Figure 6.3 shows that husbands and sons of women borrowers are the users of 78 percent of the microloans to women. In 60 percent of cases women pass on their entire amounts or most of the loans to men and are left with little or no control over the capital or the investment.

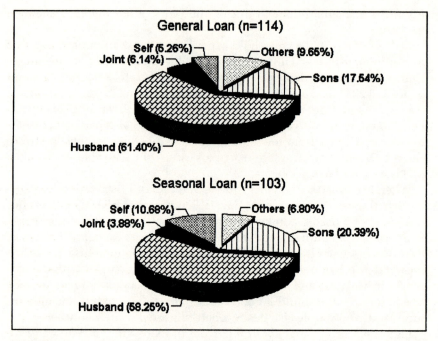

FIGURE 6.3   Users* of Loans to Women in Pas Elashin, Bangladesh, 1994–1995

*50% or more of loan is used or controlled by indicated user

The use of loans to women by men in different microlending projects in Bangladesh has been noted in several other studies (Rahman 1986, Goetz and Sen Gupta 1996; Todd 1997). The number of women borrowers who pass on their loans in my study (60 percent) is more than double that reported in other recent studies. For example, Todd reports 25 percent, and Goetz and Sen Gupta (1996) report that women borrowers retained full or significant control over loan use in 37 percent of the cases, partial control in about 18 percent, very limited control in 17 percent, and no control over their loans in 22 percent. These differences are attributed mainly to how one defines "user" and to the nature of my qualitative research and my intimate knowledge about loan use in the households of my informants. In microfinance studies, researchers without a long-term research plan and strong rapport with informants have rarely had the opportunity to draw people out regarding the complexity of loan use in the household arena. More important is that informants may disguise the information about their real use of loans and the identity of the users for fear of offending the workers of the lending institution who may take action against them and jeopardize their future loan prospects (Johnson and Rogaly 1997:83).

The data show that husbands—household heads—control about 60 percent of the microloans to women; 19 percent of women borrowers pass their loans on to their sons, and about 8 percent of loans go to other male relatives residing in the homestead, in the village, or in the woman's natal village or to a son-in-law in another village (mostly husbands' agnatic kinsmen, but sometimes to the woman borrower's agnatic kinsmen). The women borrowers who pass on their loans to relatives other than their husbands are widows or have husbands absent from the village or unable to use the loans because of advanced age.

In the village, women borrowers often showed dismay at my question of who used their loans. For most of them it was an obvious matter. They held the view that "as a son of the soil" *(bangalir sayle)* I would understand that handling money in the household is "men's job" *(beta manusher kaj)*. The women informants in the village not only gave their loans to men and became "disentitled" but also expected that as a "native" I would accept such a "culturally appropriate practice"—a public transcript—without further questioning. Such expectations from my informants is an outcome of the culturally constructed roles of women and men in society, which are also learned and reinforced through early socialization (Aminur Rahman 1992; Kotalova 1993). Lal, a fifteen-year-old borrower, put it this way: "The bank does not give money to my husband, so I go to the loan center and bring it for him. But if the bank decides today to give him the loan, then I would not need to go either to the loan center or the bank." The acceptance of socially constructed roles by both female and male not only perpetuates the patriarchal ideology but also is significant for understanding the hegemony of the society.

In Bangladesh, women in general, and rural women in particular, have only one option open to them—marriage and children. Not only is women's marriage in rural Bangladesh linked with their status and future prospects, but also their children's future marriage prospects are directly related to the security of marriage (Aziz 1979). The "habitus" (worldview) of female children in rural households is influenced and shaped through the teaching of their elders about the importance of marriage. The meaning of life (habitus) acquired by women in their early socialization does influence their marriage relations. In the study sample, there is evidence that passing on their loans to men is used by women both consciously and unconsciously as a marriage survival strategy. The case of Rafiya illustrates such a strategy.

Rafiya was married in 1990. After the marriage her husband moved to her natal household from another village to live uxorilocally (as a *gharja-mai*).[10] At the time of Rafiya's marriage her father promised a bike, a wristwatch, and a "two-in-one" (a cassette player) as her dowry. The bike and watch were given at the time of her marriage, but her father never managed to buy the cassette player for his son-in-law. For the first two years of their marriage the couple lived in a joint household with Rafiya's father's household, and her husband helped her father with his oil-pressing and oil-vending business. In 1992, after the birth of their first child (a daughter), they built their own house on the homestead of Rafiya's father. Just after setting up their own residence, Rafiya's husband insisted she should join the Grameen Bank and get loans for him to start his own business. Rafiya joined the bank at the end of 1993 and with her first loan the husband started his own oil-vending business. For the past five years Rafiya's husband has increased pressure on her to get the cassette player promised to him. Rafiya knew that her father did not have the ability to buy it and refused to ask him. In 1995, when Rafiya received her second loan from the Grameen Bank, her husband spent the total amount of 4,000 taka to buy a cassette player.

Women borrowers may be aware of inappropriate use of loans by the husbands but still give their consent. Knowing the high cost of inappropriate use of loans in the household, the question remains why there is consent to such expenses. In Rafiya's case she was well aware of the consequences of debt because of her husband's use of a loan for a luxurious item—a cassette player—but she silently consented to it to save her marriage. In the context of very limited investment and employment opportunities for women, loan-based income generation hardly provides the prospects for building an alternative institutional base that would induce women to compromise their marital household. In the structure of patriarchy, in case of a breakdown of the marital household women not only become economically vulnerable; they are also socially more vulnerable than men to being accused and scorned in society. A divorced or abandoned woman brings a bad reputation (*durnam*) to her natal household and lineage and destroys the prospects of her children's future marriages; she can seldom remarry, whereas men almost always remarry in case of divorce or widowhood (see Cain, Khanam, and Nahar 1979; Wiest 1973 and 1998).

Women in rural society rarely have access to alternative entitlements, that is, to economic resources outside their marriage. Therefore, women often tie their own interests to the success of the household unit, provided the household males respect the normative entitlements of the household (Kabeer 1991a:258). The lack of choice outside of marriage and family makes the concept of autonomy—in the sense of independent, individual existence supported by a separate income—not meaningful for most of these women. Even women who have some or absolute control over their loans—sometimes using these loans jointly with their husbands—would usually consider their income as a shared family resource and not as their own personal income (Mies 1986). In the household structure in the study village, if women's contribution in bringing capital through their credit entitlements or producing resources for the household is recognized and valued by other members of the unit, then women have influence in the matter of household decisions (Agarwal 1990; Todd 1997:80). This is explained with the example of Achia.

Since joining the Grameen loan group in 1989, Achia has borrowed money and bought a hand loom for her husband. Together they operated this home-based enterprise with Achia's loans. Achia acquired a house loan in 1993 and built a house, where they have placed the hand loom. Most of Achia's loans were used to run the hand loom business, but the household also managed to buy one cow and mortgage a small plot of land by using bank loans. Achia's husband, Bella, runs the hand loom to weave *sari* and Achia helps him by spinning thread for the loom. They work together to produce at least two *saris* each week. Bella takes the product to the city of Tangail to sell and arranges Achia's weekly loan installment. During my stay in the village, Bella always recognized Achia's contribution in borrowing money to purchase the hand loom, running the business, and helping him operate the loom. Such recognition is also obvious in their interaction with each other. But both Achia and Bella feel that although they are managing their installments on the Grameen loans from their own earnings, the interest rate of the bank is incompatible with the profit they make. They work hard but are unable to build a household resource base for a better future for their only daughter. Consequently, the household has planned to send Achia to Malaysia as a migrant laborer by using Grameen loans, selling the household resources, and borrowing funds from Bella's patrilateral-parallel cousin who is also a migrant laborer in Malaysia.

The example of Achia shows that the idea of separate control over separate earnings in the rural household unit is not very useful for understanding intrahousehold negotiations. What is meaningful is the "centrality" of the women in the management and decisionmaking of the household. When the contributions of women are valued by other members in the household, such as in the case of Achia and Bella, it empowers women in the household unit and also encourages their self-expression and self-esteem not only within the household but outside their household unit (see the example of Achia in Chapter 5).

Loans in the Household Economy

At least three observable circumstances in the study village led borrower households to divert loans for uses other than proposed projects: (1) the uncertain economic environment of the household, (2) a scarcity of resources in the household economy, and (3) the low level of loan investment supervision. The rural economy in Bangladesh in general is prone to high unemployment and uncertain returns on investments. The rural households in particular are also routinely subject to a variety of crises—natural disasters and familial crisis factors—that significantly affect a household's ability to sustain its growth and influence the household's "downward mobility" (Rahman and Hossain 1996:126). In rural Bangladesh, 66 percent of households routinely encounter natural disaster and 48 percent face a crisis of illness in the household every year, which has made rural poverty in Bangladesh not only a state of material deprivation but also "a state of vulnerability" (Rahman and Hossain 1996:113).

Informants in the village are no exception; they also experience a state of vulnerability specifically in regard to uncertain returns on loan investments and the illness of household members. The illness of household members may force the household to large and unexpected expenditures and in some instances put earning members out of action. In 1994–1995, during the field research period, three households with Grameen Bank borrowers were struck by unexpected extra and large household expenditures because of the illness of husbands.

First was Sabiha, whose husband, Falu, was involved in a fruit-vending business. Sabiha joined the Grameen Bank in 1987 to borrow money for her husband's business. Falu used Sabiha's loans to lease fruit gardens during the preharvesting season. He took care of the gardens, harvested the fruit for sale, and made a good profit. The use of Sabiha's loans by her husband in a "good business," together with Falu's hard work, helped the household to survive well until Falu had an accident in December 1994. Falu climbed a tall date tree in the neighborhood to get juice. He fell from the tree and broke his back, his right foot, and his right hand. The incidence not only put Falu—the only earning member of the household—out of work for more than six months but also forced the household to spend several thousand taka for his hospital bills and medicine. Similar expenditures arose for Ruhi, a ten-year Grameen Bank borrower, when her husband was diagnosed with a complicated heart disease, and also for Rani, whose husband was badly injured in an interhomestead conflict in the village.

To provide medical treatment for their husbands and maintain their regular weekly installments on their Grameen Bank loan, the households of Sabiha and Ruhi borrowed from all possible sources, such as relatives and moneylenders, and reduced household expenditures by cutting consumption. After these sources were depleted, the households began to sell their household assets, such as trees and homestead lands, piece by piece to cope with the crises.

My study documents the utilization of loans to meet immediate household needs, such as payment of dowries, purchase of medicines, or immediate consumption (see Figure 6.2). Such utilization is rationalized by household members in the context of economic necessity (Jansen 1987) and is consented to by the women. In rural society, it is often the women whose future is most at stake in ensuring a daughter's smooth entry into her in-laws' household or in attending to the health of household members. But it is women who are responsible for the loans and have to pay their installments every week regardless of how the loans are used or by whom.

In 1994–1995, 32 of 217 loans to women were used in land accumulation (mortgaging-in or purchasing) and financing the migration cost of household members. When loans to women are used to build the household resource base either by land accumulation or through the remittances of migrating household members, the installments must be arranged from sources other than the approved loan investment from the bank. This may increase tension among household members. But as the return from such investment begins to pour into the household economy, it enhances women's position in the household domain and helps them raise their voices in household decisionmaking (see Todd 1997). For example, during my fieldwork, eight persons from Grameen borrower households, including three women borrowers themselves, migrated overseas as laborers. These household members used all or part of Grameen loans to finance their trips. During my fieldwork period, six out of eight (including Dilu and her mother-in-law) were successfully sending remittances, raising their household income substantially and producing a positive impact on the women borrowers themselves.

Loan Supervision

The ensuring of microloan investment by poor borrowers in entrepreneurial ventures and their regular weekly installment payments from investment profits requires constant supervision. As stated by Yunus (1992), "Borrowers would have to be constantly observed. The moment you [lender] stopped supervising, there would be a risk for abuse of the loan" (22). This statement from the founder of the bank establishes the importance of the supervision of loans used to poor households by the bank.

The public transcript of the Grameen Bank elaborates a strong supervisory measure by involving both borrowers and bank workers to ensure that borrowers use their loans for income generation and pay installments from their earned income. This monitoring of loan utilization starts with the involvement of the group chairpersons and the center chiefs, who are obliged to supervise the loan use immediately after disbursement by the bank. Upon their investigation they submit an official form to the bank worker in the center. The bank worker then must inspect the investment to verify the report and prepare a detailed written description about the investment for submission to the branch manager. In addition, the higher officers from the area office are also responsible for random checks on at least 30 percent of all disbursements made in the branches and areas (see Fuglesang and Chandler 1993:97).[11]

Supervision of loan use by the borrowers is rarely practiced in the study village. The data show that 78 percent of investment loans were used for purposes other those than approved by the bank. Both chairpersons and center chiefs, despite their knowledge about loan diversions, formally report these loans to bank workers as properly used. They also legitimize their untrue statements to bank workers by saying, "Everybody in the system knows where borrowers use their loans; reporting to 'sir' [the bank worker] is nothing but just a formality."

The inadequate supervision needs to be placed in a larger context, that is, the phenomenal expansion of the Grameen Bank (see Chapter 1). Currently, on average each branch of the Bank serves 50 loan centers and an area office serves 500 loan centers. The branch managers, program officers, and area managers are often in the field, but any particular loan center is visited only rarely (see Todd 1997:181). Haq, a bank worker at the study branch explained the loan supervision issues this way:

> As bank assistants, on average we are responsible for about 300 borrowers in eight loan centers in different villages. The distance between these villages varies from three to seven kilometers. During the dry season we can ride our bikes, but in the rainy season it takes hours to get there. We visit two loan centers each morning and we are expected to spend only two hours in each center to look after thirty-five to forty borrowers and at least 80 to 100 loan files. On average, this gives one loan file less than a minute per meeting and less than four minutes per month, which does not leave much time to supervise loan use. Moreover, in the center meeting our main concern is *kisti* collection and we do not have time to consider how they are paying. Collecting *kisti* from poor people is not an easy job; most days after returning to the bank from the field I feel guilty in my conscience *[bibek]* for becoming harsh with poor people. But this is our job and we have to do it.

Although the practice of transferring loans to men and the diversion of loan amounts for other purposes is widespread and generally ignored, it is contrary to the Grameen Bank's philosophy and the commonly held view of its operation by outsiders. The bank workers in the local branch often rationalize their practice of not supervising loan investments in terms of the "practical needs of the situation" and "forthcoming realities of the situation" (Bourdieu 1977). They complain about how the expansion of operations has given them an enormous workload and how pressure is placed on them by their superior officers to collect installments from poor members of the program. The bank workers also have their own hidden transcripts regarding loan supervision. They feel that according to the official transcript, bank workers are obliged to supervise borrower loan use, but in reality the "credibility" of a bank worker lies mainly in his or her successful collection of installments from borrowers, not in the supervision of the loan use. Earning this credibility is essential for bank workers to increase their social and symbolic capital—reputation as "a good bank worker"—and also required for job promotion. In the study branch, the institutional pressure on bank workers to collect installments and bank workers' zealousness in the collection of weekly installments in the loan center hardly leaves time for them to supervise the investment of loans.

Loan Repayment Schedule

The payment of regular weekly installments and collection of all installments from each loan center are pivotal to the Grameen Bank discourse in the study area. As borrower informants put it, "The Grameen Bank has become a *kistir* bank," a bank for installment collection. The evidence of the centrality of installment collection to Grameen schemes of lending is illustrated by the following example.

A dispute between two women borrowers (Yuri and Rani) in the loan center escalated into a fight between two lineages in the village; it led to the physical injury of several people from both sides of the dispute (see "Power Hierarchy in the Loan Center," later in this chapter). The manager from the study branch rushed to the scene, but his endeavor to mediate the fight through neighborhood leaders *(para matubbars)* was unsuccessful. The two disputing lineages warned of going to the police station *(thana)* to file cases against each other. That afternoon, the manager and I were invited to the area manager's residence in Nagarpur (a *thana* headquarters ten kilometers away, where the area office is located). During our stay, the area manager, the program officer (higher-ranking officers in the Grameen Bank area office), and the branch manager discussed how these lineages could be stopped from filing police cases against each other. I became very curious why the bank officials were so concerned about the possibility of a police case. The program officer explained it this way:

In the event of a police case in the village some borrower households in the village will be accused by both disputing sides. The male members of these households will flee from their villages because police may come to the village and arrest them. When the male members are away from the household the women will not be able to pay their *kisti*, which will make a problem for the loan center, and harm the reputation of the Branch and Area. Our main concern is to get *kisti* from the borrowers and we do whatever necessary to accomplish this.

The performance of borrowers in installment payments and bank workers in installment collection is the primary indicator of being "good borrowers" or "good bank workers." Individual borrowers must comply with the fifty-week time cycle in repaying the principal amount. Failure to meet this time cycle by individual borrowers not only destroys the reputation of the "good loan center," but threatens the prospects of new loans for members in the loan groups; it also diminishes the prospects for bank workers' future job promotion and brings a bad reputation to the bank branch.[12]

Figure 6.4 presents the sources of loan installment payments on general and seasonal Loans to women. The profit earned from the investment pays only 34 percent of total installments; 66 percent of installments are arranged from other sources, for example, by using capital (10 percent), borrowing from the woman's kin or her husband's kin (35 percent), borrowing from peers in the loan centers (3 percent), and borrowing from moneylenders (6 percent). Figure 6.4 shows that borrower households depend primarily on their kin to meet their installment payments, which reinforces the importance of kin networks in rural society (Aziz 1979; Jansen 1987; Kotalova 1993). Interestingly, women borrowers often draw from their own agnatic kin to meet installment payments, whereas their loans are used primarily by the husband and his agnatic group.

In the loan center, women borrowers deal with peer group pressure and coercion from bank workers for repayment. In the village, I witnessed several Grameen Bank borrowers who sold preharvested paddy, preharvested fruits (jackfruit), fruit trees, and even hens with hatching eggs to collect installments for weekly payments. The price of pulling other resources from the household and diverting funds from consumption needs to repayment of loans can cause further impoverishment for the borrowers of poor households (Goetz and Sen Gupta 1996:56).

The example of Rina illustrates a situation where the household members fail to arrange funds for weekly repayment and the consequence for household consumption. Rina's husband is a vendor who sells betel leaf in the local market, and their son is a day laborer. Rina joined the bank in 1989 and borrowed for her husband's betel leaf business until 1993. In

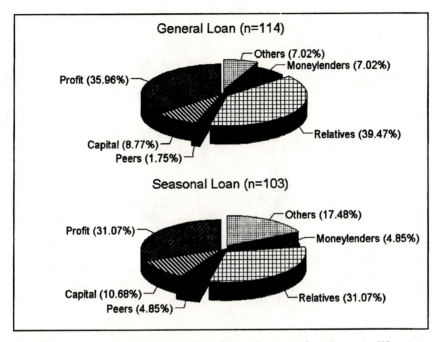

FIGURE 6.4   Sources of Funds for Instalment Payments* on Loans to Women
Borrowers in Pas Elashin, Bangladesh, 1994–1995

*50% or more of funds for installment payments are collected from indicated source

1993, Rina's only son, who is in his mid-twenties, bought a used baby-
taxi (a three-wheeled motorized passenger van) with his mother's general and seasonal loans from the Grameen Bank. To help her son buy the
vehicle, Rina borrowed an additional loan from Proshika, another NGO,
of which she is an active member, that offers credit in the study village.
The baby-taxi was wrecked in an accident in the same year. Consequently, the household lost the capital and was left with a debt burden
with both the Grameen Bank and with Proshika (the repayment schedule
of Proshika is very flexible). For the past two years Rina's household has
gone through extreme hardship to keep up with the repayment on three
Grameen Bank loans. The household pays its installments of 260 taka
every week from an uncertain household weekly income of 300 to 350
taka. In 1994, after the accident, Rina received a group fund loan and a
seasonal loan from Grameen Bank. The household used these Grameen
loans, sold most of its fruit trees, and borrowed cash from all available
sources to keep up the installments.

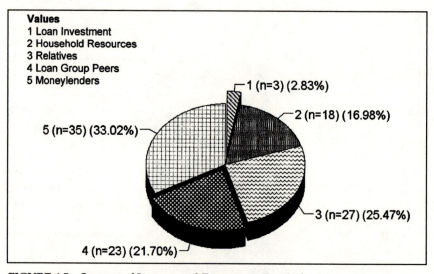

FIGURE 6.5   Sources of Interest and Emergency Funds for Women Borrowers in Pas Elashin, Bangladesh, 1994–1995 (n=106)

After payment of the entire capital amount, 85 of 106 borrowers (80 percent) reported paying the interest and emergency fund dues through short-term borrowing from sources other than their loan investment or household resources (*tan dee-ya-dichi*, "paid through borrowing").[13] Figure 6.5 details the sources of these funds. The interest and emergency fund dues are borrowed from other sources, either by the women borrowers or by men, with a promise to the lender that the borrower will return the amount (usually with interest) after receiving a new loan from the Grameen Bank.

Escalation of Aggression and Violence

Women in Bangladesh encounter various forms of violence; specifically, men's violence against women is widespread in rural society (see Arnes and Beurden 1977, White 1992, Zaman 1998). The patriarchal ideology, that is, women's absolute socioeconomic dependency on men, makes them particularly vulnerable to violence in society (Omvedt 1990). Studies on microlending institutions in Bangladesh postulate that "credit programs . . . reduce domestic violence by channeling resources to families through women, and by organizing women into solidarity groups that meet regularly and make the women's lives more visible" (Schuler, Hashemi, Riley, and Akhter 1996:1740; Schuler, Hashemi, and Riley

1997b:33). This expression represents the public transcript of the program and expresses an obvious desirable outcome of such programs. But my research suggests that "manipulation" of the lending structure by borrowers and bank workers at the level of grassroots loan operation to maintain regular installment payments and to ensure high repayment rates may actually escalate violence toward women borrows.[14]

In the study village, my research assistants and I kept track of observed incidences of aggression and violence in the loan center and in the household and followed up on many of these incidences over the duration of fieldwork. In the last stage of my research, my rapport with the informants (see Chapter 2) enabled me to probe into the matter with women borrowers. I asked them specifically about their experiences with violence. With regard to violence in general (ranging from verbal aggression to physical assault), all informants stated that they experienced violence of some kind in the household. This response is consistent with other village studies that recorded violence against women as widespread in rural Bangladesh (Arnes and Beurden 1977, White 1992).

Based on the expressions used by informants to characterize violence and aggression, I divided their responses into the two main categories—verbal aggression and physical assault—presented in Figure 6.6. Verbal aggression includes verbal, symbolic, and psychological belligerence (Zaman 1998:1) such as rebukes, quarrels, or screaming; physical assault includes "wife beating."

Among 120 women borrowers, 21 women (18 percent) claim a decrease in verbal aggression and physical assault because of their involvement with the bank. Sixty-nine women (57 percent) report increased verbal aggression after joining the bank. Another sixteen women (13 percent) recall an increase in both verbal aggression and physical assault; six borrowers in this group reported encountering men's violence because of the women's refusal to give their loans to men or for challenging men's proposals for using the women's loans. The escalation of the violence against women borrowers in the loan center and in the household can be seen as a repercussion of current practices of grassroots lending to the poor. I discuss this in the light of the evidence of the study community loan operation and the power hierarchy in the loan center (see "Networks of Borrowers and Bank Workers" in Chapter 5).

Repercussions of Group Liability

In the previous section, I stressed the centrality of meeting weekly installments and the importance of maintaining the credibility of the loan center. The credibility of a center and the potential for new loans for its borrowers is jeopardized when even one borrower fails to maintain her

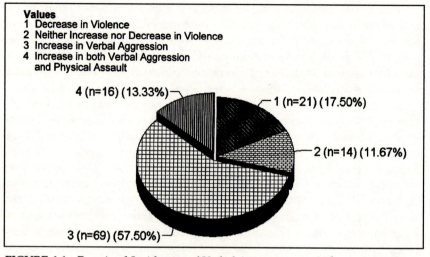

Values
1 Decrease in Violence
2 Neither Increase nor Decrease in Violence
3 Increase in Verbal Aggression
4 Increase in both Verbal Aggression
   and Physical Assault

4 (n=16) (13.33%)

1 (n=21) (17.50%)

2 (n=14) (11.67%)

3 (n=69) (57.50%)

FIGURE 6.6   Perceived Incidences of Verbal Aggression and Physical Assault in Pas Elashin, Bangladesh, 1994–1995 (n=120)

regular payment. The Grameen Bank has been working in the study village over fifteen years. In all five women's centers in the village there are often one or two borrowers who because they are unable to arrange their installments do not come to center meetings. In such a situation, other regular borrowers in the center are forced to sit on their bare feet on a mud floor for several hours until all installments are collected. If the absent borrower is available in the village, her peers must persuade her to come to the center. The appearance of the absentee usually releases an outburst of anger toward her by fellow borrowers and the bank worker. If the absent borrower is unavailable in the village or available but absolutely unable to make her installment, then a number of strategies may be followed: (1) peer members in the loan group or center may pay the installment from their own funds, depending on the amount needed and on the defaulter's relationship with the other members; (2) a bank worker may use other borrowers' funds brought to the loan center to repay their GFA loans (weekly payment for this loan is not obligatory); (3) the bank worker may lend all or part of the installment to the defaulting borrower in order to adjust her account; (4) the bank worker may leave the center without collecting the default installment (this rarely happens); or (5) in extreme situations, peers may decide to take the defaulter's salable household items or personal assets and sell or mortgage them out to collect the installment.[15]

One possible consequence of a default by a borrower is that all the other borrowers who paid their installments in a timely manner must wait in the center and experience a delay before they can return to their household. In the household, the male members give the installments to the women and expect them to pay the installments to the bank worker and promptly return home. The forced delay of women in the center produces disorder in household chores and may generate tension among household members. Increased tension among household members may turn into domestic violence in which women become victimized. An excerpt from my field notes illustrates:

Once I missed a center meeting, so in the afternoon I went to Romeza's house to collect information about the meeting. I found Romeza sitting on her veranda (the front balcony of the house), pale and depressed. My initial inquiry about what happened went without response for some time, but Romeza's husband's elder brother's wife, who lives on the same homestead, informed me that Romeza had a fight with Jinnah (Romeza's husband). At that point Romeza protested by saying that she did not fight with her husband but it was the husband who had beaten her. Romeza then explained that the previous night Jinnah had borrowed the installment *(kisti)* from one of his friends in the neighboring village and promised to sell his labor to the lender. In the morning Jinnah gave the *kisti* to Romeza and asked her to pay it to the bank worker and return home to prepare his morning meal. But Romeza was delayed in the center because one borrower of her group, who comes from a distant village, did not show up in the meeting. Jinnah twice sent one of their daughters to the center to bring Romeza home. In the loan center Romeza tried to explain her urgency to other borrowers and asked permission from the bank worker to return home. The bank worker refused to accept her installment and did not allow her to leave the loan center until the *kisti* problem was resolved. Romeza, along with all the other borrowers, was forced to sit a couple of extra hours in the center before she could return home. Jinnah waited at home. He was furious toward Romeza and refused to accept any explanation about her delay in the center. They argued, Romeza was beaten, and Jinnah left the house without eating his food.

As the "guardian" (normative conception) of the household, it was Jinnah who asked Romeza to join the bank and borrow money for his own business. Jinnah is aware that when an installment repayment problem arises then other borrowers must wait in the loan center until they solve this problem. But he explains his violent behavior toward Romeza as a repercussion of his frustration and anger over which he has no control.[16] Jinnah used Romeza's loan in his brown sugar business but could not

make enough profit from this investment to maintain regular installments from it. Jinnah used part of his capital each week to pay Romeza's
installment. In this process he exhausted the capital borrowed from the
bank. The household arranged installments from other sources, including borrowing, for four weeks. Romeza had to pay installments regularly
to become eligible for the next loan in six weeks.

Romeza was sympathetic toward Jinnah's frustration. She rationalizes
her husband's violent behavior by explaining the societal norm, that is,
"a man in the village is not supposed to prepare his own meal." Her
delay in the loan center happened because one of her peers was absent
and the bank worker refused to accept her installment. Romeza stressed
that such delays would make any man angry who waits for his wife to
prepare his meal. She said she felt very bad because she failed to prepare
the morning meal for her husband, who left home without eating any
food (*khalimukhe*, literally "empty mouth," a phrase used by the local
people to say nothing has been eaten).

The example of Jinnah's verbal aggression and physical assault on his
wife Romeza and Romeza's reaction to Jinnah's action against her suggests that men's aggressive actions in the study village are condoned
within certain limits and even supported by the women themselves.
Sometimes women actively protest men's violence (see Schuler,
Hashemi, Riley, and Akhter 1996:1733), but often, like Romeza, they put
up with men's violence because of their social and material survival dependency on normative-based entitlements. Lending to women by using
the existing patriarchal structure of the society often fails to provide any
acceptable alternatives for women—social, economic, or legal entitlements—that are supported by the society, including active individual or
organized protest against aggression and violence (Sen 1981; Agarwal
1994; Kabeer 1991a; Wiest 1998).

Power Hierarchy in the Loan Center

In Chapter 5, I discussed the nature of the power hierarchy and the importance of networks of relations among borrowers and bank workers
for the local-level loan operation. In this section, I discuss the implications of this power hierarchy for the escalation of hostility and violence.
The Grameen lending policy states that when the individual borrower
completes payment of one of her existing loans, she becomes eligible for
a new larger loan within two weeks. The new loan must be approved by
both the group chairperson and the center chief. In the loan centers, problems often arise in receiving the loan in a timely manner or in getting the
expected amount (that is, more than the repaid loan). Such problems
often occur for two reasons: (1) the loss of credibility of a particular loan

center within the bank, for example, from irregularities of any members in the center; or (2) a woman's adverse personal relations with other members or with the center chief, who has authority over approvals in the center. In a situation where a woman pays off her outstanding loan but does not receive the subsequent new loan according to established practice (which is becoming very common in the study area), she faces serious consequences of verbal aggression or physical assault from her spouse or male relatives. If the concerned borrower experiences a delay in receiving the new loan or must accept an unexpectedly low amount because of a fellow borrower's unwillingness to consent to the loan proposal, then the problem of the loan center may broaden the dispute and lead to fights among different households or lineage members in the village. Here is an example from the study village:

Yuri received her first loan of 3,000 taka in December 1993. At the end of fifty weeks, Yuri asked her husband, Naim, to manage funds to pay the outstanding dues (interest and emergency fund) on her first loan, assuring Naim that she would give him her second loan (4,000 taka) two weeks after the repayment. Naim borrowed the amount from a moneylender in the village on condition that he would return the amount with interest in a couple of weeks. In early February 1994, more than five weeks after Yuri had paid all her dues on the first loan, she failed to acquire the second one. The center chief refused to consent to her new loan and the bank worker would not listen to her appeals. Naim could not keep his promise with the moneylender but was pressured to return the money. This situation generated tension in the household and resulted in disputes; Yuri was physically beaten by her husband several times for her failure to acquire the new loan. Yuri and other peer members reported that Yuri could not get the second loan because of her refusal to lend Rani 1,000 taka from the expected new loan.[17] Yuri's refusal made Rani angry, so she asked Yuri's center chief (who is also Rani's eldest daughter) and the bank worker not to extend a second loan to Yuri. Ultimately, Naim brought the issue to the center meeting where he confronted Rani and asked for an explanation of her activities against Yuri. Rani and Naim quarreled and exchanged harsh words. The bank worker (female) failed to stop the argument and left the center without collecting the installments. For Lal (Rani's husband), Naim had not only humiliated his wife by using harsh words against her before other borrowers—in a public place—but also humiliated the honor *(ijjat)* of his homestead by doing it on his (Lal's) own homestead (see Aziz 1979). Lal was angry and challenged Naim in revenge. A fight broke out the same day between Naim and Lal and later spread among their two lineages (see Zaman 1991).

Rani, who belongs to a different loan center, rationalized her acts toward Yuri by stating that she organized and recruited all members in the center and sacrificed her own courtyard to build the center house for weekly meetings. If someone in the center fails to pay their installment, Rani manages the amount and pays it to the bank worker. To manage such unexpected but very common crises in the loan center, she must keep cash money at her disposal. Sometimes she arranges the cash through borrowing from other members who receive new loans, but she always pays them back on schedule. The statements of many other members and my own observations not only contradict Rani's explanation but also signal the importance of borrowers' personal networks in the loan center. Rani maintains a strong network with several other members in two women's loan centers situated on her homestead. If Rani's household fails to arrange weekly installments, then she uses her network to borrow money from other members in the center to pay her own or her daughter's installments.

Eighteen percent of my informants reported they experienced decreased violence in the household because of their involvement with the credit program. Loans to these women are often used successfully in the household economy, and these loans are considered a new economic resource for the household, bringing benefits for all members in the unit. But when borrower households enter a debt cycle because of low returns on investments, household crises, or natural disasters, then the loans to the women become burdens to the unit rather than a household resource. In these cases, the capacity of the women to bring resources to the household through their bank loan entitlements becomes ineffective. Six borrowers in the study village encountered men's violence because of their refusal to give their loans to the men or for challenging the men's proposals for loan use. This suggests that women's control over their loans—a defiance of the patriarchal ideology—undermines men's authority in the household. Women may be victimized as a consequence.

The informants in my study commonly view men's violence against them as an expression of men's frustration arising from the pressure to maintain timely repayment in the loan center. The examples of Romeza and Yuri suggest that women become victims of violence primarily because they are not in situations to use their power—acquiring credit—in a positive way. In the household they have less power than their husbands, and in the loan centers they have less power than influential borrowers and bank workers, who are mostly men. Most women who encounter violence in the household, like Romeza or Yuri, often blamed either the peer group borrowers or the bank workers instead of their own men for such behavior. Not only are women borrowers conscious of the increased violence, but a few women in the study village are also gaining power by controlling their loans to resist men's violence against them.

The focus of the institutional sustainability of the bank (financial sustainability) emphasizes the self-sustainability of each local branch through loan investment and loan recovery. To meet the challenge of financial sustainability, grassroots bank workers initiate "practical" strategies (Bourdieu 1990), as illustrated in previous chapters. They employ coercive methods and use local power hierarchies in installment collection and loan investment instead of the borrower empowerment and solidarity envisaged by the bank in its public transcript. The women borrowers and their household members are frustrated with the structure and strategies of lending (e.g., the roles of influential members in loan center decisions) and strategies for loan recovery (e.g., keeping all members of the center in the center until all installments are collected). Financial sustainability and institutional and borrower sustainability are discussed in the next chapter.

Notes

1. To become eligible for a house loan, the borrowers must be group members for at least two years and have good repayment records on their loans. The women borrowers must also provide documents proving land title for building a house.

2. By the end of 1996, the Grameen Bank had modified the repayment terms. Now the interest payments are spread over fifty weeks and accepted with the installment payments. Collection for an emergency fund was terminated in 1996.

3. In June 1997, UNDP organized an international workshop in Bangladesh titled "Emerging Issues on Gender and Microfinance," in which I participated. After field visits to several microlending organizations, including the Grameen Bank, the general sentiment of workshop participants was that the mechanisms by which microfinance is delivered may be "disempowering" for women even though they may have a positive impact on poverty reduction (see UNDP 1997: 11–13).

4. In the study village the loan center proposals are formally submitted in writing. The proposal is drafted by the bank worker and must be signed by both the group chair and the center chief.

5. Based on my observation in the study branch and in seven other branches, I term this interview "ritualistic." In all these branches the managers invariably asked every borrower the same questions and maintained the same sequence in posing these questions.

6. When loans are approved for a specific purpose but subsequently these loans are used for another purpose, whether income generation or household consumption, I consider there to be a loan diversion.

7. *Dhekki*—a heavy wooden plank used in a pedal-operated husking implement—are traditionally used by rural women to husk paddy and make rice. *Dhekki* are now being replaced by power-operated rice mills. During my research, I found only three *dhekki* in the study village; none of them belonged to Grameen borrowers.

8. The term *bhalo shadasha* is used by bank workers for the borrowers who maintain the best performance in their installment payments and loan center meeting attendance.

9. *Taka lagano* is a traditional moneylending scheme in rural Bangladesh in which the investors provide cash to the borrowers and the borrowers pay it back after the harvest in the form of paddy instead of cash. This type of lending is also known as *dadan* (see Schuler, Hashemi, Riley, and Akhter 1996).

10. When the husband leaves his father's village and settles with his wife's father's household or homestead (uxorilocal residence pattern), it is called *gharja-mai*. In rural Bangladesh patrivirilocality is the common practice and uxorilocal residency is a matter of shame that reduces a man's status in society because of his social and material dependence on in-laws. This reduced status is carried for generations (see Wiest 1991; Aminur Rahman 1992; Indra and Buchignani 1997).

11. The supervision is checked and rechecked by using the "Loan Utilization Form," according to Fuglesang and Chandler (1993:97). In the study village I never observed use of a Loan Utilization Form.

12. In the monthly descriptive report to the head office, the branch manager must include a section explaining how many loans in the branch have gone beyond the fifty-week time cycle and what strategies are followed by the bank workers to bring these loans back into a regular time cycle.

13. Todd (1997) documented that "most (64%) borrowed to make the interest payment and then repaid this borrowing out of their new loan" (165).

14. The term "violence" in the context of this study includes a range of responses, from verbal aggression to the physical assault commonly referred to as "wife beating."

15. The first two strategies are commonly used to resolve individual weekly defaulting problems, whereas the third and fourth are seldom used. In my ten-month stay in the village, during which I attended more than 100 center meetings, I experienced three cases in which peers used the last strategy to cover the defaulter's installment.

16. It is commonly believed in the study village that when a person gets angry then he or she is no longer the same person because *saitan* (the devil) takes control over the angry person's actions.

17. Rani is a Grameen borrower who established two loan centers on her own homestead courtyard and recruited most of the members in these centers, including Yuri.

7

Microlending and Sustainable Development

The extension of microcredit to the poor as a new model for economic development (Morduch 1997) has emerged from the programmatic success of the Grameen Bank in Bangladesh. Poor borrowers, specifically women in Southern countries, maintain high repayment rates on their microloans. For example, both the Grameen Bank and the Bangladesh Rural Advancement Committee (BRAC) have over 90 percent recovery rates on their loans to women. This fiscal performance of microlending institutions has encouraged the institutions and development organizations to impose interest rates high enough to cover the cost of services provided to the clients. It has also led to the philosophy that microcredit for the poor enhances the long-term economic viability of service-providing institutions. The issues discussed in this chapter are (1) the interrelationships of the Grameen Bank microlending, cost recovery, and profit making in the context of capitalist finance; (2) how the bank's ownership by its borrowers is important in promulgating bank policies, specifically, in transferring the transaction costs of microlending from the institution to the borrowers; (3) the importance of expanding credit programs and scaling up outreach for achieving the goal of institutional economic sustainability and the implications of this for borrowers and bank workers; and (4) the role of bilateral and multilateral donors in the process.

Sustainability and Profitability

The achievement of financial sustainability has become a key concern for institutions providing microlending services to poor people. The performance of lending institutions and their financial and economic viability is determined by cost recovery in the programs. Havers (1996) provided a financial sustainability index (FSI) model that is helpful in illustrating my point:

$$\text{FSI} = \frac{\textit{total income earned from a credit program during the period}}{\textit{credit program cost during the same period}}$$

The sustainability index is based on the imposition of appropriate pricing policies by the lending institutions for earning sufficient income to achieve the goal of financial sustainability. Rosenberg (1996) argued that microlending service-providing institutions are required to extend loans based on an "effective annualized interest rate (R)" to cover their full lending cost (1). The annualized effective interest rate on microloans to the poor—like any other loans in a capitalist economy—depends on five expenses and the costs of delivering services. The expenses are administrative expense (AE), loan loses (LL), the cost of funds (CF), the desired capitalization (K), and investment income (II). Microcredit projects require their clients to pay the annualized effective interest rate and bear the costs of the loans in order to become financially sustainable. The greater the positive value of the FSI, the more sustainable the institution.

Jackelen and Rhyne (1991), in their study of a range of microcredit organizations, identified three levels in an organization's financial viability: (1) subsidy dependent, in which the costs of the organization are funded through grants and subsidies from donors; (2) operationally efficient, in which the nonfinancial costs of operation—salaries and other administrative costs—are covered out of program revenues, that is, interest income from loans and fees; and (3) fully self-sufficient or profitable, where the institution is generating positive (inflation-adjusted) returns on assets and the financial costs of operation of loans and income can cover the costs of loans.

Jackelen and Rhyne (1991) place the Grameen Bank of Bangladesh at the second level of financial viability. So far, however, the Grameen Bank has been a subsidy-dependent institution. The bank has received grants from foreign donors as well as implicit subsidies in concessionary interest rates for borrowing capital from international agencies and from the Central Bank of Bangladesh to relend to poor households. The Grameen Bank has experienced steady increases in the amount of subsidized funds obtained, but with a recent shift toward borrowing from the Central Bank. The Central Bank charged the Grameen Bank only a 3 percent interest rate until 1994, and then the rate rose to 5.5 percent, whereas the interest rate on loans from international donor agencies—IFAD, SIDA (Swedish International Development Agency), NORAD—has held steady at 2 percent (Grameen Bank 1996:130–131). Since the early 1980s the bank has also received interest-free foreign capital from donor agen-

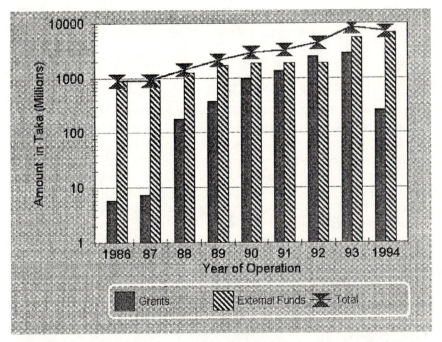

FIGURE 7.1   External Funds and Grants Received by the Grameen Bank,
Bangladesh, 1986–1994

SOURCE: Adapted from Khandker, Khalily and Khan 1994

cies. For example, in 1994 it received a grant of US$74 million from for-
eign donors (Morduch 1997). Figure 7.1 shows the sources of external
capital in the Grameen Bank from 1986 to 1994.

Morduch (1997) calculated that the Grameen Bank is "relatively far
from full financial sustainability" (1). The total interest subsidies (the
sum of subsidies on loans and foreign grants for lending) of the Grameen
Bank has risen from $4.3 million in 1987 to $24.2 million by 1994. A study
by the World Bank, however, shows that in 1991–1992 the household incomes of Grameen borrowers increased about 17 cents for every dollar
the bank lent (Pitt and Khandker 1995, cited in Morduch 1997:8). Morduch finds that during the same time period (1991–1992) the subsidies to
the Grameen Bank amounted to 21.5 cents for every dollar the bank lent
to its clients. This subsidy was nearly five cents more than the per dollar
impact on household consumption measured by Pitt and Khandker
(1995). Based on his own calculation, Morduch (1997) commented: "Had
the subsidy been simply transferred directly to households, they would

have been as well off (at least in terms of current consumption and ignoring the costs of making the transfers)" (8).

The Grameen Bank and Capitalism

The Grameen Bank model resembles Western banking institutions. In its
practices of banking, the Grameen Bank upholds the ideology of capitalism, that is, investing capital for maximizing profit. During the early
years of bank operation the emphasis was to help the rural poor in
Bangladesh by giving them easy access to credit, enabling borrowers to
build sustainable livelihoods and eradicating rural poverty from the
country. In the mid–1980s and 1990s the expansion of the Grameen Bank
in most regions of Bangladesh (see Figure 1.3) and its international reputation for loan recovery changed the bank's emphasis from borrower sustainability to profit making and institutional financial sustainability. The
bank tries to achieve its goal of financial sustainability through employ-
ing strategies of recovering the full lending cost from its borrowers.
Yunus (1995) postulated, "A sustainable system can be built only on the
basis of users undertaking responsibility" (13). Such a policy leads the
bank to operate its lending to the poor on the basis of cost recovery and
profit making, not on the altruistic motives that underlay its formation.

Until 1991, the Grameen Bank followed the commercial market interest
rate in Bangladesh and charged 16 percent annual interest on its microloans to borrowers. In 1991, the Grameen Bank raised the salaries of its
workers by around 25 percent, adding an additional cost to the lending
program of the bank. The increased cost became a serious hindrance for
the profitability of the bank. The bank responded to the problem in terms
of the rules of capitalist finance, which dictate earning profit by any
means (Auwal 1994), by increasing its interest rates on investment loans
from 16 percent to 20 percent; it "thereby loaded the increased cost on the
borrowers" (Fuglesang and Chandler 1993:127).

Yunus (1994c) endorsed the basic features of capitalism, for example,
profit maximization and market competition, and asserted "capitalism"
was a philosophy with no challenger in the current global economic system. His vision of capitalism for the Grameen Bank, however, is "socially
conscious–driven," focusing on the freedom of individual thought and
action instead of "free enterprise." Auwal (1994) investigated the
Grameen Bank's rationale for supporting the ideology of capitalism in
his doctoral work:

> By siding with capitalism and professing to use it in the service of the poor,
> Yunus attempts to win friends from the West. In this way he builds a sym-

bolic bridge between developed countries that generally rely on capitalist economies and the developing nations that, in keeping with the Grameen Bank model, are looking to capitalism as a way to solve their long standing economic problems. (150)

The annual interest rate of the Grameen Bank on its small loans is now 20 percent, which is much lower than the interest rates of moneylenders in the same areas of operation, who may charge as much as 100 to 200 percent on their investment capital. In rural Bangladesh, however, these moneylenders are small in number and have neither standardized nor institutionalized interest rates for large-scale operations. The Grameen Bank institutionalizes its interest rate on a mass scale by reaching more than 2 million borrowers. The oldest man in the study village put it this way:

The Grameen Bank is a kind of British Raj[1] in this country who unfairly takes advantage of poor people's poverty. It replaces one evil by another, for instance, moneylenders charge exorbitant interest rates on a smaller scale, the Grameen Bank charges lower interest rates but on a mass scale. Instead of eliminating moneylenders from rural Bangladesh, the bank is now creating a new class of moneylenders within its own borrowers. For poor people, particularly those who are followers of Islam, there is no difference between the moneylenders and the Grameen Bank.

The Grameen Bank has been privileged to borrow funds at subsidized rates of interest from the Bangladesh Central Bank and other sympathetic funding agencies in the West to relend to rural poor households in Bangladesh (see Figure 7.1). Yet, in 1994–1995, the annual net interest rate charged by the Grameen Bank was 20 percent, which was 8 to 10 percent higher than the commercial market rates in the country.[2] The bank workers in the study branch rationalize the imposition of higher interest rates in comparison to commercial market rates on the basis of the public transcript of the bank. One bank worker said, "It is the board of directors of the bank (the majority of whom—nine out of thirteen—are representatives from women borrowers) who decides about the bank's policy. The board decides the annual interest rate on individual loans. The borrowers are also the owners of the bank who will receive dividends from the bank's profit." In the study village, none of the borrowers agreed with the view of this bank worker. Ainal (a male borrower) explained:

The borrowers have no power in bank policy matters. It is Dr. Yunus, the managing director, who decides about everything; the representatives of the borrowers are there to support his view. Women borrowers who are representatives on the board are not brave enough to talk in front of Dr. Yunus. Moreover, area and zone managers choose the members who are elected to the board. They will not allow me nor any outspoken person to become a member of the board.

Ainal rationalized his statement about the board—a hidden transcript—by elaborating on the power relations in the board of directors, which, according to a public transcript, runs the bank. The nine directors who come from the Grameen borrowers are women, the poorest people in the society with absolutely no formal education. In the board meeting at the head office these women sit with five highly educated and powerful men[3] with high status in the society. In the face of such power relations it is unrealistic to expect that these women on the board will speak out from their own understanding and experience.

The cultural norms of the society also support the explanation of the informants. Women are expected to be passive and shy (Mandelbaum 1988, Blanchet 1989). A few women borrowers in the study village are aware that the bank is owned by its borrowers. None of them can explain the organizational structure of the bank, how the bank runs, or by whom it is run. A few male borrowers who, like Ainal, may be aware of both the organizational structure and the power structure of the bank are unable to become a part of the bank's decisionmaking structure. Men borrowers of the Grameen Bank are not allowed to be elected to the board, and outspoken persons are cut off in the selection process.

The policy of the bank states that borrowers from the different zones of the Grameen Bank are to elect nine directors to the executive board for three-year terms. Several informants in the study village spoke openly about the influence of local bank workers in selecting women of their own choice to become representatives on the board. Bank workers at the study branch always disputed the portrayal of the borrowers, but when they failed to send one of their women borrowers to the board they constructed their own hidden transcript on the matter. In the Summer of 1997, when I returned to my study village for follow-up research, the bank workers shared with me their experience at a recent election of board representatives. In this election, Sofia, a sixteen-year borrower of the bank, won her candidacy in the local area office for a position on the board. There are eight branches under the local area office and Sofia was elected as a candidate by the borrowers of these eight branches offices to compete in the zone. Ten representatives from ten area offices in the zone are sent to the zone competition, and out of these ten one is sent to sit on the board. During the zone competition the zone manager did not support Sofia's candidacy and the representatives from other area offices did not vote for her. The bank workers in the study branch were disappointed, because if Sofia had been elected it would have brought status and encouraged pride for the study branch. The bank workers felt that the "Zonal Sir" (zone manager) did not support Sofia because many senior officers in the zone knew Sofia was an outspoken person, a personality trait that is thought of as uncongenial to other directors on the board.

According to the Grameen Bank official transcript, borrowers own 92 percent of bank shares and hold its ownership. The documents in the study branch show that all borrowers in the village had purchased shares in the bank, but only fifty-five women borrowers (46 percent), and twenty-seven men borrowers (80 percent) were aware of purchasing their shares from the bank. None received dividends during the bank's operation years. Why a large number of borrowers are unaware of their purchase of shares from the bank was explained by one bank worker:

> Borrowers who become members of the loan groups and receive loans must purchase shares of the bank before accepting their second loans from the bank. During the first loan cycle all five borrowers in the group receive loans. According to bank policy 5 percent of each individual loan is levied and put into a joint group fund account (GFA). Before the second loan is sanctioned for the group, the bank worker transfers 500 taka from the GFA to the share purchase account (SPA) and issues share certificates to all five members. The transfer of money from GFA to SPA is done with the consent of the group members. Because the borrowers do not pay the price of their shares from their own sources but from GFA, most of them would not remember purchasing their shares.

The Grameen Bank as an institution serving the poor and owned by the poor is privileged (compared to other banking institutions) in being allowed to formulate its own policies without much restriction from the Central Bank of the country. Such privilege gives the Grameen Bank the opportunity to formulate and employ its own strategies for maximizing profit. But these efforts toward making profits by the institution have economic, social, and human costs for all actors involved in the program.

Transaction Costs, Outreach, and Sustainability

The Grameen Bank extends loans to poor women by creating a structure of joint liability. In the study village this joint liability works in two ways: (1) it is an effective alternative to conventional material collateral that enables the bank to transfer default risks from the institution to the borrowers; and (2) it reduces the transaction costs of providing a large number of small loans by concentrating the clientele in groups, at regular village-based meetings, rather than dealing with individual borrowers at different times.

The microloans of the Grameen Bank are by definition small in amount. The income these small loans generate through interest payments is also small. Therefore, to generate profits to make the institution economically viable, the bank emphasizes scaling up the "outreach," that is, the number of loans made and the number of borrowers reached (Otero and Rhyne 1994). The transfer of lending transaction costs and risks through joint liability, expanding credit delivery services, and maintenance of high repayment rates has a cost. The poor, specifically women, the most weakly positioned category of social actors in Bangladesh rural society, pay this cost (see Chapters 5 and 6).

In the study branch the trade-off between maximizing profit for the economic viability of the branch and increasing investment and recovery rates on invested loans is clear. Since the mid–1980s, there has been pressure from senior officers on grassroots-level bank workers to increase the investment of the branch. The increase in loan investment is also reflected in the yearly loan disbursement profile of the study branch. Figure 7.2 shows that the investment profile has increased more than threefold from 1991 to 1994. The pressure to increase investment, and its consequent implications for the borrowers and the bank workers, became a concern for a few managers. I present here my translation of an excerpt from one such field manager's monthly descriptive report to the managing director (Yunus), released to me by the head office:[4]

> Recently, there is an intense competition among different managers to increase their "outstanding" loans [investment]. Whenever we meet our fellow Managers, the only question we ask is about the investment profile of the branch. Increasing our investment is important for the bank but we must not forget the capabilities of our members; increasing investment must not be our main objective. We have been educated in the Grameen Bank that our primary consideration is the welfare of our members, but in many instances investment has become prime and members are becoming secondary. If we continue with our present attitude, then the result will be serious for a poor country like Bangladesh.

One bank worker in the study branch once explained to me that in the Grameen Bank system there is always "a hidden agenda." Each branch, each area, and each zone of the bank must strive for a substantial profit margin. To gain this profit margin both the disbursement and the recovery of each unit must always be kept at an optimal level. The experience of two bank workers in the study branch (L and R) is relevant to this discussion.

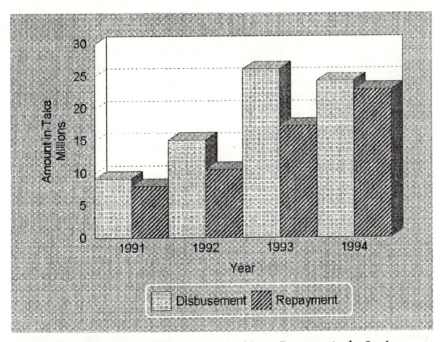

FIGURE 7.2   Yearly Loan Disbursement and Loan Recovery in the Study
Branch, 1991–1994

SOURCE: Evaluation and Monitoring Department, Grameen Bank, 1995

In 1990–1991, L and R were employed in two different branches in the
Tangail zone. Their respective managers instructed them to increase loan
disbursement in their loan centers either by recruiting new members or
by augmenting the amount of small loans among borrowers. These two
bank workers, who are also local leaders for the Grameen Bank Workers
Association (*karmachary samity,* "labor union" or "workers' association"),
are aware that increasing disbursement without considering the capabilities of the borrowers could cause some defaulting. The increase in defaulting would ultimately be blamed on the bank workers, because they
are responsible for recovering defaulting loans. They decided to defy
their managers' instructions, but in doing so they paid a price; their pro-
motions were delayed for six months.

According to the philosophy of the bank, bank workers must not exceed borrowers' capabilities when approving loans and must not recognize a loan group that includes members who fall outside the official selection criteria. The practice of increasing disbursement and disbursing
loans to those who do not meet the official criteria contradicts the bank's

operational policy. The bank workers explain that to understand why they carry out instructions by their superior officers that contradict the philosophy of the Bank, one has to understand the chain of hierarchical command in the system. The operational instructions at the grassroots level come from zone managers to area managers and then to branch managers, who pass them to bank workers to carry out in loan centers. In this hierarchy, one person's job prospects are heavily dependent on the confidential reports (CR) submitted by the immediate superior officer; therefore, no one would dare to defy the command of his or her immediate boss.

The instruction that contradicts the objectives of the bank—increasing investment—is transmitted verbally and it is not indicated in the public transcript. The normative behavior for the bank workers, however, is to follow the instructions of superior officers without raising any questions, whether these instructions come through written memos or are passed on verbally. The bank workers state that like their colleagues L and R, they have learned from experience the cost of defying a superior officer's instruction. Rakib explained the situation with an analogy: "In this country, when one rides a public bus it is hard to ignore a two-line instruction for traveling passengers that hangs above the driver's seat. The first line of it reads, "When this bus is running, report your complaint to the driver"; the immediate second line reads, "Do not talk with the driver when he is driving." By putting forward this analogy Rakib stressed that "we, the bank workers, are like the passengers on a bus who may have questions or concerns about the system, but are unable to express their concerns because the bus is running."

Consequences of High Loan Disbursement and Loan Recovery

Both high disbursement and high repayment rates in reality work against the poorest in the society. Currently, many clients of credit programs of the Grameen Bank are coming not from the extremely poor but from the better-off sector of the rural population. The exclusion of the extremely poor from microcredit programs is now becoming evident in various studies on different microcredit programs, including the Grameen Bank in Bangladesh (Hulme and Mosley 1997; Ito 1997; Matin 1997; R. I. Rahman 1997).

Bank workers at the study branch are aware that as there is no grace period between loan disbursement and the beginning of installment payments the borrowers are unable to pay their first few installments from the earnings of their loan investment. Therefore, the poorest women, without multiple sources of income, are considered as high risk by the bank workers and tend to be excluded from their loan entitlement

(Ebdon 1995). Afzal, a senior bank officer working in the study area, commented,

> Fifteen years ago, after my graduation from the university, I joined the Grameen Bank. My dream was to help the rural poor and contribute to the eradication of poverty in the country. During the last fifteen years the bank has changed tremendously. Now, you find many well-off people in the program. I have borrowers who not only own arable land but also own a transport business. Schoolteachers and college students are borrowers. When I meet these borrowers during my loan center visits, I feel myself poorer than Grameen borrowers. The vision of the Grameen Bank is to provide microloans for small businesses, but now we give loans as big as taka one lakh [100,000] or more.

In the Summer of 1997, during my follow-up research, I witnessed a leasing loan disbursement at the study branch. It was a transport loan of 150,000 taka (approximately US$3,500) approved for a male borrower. This borrower is from a neighboring village of the study branch and he lives in a joint household that owns about fifteen acres of arable land (a large quantity of land in the study area). One elder brother of this borrower is an officer in a major department of the national government. The household owns five fish ponds for the commercial production of *renu* ("fry," or newly hatched fish). During the harvesting of the fry the household rents vehicles to transport the fish to different areas for marketing. The Grameen leasing loan to one household member will enable the household to buy a truck for use in transporting the fish. During the off-season the household plans to rent out this vehicle and earn the required income for the loan repayments.

Bank workers at the study branch and other senior officers in the area office whom I interviewed regarding this loan said that the decision to approve this leasing loan for a transport business to a well-off borrower is appropriate and rational. Azam, a bank worker, explained that this particular borrower comes from a household that has various existing sources of incomes. The client lives in a joint household and his elder brother, who is respected in the study area, has assured the bank of timely installment payments. Even if the project fails, the bank can get back its investment from the household and from the borrower's brother.

This contrasts with the case of Ruki, who after three years of trying to get a leasing loan from the bank to buy a used baby-taxi for her husband, is still unsuccessful. Ruki's husband drives a baby-taxi, or three-wheeled motor car, in the area, paying rent for it on a daily basis. Ruki joined the loan group in 1989; she received her general and seasonal loans regularly from the bank and invested most of her loans in other villagers as a traditional moneylender *(taka lagano)*. Ruki has also mortgaged-in a small plot of land with one of her loans. Since joining the bank, she has paid her weekly installments using her husband's income from his baby-taxi earnings. Ruki always maintained that if her household had a baby taxi of its own the family could have earned enough income to pay the installment without any problem. The branch manager's concern is that Ruki's household has no land of its own or any potential existing sources of income except her husband's driving skill. If the project fails, branch's reputation would suffer. Therefore, the manager would not approve the leasing loan for the baby-taxi even though most of the members in the loan center supported Ruki's proposal.

The bank workers at the grassroots level are responsible not only for increasing their disbursement of loans but also for maintaining the high repayment rates. In such a complex situation, a bank worker prefers clients who have existing income or assets instead of extending loans to the extremely poor. In the study village, before recruiting new borrowers the bank workers first investigate the earning sources of the household, the number of earning male members, and whether the household can pay the installments from earnings other than the earnings of the loan investment. In the Grameen Bank the inclusion of well-off clients in microcredit programs reached such an obvious point in 1994–1995 that it became a concern for the central administration in the head office. The matter was discussed at the 1995 annual conference of the Grameen Bank zonal managers; they concluded that well-off borrowers must be phased out from the credit program (Grameen Bank 1995b).

Spiraling Debt Cycle

In the study village, borrowers of Grameen microloans have limited opportunities to become self-sustaining and leave the credit program. Most of the enterprises supported through Grameen microcredit appear to be not economically feasible given the lending structure of the bank. For example, in 1994–1995 the bank approved 39 percent of its total microloans to women borrowers in the village for rice husking projects and another 16 percent as cow loans (to buy cows either for fattening or for milk production). But no loans were used for paddy husking, and only 8 out of 217 microloans (3 percent) were used to buy cows (Figure 6.2). Borrowers who buy cows with Grameen loans often pay installments on these loans from sources other than their project investment, because investments in these sectors (cows) do not give an immediate return, but the installment payments start within two weeks of loan disbursement.

In the village, 78 percent of loans to women are diverted from approved projects and used for other economic activities or meeting household needs (13 percent of microloans were exclusively used to meet household needs). In the study area, the investment of loans in small businesses by household members often resulted in diminishing profitability (see "Loan Projects and Actual Use of Loans" in Chapter 6). In addition to encountering limited investment opportunities and diminishing profitability, poor households in the study village need to cope with the vulnerability to economic stresses caused by a variety of factors, including (1) structural dimensions of the rural economy, such as seasonal price fluctuation; (2) familial or life-cycle effects, such as variable household dependency ratios over time; and (3) unexpected and sudden crises, such as death or illness in the family or natural calamities (see "Loan Repayment Schedule" in Chapter 6 for details).

Credit has been seen as a resource to borrower households, but credit is also debt and is a risky strategy for the poorest and most vulnerable to economic stress. Outstanding repayment pressure places an additional burden on poor households, and if such obligations coincide with other crisis contingencies, then even the small weekly payment strains those households without a regular cash flow. The seasonal economy, fewer employment opportunities, and uncertain economic returns on investment in the study village create cash flow problems and lead to extensive informal borrowing among group members and their kin to service the regular and fixed weekly installments. In 1994–1995, the data show that only 33 percent of installments on loans to women were paid by the household from investment profits; 10 percent were paid by using the principal amount; and 57 percent were paid from other sources—relatives, loan peers, moneylenders, and others (see Figure 6.4). In addition to the installment payments, 80 percent of interest and emergency fund contributions for women borrowers are paid through informal loans from kin, neighbors, loan peers, or moneylenders (see Figure 6.5).

The payment of the installments from the capital or borrowing of funds either for installment payments, as Rina did (see "Loan Repayment Schedule" in Chapter 6), or for the interest and emergency fund dues for new loans, as Yuri did (see "Power Hierarchy in the Loan Center" in Chapter 6), is directly linked to the creation of debt cycles. The borrower must return the amount to the lender immediately after receiving a new loan from the Grameen Bank. The payment of this amount leads the household member to start his or her venture with a deficit in the capital. This deficit becomes greater with each new loan cycle and creates a spiraling debt cycle for women borrowers' households. The example of Ali and Khatun illustrates the process of building debt cycles in the household.

Ali and Khatun, husband and wife, joined the first male and female Grameen loan groups in the village in the mid–1980s. Since joining the group the couple has accepted about twenty-five loans from the bank. Until 1985, they used Grameen loans in their domestic oilseed-pressing business. The loans were small, their business was then profitable, and the household managed the installments mostly from profits without hardship. In 1986 and 1987, the household used part of the Grameen loans for a daughter's dowry, starting a deficit cycle on the capital borrowed from the Grameen Bank. In 1988, Ali and his loan group accepted a collective loan of 70,000 taka for buying and storing mustard oil seeds during the harvesting season to sell in the off-season for profit.[5] During the loan year, the price of oilseeds went down and the collective project failed. The center members lost most of their capital and had to pay both the loan principal and the interest from other sources, including new loans. For the past four years Ali's household has survived on his oil business in the local market and taking new loans to pay old loans, increasing the household's debt cycle. In 1994–1995, the total loan (general and seasonal) of the household was 36,000 taka, on which they were paying installments through loan recycling and thus becoming permanently trapped in a spiraling debt cycle.

All of the borrowers, except one women, in the study village are followers of Islam. For them a debt burden with the bank is not only a burden in the material sense but, according to the informants, they believe this burden will continue in their life in the hereafter. In rural Bangladeshi Muslim culture, debt is considered unethical. No one should die with debts, and a deceased person's debt must be paid off by his or her heirs before they can bury the body. Tusta, a frustrated borrower, explained to me that most Grameen borrowers remain in debt all through their life. Many of these borrowers die with debts outstanding; they are punished during their lifetime and after death.

In response to my probing about a solution to the problem of spiraling debt cycle, most informants (borrowers) stated that they are only able to get out of the debt cycle by using their savings in the group fund account (GFA; the fund in which 5 percent is levied and deposited from every Grameen loan). In 1994–1995, individual borrowers had no access to this account. The informants explained that if the Grameen Bank were to decide to return individual borrower's savings held in the GFA, then most borrowers could pay off their debts. Once borrowers are cleared from their debts, they probably would either stop accepting new loans or accept loans in small and manageable amounts.

In 1994–1995, Grameen borrowers (primarily men) in different older program areas of the bank brought their "hidden transcript" of the program to formal protest. They organized demonstrations against the bank and asked the bank to comply with their demands. They demanded individual borrower access to the GFA, application of commercial market interest rates to Grameen loans, calculation of interest on a weekly basis instead of fifty-week basis, and reduced pressure for different types of compulsory savings.

In a few areas in the Tangail zone some borrowers stopped attending loan center meetings and stopped paying their weekly installments. In the study village borrowers did not participate directly in the formal protest but both women and men borrowers extended their moral support. In August 1995, the central administration of the Grameen Bank decided to accept some of the borrowers' demands and gave individual borrowers who have completed ten years or more with the bank access to their GFA (Grameen Bank 1995b).

This became a new policy of the bank in October 1995. Under the new policy, twenty-six women borrowers in the study village gained access to their GFA. In January 1997, the study branch transferred more than 200,000 taka from borrower GFAs to their individual savings accounts and then adjusted borrower debts with the bank. After the implementation of the new policy several borrowers in the study village have either stopped accepting new loans or have reduced their loans to manageable amounts. For example, the household of Ali and Khatun received 22,000 taka from their GFA and used the amount to pay off their debts. Now Ali has stopped accepting new loans and his wife, Khatun, only accepts loans in reduced amounts.

During my fieldwork, I found at least five women borrowers in the village who no longer accepted new loans from the bank but continue to pay weekly savings and continue their membership with the group. One of these women is Taj, who joined the bank in 1984 and continued to accept loans until 1993. During these years she accepted loans and her husband used her loans in his jute trading. Taj never encountered problems paying her installments, because her husband has always made the installments available to her. Two of their sons now work with two local NGOs. Their only daughter is married. Since 1993, Taj has not accepted new loans because her husband felt that the high interest rate of the Grameen loan makes it unprofitable to its borrowers. But Taj, like many other borrowers in the study village, continues her membership with the bank. She explained that during her involvement with the bank she sacrificed a great deal for the bank *(banker jonno anek karesi)* and she will not discontinue membership with the bank. Moreover, the Grameen Bank is a good source for borrowing money in case the household needs to borrow money for specific purposes, for example, for purchasing or mortgaging-in land.

Currently, there are several borrowers in the study village who have paid off their debts and reduced their borrowing or stopped accepting new loans but continue their membership with the group, as reflected in

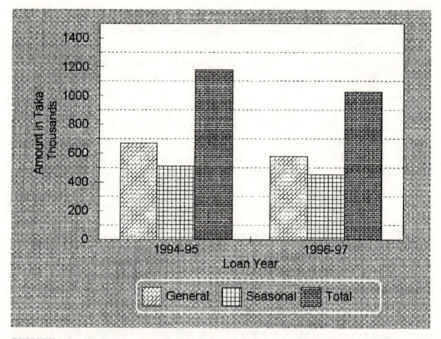

FIGURE 7.3   Disbursement of General and Seasonal Loans Among Women
Borrowers in Pas Elashin, Bangladesh, 1994–1995 and 1996–1997

the change in the investment profile of the study branch in the loan years
1994–1995 and 1996–1997 (Figure 7.3). The reduction in the branch's investment produces a negative impact on its profitability and financial
sustainability.

The Grameen Bank in the study area has tried to face the problem of
decreasing investment by introducing two new types of loans in
1996–1997—cattle sharecropping *(pashu barga)* and leasing loans—for income generation. The cattle sharecropping loan is a loan of 6,000 taka
given to individual borrowers to buy cattle; it is repayable after a six-
month term. The borrowers pay both principal and interest in the total
amount of 7,500 taka in one installment after the term is over. In
1996–1997, twenty-one women borrowers in the village received this new
type of loan, most of whom were already in debt cycles. During my follow-up research, I encountered a few situations where borrowers are encountering problems in repaying the cattle sharecropping loans. They
have either recycled these new loans to make their installments on other
loans or have used part of the amount for household consumption needs
instead of buying cattle, and now they cannot pay back the large amount
in one installment.

Women borrowers in the study village are now also eligible to receive the newly introduced leasing loan of the Grameen Bank. These are technically leases of more than 100,000 taka (approximately US$2,400) that the Grameen Bank offers for income-generating assets, such as transport vehicles. In the study village, the bank does not yet extend this loan but will very shortly (the branch is in the process of getting approval). The provision of leasing loans (larger amounts compared to microloans) to women borrowers is a probable solution to the decreasing investment trend of the bank, but the impact of these loans on women borrowers is yet to be studied.

The Donor Perspective

There is considerable pressure from donors and Western financial institutions for rapid scale-up of services to reach the goal of institutional financial sustainability. Von Pischke (1995) stated, "Using vehicular vernacular, this urge is based on the fender-bender or bumper-crumpler strategy of assistance to the poor: *to make a dent in poverty*" (4). J. Avina (1993:364) examined the relationship between NGOs and donors with respect to institutional development and identified a donor's priorities in expanding outreach. The donors themselves are also under pressure to show performance to taxpayers and to be accountable to them. The donors must show a record of orderly disbursement and quantifiable outputs using disbursement levels to evaluate their own institutional performance.

Wood and Sharif (1997) wrote in their recent book that there is strong feeling among NGO participants and other observers that donors such as the World Bank, USAID, and the United Kingdom–Overseas Development Assistance (UK-ODA) are keen to push multisectoral, social development–oriented NGOs into the narrower function of microcredit. The premise behind such an influence is that as NGOs increase in scale of operation and significance, so does their ability to sustain costly social development activities at existing levels. If NGOs wish to continue to be attractive to donors in a larger scale activity, then they have to show that they are sustainable as institutions in the longer term by securing cost recovery through microlending and other financial services.

The emphasis on financial sustainability by the donors is changing the ethics of the NGOs, or at least is creating an internal tension between "compassion and capitalism" (Greeley 1997:95). There is less space to allow agendas of both social development and institutional financial sustainability. These concerns are reinforced by the enthusiasm with which donors promote this alternative to public sector spending and mold the agendas of agencies that were, at one time, providing an alternative vision to the mainstream.

Notes

1. "British Raj" refers to British colonial rule and is a symbolic expression of an exploiter.

2. In 1994–1995, the gross interest realized from borrowers was much higher than the bank's claimed interest rate of 20 percent. Following Grameen repayment rules, borrowers returned the borrowed principal in fifty equal installments, i.e., they paid 2 percent of the principal each week. Only after the full payment of the principal the bank workers calculated and charged 20 percent interest on the total principal and for the full year. In other words, the bank charged interest on borrowers' partially paid-off principal. The calculation of interest based on borrowers' paid-off principal every week yields a weekly gross interest rate of 0.60922 percent, and the actual annual interest realized from borrowers was 31.68 percent.

3. In 1994, three of the four directors who were not Grameen representatives and the chairman of the board (who is not a director but a member) had Ph.D. degrees. All were men and all except Yunus held high official positions in the government bureaucracy (either additional or joint secretaries in various ministries of the Bangladesh government).

4. At the end of every month the managers of the branches must send a descriptive report to the head office. This report contains a description of the situation of the branch. In the early 1990s in many of the reports managers described in detail their strategies for increasing branch investment.

5. During harvesting periods the price of a seasonal crop is much lower than its price in the off-season. Storing seasonal crops for their marketing in off-season for profit is a traditional business in rural Bangladesh.

8

Conclusion

In this research, I have studied women borrowers' involvement with the microcredit program of the Grameen Bank; examined the grassroots lending structure of the bank; and analyzed the implications of this lending for the borrowers, their household members, and bank workers. The study focuses on the processes of village-level microcredit operation; it addresses the realities of the day-to-day lives of the informants—women borrowers and bank workers—and explains informants' strategies for involving themselves in this microcredit scheme. My work illustrates the power dynamics of the everyday lives of the informants as they affect women borrowers' relationships in the household and the loan centers and bank workers' relationships in the loan centers and the bank. In the concluding chapter, I present a brief review of the study, its theoretical implications, and several policy recommendations.

Review of the Study

In the mid–1970s, the Grameen Bank started its group-based credit scheme for landless poor households to alleviate rural poverty in Bangladesh. Since the early 1980s, the bank has focused primarily on women—as efficient agents for household welfare and better credit-risk clients (Kabeer 1995:111)—and has launched the "Sixteen Decisions" social development program for Grameen borrowers. The group lending structure and the effective use of joint liability among borrowers enable the Grameen Bank to maintain its high repayment rates on invested loans, to generate interest revenue, and to bring institutional financial sustainability into microcredit discourse. In the late 1980s and in the 1990s, the achievement of institutional financial sustainability has become the central agenda for the bank's microlending program.

The programmatic success of the bank has internationalized the microcredit concept and has made microlending initiatives for poor people, specifically for women, a new paradigm to achieve the goal of equitable and sustainable development. Currently, microcredit is a widely discussed topic among academics in the field of equitable and sustainable development, development workers, and development critics. The discourse on microcredit spans a wide range of debate regarding the potential that credit holds for poor people, specifically for poor women; it has even been promoted as a "panacea" for involving women in development (Scully and Wysham 1996:6).

The findings of my study, however, suggest that women become the primary target of the microcredit program because of their positional vulnerability; they are seen as submissive, shy, passive, immobile, and easy to discipline. The positional vulnerability of women meets the requirements of the microlending structure, which demands the regular attendance of borrowers in weekly meetings at the loan center and a rigid schedule for repayment of loans.

The grassroots lending scheme of the bank involves the formation of solidarity groups in which women borrowers in loan groups and centers are jointly liable for individual loans in the loan center. The study suggests that the current practice of joint liability of group members gives the lending institutions an alternative to conventional loan collateral. The joint liability facilitates three important aspects of institutional lending in its implementation by the lending institution and by the borrowers themselves: (1) it enables the lending institution to transfer default risk from the institution to borrowers, (2) it reduces the microloan transaction costs, and (3) it ensures the high repayment rates and high rate of profit required to achieve institutional financial sustainability.

The economic and financial arguments for joint liability in the credit program are complemented by the social development objectives of the bank—building trust and mutual self-help and increasing solidarity and unity among peer loan group members. The bank emphasizes homogenous peer loan groups for building and maintaining solidarity of group members. The assumption of homogenous loan groups in the study community becomes unrealistic for several practical reasons: I(1) the women who organize loan centers come from different lineages, which may be factional within the village power structure and the community social hierarchy; (2) the starters of loan centers assume power, as recognized by the grassroots bank workers, so that influential members often become de facto dominators in loan center decisions; (3) more than 90 percent of borrowers have relatives in the Grameen loan centers who build their own small factional groups within a larger solidarity group; (4) the dynamics of rural poverty make individual borrowers vulnerable to crises in cash flow that may push a "good borrower" to become a "defaulter"; (5) the volatile economic environment in rural society and the lack of appropriate insurance backup make the earnings of Grameen borrowers unsustainable in the long run; and (6) poor women are rarely able to fulfill the obligation of their joint liability to pay defaulters' loans and continue to maintain group solidarity.

The failure in building mutual trust and support with each other in loan centers compels peer loan group borrowers and the bank workers to impose certain forms of repayment discipline—coercion and even debt recycling—that contradict the social objectives of generating trust, mutual support, and solidarity. In reality, women borrowers in the loan centers build and maintain factional instead of solidarity groups for their own strategic reasons. Factional loan group formation and group power hierarchies in loan centers have their roots in the rural culture in Bangladesh. In rural Bangladesh society, factions *(dal)* are an integral part of "patron-client" relationships between the rich and the poor. The powerful and rich classes create factional groups and use these groups to protect social and political interests and to control landed property (Bertocci 1974; Islam 1974; Jansen 1987; Zaman 1991).

Loans to women and the empowerment of women—raised self-confidence and increased status in households—are linked to each other. The link between empowerment and credit is generally assumed to be the expected outcome of the improved capacity of women to invest their loans profitably and benefit from the return of their investment (UNDP 1997:7). But this study shows that rural women are vulnerable to the patriarchal ideology expressed most obviously in prevailing social norms and intra-household gender relations; they are often unable to use loans by themselves in the structure of patriarchy and the rural market economy. The absence of investment opportunities for rural women and the lack of control by the lending institution itself (i.e., lack of supervision) as to how these loans are used and by whom lead women to pass on their loans to others (generally men) and to lose control of their loans.

The poverty reduction potential of microcredit schemes is commonly perceived as a process through which poor households "graduate" from their poverty situation. This graduation has been simplified to breaking from a "vicious circle" of low income and low investment to a "virtuous circle" by injecting capital in the form of credit to generate productive employment, higher incomes, and more investment (see Mayoux 1995:11). This model of poverty and the focus on credit as the solution is too simplistic because of a range of factors other than investment that reproduce poverty and its qualitative dimensions (H. Z. Rahman 1996).

Apart from facing limited investment opportunities in activities in the rural economy, poor households are also vulnerable to economic stresses caused by a variety of factors: I(1) structural dimensions of the rural economy (investment and return), (2) familial or life-cycle effects and shifting household consumer/worker ratios over time, and (3) sudden crises such as death or illness in the family or natural calamities. These forms of economic stress introduce fluctuations in income consumption and threats to productive resources and require households to use a range of coping strategies. The many factors influencing economic well-being and the inherent vulnerability of poor people suggest that "promoting" households through credit services is likely to be more successful if household coping strategies are effective.

Credit as a debt for the household constitutes a risky strategy. The pressure of regular weekly installment payments required by the Grameen microcredit scheme can place additional burden and strain on those households that lack regular cash flow. The cash flow problems may lead to extensive informal borrowing to service the regular and fixed weekly installments. The microlending and repayment regularity by grassroots borrowers may also encourage a new form of legitimate moneylender who entraps the most desperate of the poor in an upward spiral of debt. The institutional debt burden on individual households in turn increases tension and anxiety among household members, produces new forms of institutional domination, and increases violence toward many clients of the project. The increase in intrahousehold tensions as a result of the desperate need for cash to make weekly loan repayment in reality may contain the disempowering elements of the credit scheme. The emphasis on financial sustainability by the donors compels development agencies to change their ethics, or at least it creates an internal tension between "compassion and capitalism" even if it is a socially conscious development (Greeley 1997:95). The intense pressure from donors (Wood and Sharif 1997) on microlending institutions for institutional financial sustainability curtails the social development goals (e.g., the consciousness raising or institution building) of agencies that were, at one time, providing an alternative vision to mainstream development.

Theoretical Implications

Targeting women as institutional microlending clients and channeling resources through women in the household to achieve poverty alleviation appears to serve a range of policy goals in keeping with microcredit rhetoric: (1) poverty alleviation and household welfare, (2) equitable development with empowerment of women, and (3) institutional needs of profitability and sustainability (Kabeer 1997:2). The findings of my research, however, indicate that loans alone (which are also debt -liabilities), without viable opportunities for women to transform the power relations and create their own spaces in the prevailing power structure, make equitable development and empowerment of women unattainable in the society.

The primary concern of the different schools addressing women's issues in development (WID or GAD) has so far been the incorporation of women in economic development within the neoliberal agenda (market approach). To a limited extent, these schools have also explored the strategies in which attention to women's concerns require changes in the way the agenda has delivered. But they have not questioned the limitation of the neoliberal agenda per se (Mayoux 1995:51). My study explores the limitation of such an approach. The Grameen Bank recruits women in the study community for its lending—a market approach—by adopting the existing patriarchal structure of the society. Loans to women are often considered by household members as a household resource instead of a resource to women. The patriarchal norms (Gramsci 1971) entitle men to claim their control over these new resources, or women themselves may pass on their loans to men as part of their own "habitus" (Bourdieu 1977). Therefore, the gender issue in the microcredit project of the Grameen Bank is not a matter concerned just with women; it must be understood and addressed through gender relations in the household and the wider community (Kabeer 1994).

Microcredit to women is an entry point that gives women entitlement to economic resources. Nevertheless, the structure of patriarchy and norms of the village society disentitle women from a newly entitled economic resource in the household—loans—in exchange for their entitlement to the normative commitment to them by the household and the society. Formulation of a disentitlement concept and its incorporation in the analysis of entitlements and normative entitlements expands the theoretical discourse of microlending to women in patriarchal societies such as rural Bangladesh. The incorporation of disentitlement in the analytical framework of microcredit to women also provides the scope to address the issue of inequality in access to power at different levels, such as in the household, in loan centers, and in the bank.

Power dynamics are central to this research. Individuals hold relatively less or more power and use it to achieve their own goals (Naiman 1995:17). The women borrowers are not powerless, although their power is far less than that of men in the household or bank workers in loan centers. The grassroots bank workers also have less power than their superior officers or the institution itself. The development of the "hidden transcript" (Scott 1990) of the grassroots informants symbolizes their power dynamics. The hidden transcript of the people with less power may also carry the potential for formal protest formulation and its expression through public demonstration. The transformation of hidden transcripts of the informants into public forms of demonstration represents the micropower of the people with less power that may challenge the power of the powerful.

The "practical intelligibility" of the informants and their endeavor to alter the "habitus" to meet the forthcoming realities of the situation presented in this study is based on the informants' conscious and unconscious rationality (Bourdieu 1977). Informants' action according to their practical intelligibility exemplifies the maneuvering of their power—whatever little they have in their possession—to meet the requirements of the situation. Maneuvering of this power by the informants not only enables them to meet the demands of the situation but also enables them to increase their social, cultural, and symbolic capital.

Policy Recommendations

In microcredit discourse and microlending practices, success is primarily determined through profitable lending by institutions and their achievement of financial sustainability. Although institutional financial sustainability is desirable, the service-providing institutions must also consider whether the attainment of this sustainability involves too large a cost, that is, social and economic impoverishment of borrowers. If the aspirations for financial sustainability and the objective of serving poor women are contradictory, it is likely the donors will sacrifice the latter, especially when the donor and international development community's attitude and support reward the former. The ethnographic data and anthropological analysis of the microcredit of the Grameen Bank in my research has raised several questions relevant to microcredit policy and future research.

First, institutional sustainability is undeniably an important issue. The lending institutions try to increase their interest revenue to achieve sustainability through various strategies: (1) expanding programs, (2) extending multiple loans, (3) increasing size of loans to individual borrowers, and (4) maintaining a high rate of repayments. With expansion, however, institutions often lose their visions of lending. With multiple loans and increase in loan size, the likelihood increases for women to lose their control over loans and assume the burden of the debt. The institution may attain the high rate of repayments through methods of organization that contain the elements of disempowerment of women, for example, coercion and women being disciplined by male workers of the institution. These are sensitive issues in microcredit programs for women that must be identified and recognized by the lending institutions and addressed in the planning and implementation of the programs.

Second, in addition to borrower discipline, the discipline of the lending institutions is also vital for the success of microcredit to the poor. The lending institutions must assess borrowers' debt capacity prior to extending their loans to women. The organization of women and imposition of discipline on women borrowers are necessary for regular repayments. Nevertheless, my study recommends the imposition of discipline on the lending institutions for at least two reasons: (1) to ensure that the disbursed loans are not beyond the debt capacity of the women borrowers, and (2) to maintain lending institutions' commitment to social development aspects and the empowerment of women and not only to use the organization of women for loan operation in the weekly meeting.

Third, the women borrowers encounter a lack of investment opportunities and alternatives for women who lack basic entrepreneurial skill. The rigid installment payments are an obstacle for women's use of their loans and making of repayments from income earned. Since returns from investments are not always earned on a weekly basis, such as in investment on cow fattening, borrowers may use part of the capital to pay the installment. The study recommends changing rigid and fixed weekly installment payments and setting up project-based repayment schedules.

Fourth, the study recognizes that the other important aspect of the institutional constraint on the empowerment of women is the mechanism through which credit is delivered. The Grameen Bank focuses and recruits only women into its program but delivers its lending services primarily by male workers. The study recommends that the management of the bank pay attention to staff capacity building in its recruitment policies for more effective service delivery and pay attention to generation of staff incentives that help meet organizational goals regarding the empowerment of women. A further point is that efforts to address issues of women's empowerment are time consuming and divert bank workers from their principal task of ensuring adequate repayment of loans. Thus, there is a potential trade-off between the financial sustainability of microcredit institutions and women's empowerment that must be considered in the planning of the program.

Microcredit and microenterprise development projects are going to be *the* significant component of the twenty-first century's development initiatives in both poor and industrialized countries. The actual experience of renowned institutions such as the Grameen Bank in Bangladesh documented in my research can bridge the gap between outsider examinations of the Grameen Bank and views of actual participants. It will broaden the understanding by policymakers of the microlending process and provide a fuller comprehension of development initiative impacts. The Grameen Bank has shown past capacity to bring changes in its policies; it therefore holds the promise to incorporate the policy recommendations of this research for the betterment of the institution and its poor borrowers.

Appendix A:
Glossary of Non-English Words

amanabik	inhuman
ansar	paramilitary unit in Bangladesh
apa	elder sister
ashalin	immodest
Asharh	third month of Bengali calendar year
bahir	outside
bangalir sayle	son of a Bengali family, a native
bangla	Bengali language
bari	homestead
bazar	market
bebsa	business
bel	a local fruit
bel diya bel bhanga	a local phrase meaning to punish a person by using the person's people
belati shahib	Englishmen
bepari	an occupational group (lineage)in the study village whose members work as oilseed pressers (low—caste Muslim in Tangail district)
beta	male person, a term used in the study village as a synonym for son or nephew
beta manush	menfolk
bhai	brother
bhai moga hoye geche	brother has become skinny
bhalo	good
bhanga	to break
bhitor	inside
bhumihin	landless
bibek	conscience
bichar	trial
bideshjaoya	going abroad
bidhimala	constitution or bylaws
bon	sister
chacha	paternal uncle
chachi	aunt
Chaitra	last month of the Bengali calendar
chula	cooking unit

dada	elder brother, a term used in Bengali culture to address senior persons in general
dadan	traditional moneylending in rural Bangladesh
dal	factions or social groupings
dhan	unhusked rice
dhekki	a heavy wooden plank, pedal-operated husking implement
dokhhin	south
durnam	bad reputation
fufu	father's or father's cousin's sister
gas katar bebsa	business of timber cutting
geram	village
ghar	home, household
gharjamai	uxorilocal residence pattern
grameen	rural or village
gusti	lineage
hat	weekly market
ijjat	honor
jaa	husband's brother's or husband's cousin's wife
jonno anek karesi	done a great deal
kaj	work
karmachary samity	labor union, workers' association
kendra ghar	loan center
khalimukhe	literally, empty mouth, a term used by the local people to mean that no food has been eaten
khana	household, eating unit
khanaprodhan	male household head
kisti	installment
kulee	porter
kurbanir eid	Muslim religious festival
lajja	shame
lajjar bepar	matter of shame
lash	dead body, corpse
mahila	woman
malrakha	buying seasonal crops during harvest time and storing them for off-season sale
mama	maternal uncle
matubbar	village leader
mauza	locality, ward
mullah	rural religious leader
murubbi	eldest male in the lineage
nari	woman
natun	new
opomanito	humiliation
opomanito-hoy-se	felt humiliated
paka rasta	concrete road
para	neighborhood, hamlet
pashu barga	cattle sharecropping

purdah	seclusion
renu	fry, newly hatched fish
saitan	devil
samabay samity	cooperative society
samity	association or society
sari	women's dress in Bangladesh
shadasha	member
shalish	village court conducted by village leaders
shamaj	village council
shamparka	relations
sholo sidhanto	sixteen decisions
swanirvar	self-help
taka	Bangladesh currency
taka lagano	traditional moneylending system in rural Bangladesh
tan dee-ya-dichi	borrowing
tempo	a three-wheeled motorized car, also called a baby-taxi
thana	local police station
union parishad	local administrative unit with usually twenty to thirty villages under its jurisdiction
vushan	clothing, etiquette

Appendix B:
The Sixteen Decisions

1. *The four principles of Grameen Bank—Discipline, Unity, Courage, and Hard Work—we shall follow and advance in all walks of our lives.*

2. *Prosperity we shall bring to our families.*

3. *We shall not live in dilapidated houses. We shall repair our houses and work towards constructing new houses at the earliest.*

4. *We shall grow vegetables all the year round. We shall eat plenty of them and sell the surplus.*

5. *During the planting seasons, we shall plant as many seedlings as possible.*

6. *We shall plan to keep our families small. We shall minimize our expenditures. We shall look after our health.*

7. *We shall educate our children and ensure that they can earn enough to pay for their education.*

8. *We shall always keep our children and the environment clean.*

9. *We shall build and use pit latrines.*

10. *We shall drink tubewell water. If it is not available, we shall boil water or use alum.*

11. *We shall not take any dowry in our sons' weddings, neither shall we give any dowry in our daughters' weddings. We shall keep the centre free from the curse of dowry. We shall not practice child marriage.*

12. *We shall not inflict any injustice on anyone, neither shall we allow anyone to do so.*

13. *For higher income we shall collectively undertake bigger investments.*

14. *We shall always be ready to help each other. If anyone is in difficulty, we shall all help him.*

15. *If we come to know of any breach of discipline in any centre, we shall all go there and help restore discipline.*

16. *We shall introduce physical exercise in all our centres. We shall take part in all social activities collectively.*

SOURCE: Fuglesang and Chandler 1993:121

Appendix C:
Grameen Bank Bidhimala
(Bye-laws/Constitution)

1.0   Grameen Bank

1.1   The objective of Grameen Bank is to introduce and institutionalize a non-traditional banking system in rural areas which would provide credit facilities under special terms and conditions. This project attempts to serve those rural people who are not covered by the traditional banking system. The success of the project depends entirely on sincere efforts to follow the rules and regulations prescribed below:

2.0   Landless group

2.1   Grameen Bank will provide credit facilities to the rural landless and asset-less people through the formation of a particular organizational structure. The primary and most important element of this structure is the group.

3.0   Group Formation

3.1   Only the landless and assetless poor will be eligible to form a group. Any member of a household owning less than 0.5 acre of cultivable land and whose total assets do not exceed the value of one acre of medium quality, single-cropped land in that area will be eligible to join.

3.2   A group must be composed of five people.

3.3   All members of a group must come from the same village.

3.4   A group shall be formed with persons who are like-minded, are in similar economic condition and enjoy mutual trust and confidence.

3.5   There shall not be more than one member from the same household in any one group. If more than one person from the same household intend to become members of landless groups, they can do so by becoming members of different groups.

3.6   It is not desirable to form a group with close relatives (e.g., father, brother, uncle, father-in-law, etc.).

3.7   There shall be a Chairman and a Secretary in each group. They shall be elected by the group members. Election will be held at the time a group is formed and subsequently in the month of Chaitra (the last month of the Bengali calendar year) every year. Chairmen and Secretaries elected in the month of Chaitra will assume their offices from the first of the month of Baishak (the month following Chaitra).

Duties and Responsibilities of Members

3.8   The Chairman and Secretary of a group will maintain constant contact with the Bank. The Chairman and Secretary shall be responsible for recommending loan proposals by the individual members, ensuring proper utilization and timely repayment of the loans.

3.9   All members of the group shall remain present during the weekly meetings.

3.10   At the weekly meeting, each member of the group must deposit at least one taka in a savings account. This will be deposited in the Bank in a group savings account.

3.11   In the weekly meeting the Chairman will maintain discipline, collect weekly installments and deposit it with the bank worker/assistant who is present at the meeting.

3.12   Every member of the group must be fully aware of his responsibilities as a member and of the rules regulations governing the activities of the group. Every member must endeavor to maintain discipline within the group and to observe the rules and regulations of the Bank. All members shall always be vigilant over each other regarding proper use of bank credits and regular repayments of their installments. They shall also make sure that every member attends weekly center meetings regularly.

4.0   Loan Disbursement and Repayment Procedure

4.1   After the Bank is satisfied concerning the eligibility of prospective members, a process of continuous group training will begin. After the training, the Area Manager or Program Officer will conduct a group recognition test. After passing the group recognition test, the group's meeting attendance and discipline will be observed and, if satisfactory, they will be able to apply for loans.

4.2   The bank will consider loan applications for different economic activities from the members of recognized groups. Group membership alone will not entitle a member to get bank loans. Members shall be considered qualified for loans in a staggered 2–2–1 format only if they fully abide by the rules and regulations of the bank.

4.3   Members who do not receive their loans initially will be granted loans in their turn if the members who have already received their loan make regular payments and if all group members abide by the rules of Grameen Bank.

4.4   All loans received from the bank will be repaid in weekly installments.

4.5   The bank shall charge an interest rate on loans which it specifies.

In all cases, loans shall be utilized such that they yield daily or weekly income streams which make it possible for members to repay the entire loan in weekly installments.

Group Fund

4.6   (a) Five percent of all loans disbursed shall be deducted and deposited in a group fund. This shall be known as "Group Tax-I." It shall be deposited in an account owned by all members of the group. The member from whose loan this amount is deducted shall have no personal right or claim over it. This deducted money as a whole shall be treated as a fund belonging to the group. All members shall have equal rights to this fund.

Withdrawals from this fund shall be made under joint signatures of the Group Chairman and Secretary. While withdrawing money from this account, the Group Chairman and Secretary must be present at the bank.

If any member of the group intends to leave the group voluntarily or is expelled at any time, he shall not receive any share of this money.

(b) During the seven days of continuous group training, seven taka will be deposited in the group fund. In addition to that, weekly savings, group tax, fine interest paid by the bank shall be deposited in the account known as the group fund. Under normal circumstances, up to a maximum of 50% of the amount in the group fund may be borrowed and invested by the group in a collective income-generating activity it undertakes on its own or in partnership with another group. Individuals within the group can also take loans for any purpose which has the approval of all the members (provided it does not exceed 50% of the amount in the fund).

(c) When taking individual loans from the Group Fund, a special meeting of the group members must be held in the presence of a bank worker. Money from the Group Fund may only be withdrawn on the basis of the approval of all members at that meeting. This meeting shall also make a clear decision regarding term, repayment procedures, etc. of the loan.

(d) When an individual takes a loan from the Group Fund, 5% of the loan amount shall automatically be deducted. This deducted amount shall be called "Group Tax–2." Like Group Tax–1, it shall be deposited in the Group Fund.

If a member voluntarily leaves a group, or is expelled, he shall have no claim on any part of the Group Fund constituted by "Group Tax–2."

(e) Each group shall fix its own rate of interest on loans from the Group Fund (the group may also advance loans without charging any interest, if it so desires). The rate so fixed shall apply to all loans. In other words, under no circumstances shall the rate of interest charged on loans vary from individual to individual.

(f) The group is fully responsible for the recovery of loans from the Group Fund. It is important to note, however, that failure to repay this loan according to the terms and conditions set out in advance shall be considered a breach of discipline by the bank.

(g) When a member leaves a group, he will be entitled to a refund of the entire amount he has deposited in the Group Fund under the weekly savings plan of 1 taka per week. This personal savings cannot be withdrawn under any other circumstances.

(h) If any member is unwilling or unable to repay their bank loans, that loan shall be completely repaid from the Group Fund deposits.

(i) If any loan taken from the Group Fund remains unpaid after the specified repayment period has expired, no new loans may be taken from the Fund.

(j) If all the members of a group leave the bank willingly, or they simply fail to maintaining the group, their Group Fund (with the exception of the weekly savings) shall be deposited in the Center's emergency fund.

4.7   *Emergency Fund*

After payment of the total interest accrued on any bank loan, an amount equal to one-quarter of that amount shall be deposited in a special fund. (In 1991, this changed to: "... an amount equal to 5 taka per 1,000 of the loan amount, excluding the first 1,000 taka"). This fund shall be called the "emergency fund." Money accumulated in the Emergency Fund shall be used the following purposes:

(a) To repay the bank loan of any member who becomes unable to repay to loan due to any accident (e.g., the death of a cow purchased with loan money, damage to a rickshaw in an accident, etc.).

(b) To utilize the Fund in such other activities which may facilitate the repayment of loans of the member making arrangements for veterinary services, adoption health, care programs for the members, etc.). Expenses for such programs shall not exceed 50% of the total savings of the Emergency Fund.

(c) The bank shall pay a fixed rate of interest on the monies deposited in the Center's emergency fund, which shall be deposited in a "Central Emergency Fund." If a member dies, the member's designated relatives shall receive grant from the Central Emergency Fund.

4.8   All loans taken from the bank shall be repaid in weekly installments according to the terms and conditions of the loan.

Until such time as the loan is paid back, the bank workers and bank assistants shall, from time to time, inspect all the properties and materials purchased with the loan. The borrowers must extend full cooperation in carrying this out.

4.9 Loan money must be utilized within one week of its receipt by the member for the approved purpose Those who cannot utilize it within one week must deposit it in the bank until such time as they wish to invest it for the approved purpose. Any exceptions to this rule require prior approval from the bank.

4.10 All properties and materials purchased with the loan money shall be regarded as the property of the bank until the loan is repaid in full.

4.11 Credit facilities offered by the bank to the members shall primarily depend on the regular attendance of all group members in the weekly meetings, their discipline and their payment of weekly installments. Failure of members to attend weekly installments, absence from meetings, underpayment of loans, non-repayment of loans, etc. shall disqualify the group form use of banking facilities.

5.0 Joining a Group

Any person, who is qualified under the provisions set out above to join the bank, may become a member of a group at any time provided that the group unanimously agrees and that the number of members in the group is below five.

6.0 Fines

If a member is found indulging in activities which are subversive of discipline (such as, absence from weekly meetings, irregularity in payment of installments, failure to repay Group Fund Loans, etc.), the remaining members may, by unanimous decision, impose of fine on him or her. The money so received shall be deposited in the Group Fund.

7.0 Leaving the Group

7.1 A member who has no outstanding loan with the bank may leave the group voluntarily at any time. At the time of leaving, the member will receive the entire amount of his personal savings.

7.2 If a member who has outstanding loans wishes to leave the group, he must repay the entire bank loan before he leaves the group.

7.3 If any member leaves the group without paying of their bank loans, the group shall be responsible for repayment of that member's loan. If an entire group is dissolved before full repayment of loans, the center shall be liable for all outstanding loans.

7.4   If the membership of any group is reduced to less than five due to deser-
        tion by one or more group members, the group concerned must bring the
        group back up to five member within 3 months by enrolling new mem-
        bers. If the required number of new members cannot be enrolled within
        the prescribed time limit, the incomplete group may merge with another
        group. Alternatively, two or more incomplete groups may merge to form
        a complete group.

8.0   Expulsion

8.1   The group members may, by unanimous decision, expel any member of
        the group for breach of discipline (such as, long absences from weekly
        meetings, unwillingness to pay installment, etc.) If the expelled member
        owes any money to the bank, it must be repaid before his expulsion or else
        the group concerned shall be liable to repay the amount involved.

8.2   (a) The center may declare a group dissolved for activities which consti-
        tute a breach of discipline (such as not attending weekly meetings, not
        paying installments, not abiding by the bank's rules and regulations, etc.)

        (b) All monies deposited in the Group Fund of a group which is dis-
        solved shall be placed in the center Emergency Fund (after all bank loans
        are cleared and individual savings refunded).

        (c) The responsibility for repayment of bank loans owed by the dissolved
        group shall rest with the center.

9.0   Compulsory Resignation of Membership

9.1   If the total quantity of land owned by a family of any member during the
        tenure of his membership in the group exceeds 0.5 acre or the assets
        owned by his family exceeds the amount fixed by the bank, he shall be
        compelled to resign from the group.

10.0   Center

10.1   A center shall be composed of several groups.

10.2   The group chairmen of the groups which compose the center shall choose
        from among themselves one "Center Chief" and one "Assistant Center
        Chief." Elections for these positions shall be held in the month of Asharh,
        and those elected shall assume office in the first day of the month of
        Shraban.

10.3   The overall responsibility for running the weekly Center meeting shall
        rest with the "Center Chief." In his absence, the "Assistant Center Chief"
        shall assume the responsibility.

10.4 As part of conducting the meetings, the Center Chief shall ensure the attendance of group members at the meeting, payment of installments and overall discipline. He or she shall assist the bank worker/bank assistant collect installments and savings and in explaining the bank's rules.

10.5 If any Center Chief fails to attend more than half of the weekly meetings during any three month period, the post of Center Chief shall be considered vacant and a new Center Chief shall be elected.

10.6 If the Center Chief becomes a "difficult loanee" at any time (i.e., if he does not pay installments for 10 consecutive weeks), he shall be disqualified from the post of Center Chief and the post shall be considered vacant. In such case, a new Center Chief shall be elected to replace him.

11.0 Functions of the Center

11.1 It shall be the responsibility of the Center to motivate its membership and to create among them a proper attitude, a sense and discipline and a spirit of cooperation (among each other and with the bank) such that they are able to take full advantage of the opportunities created by Grameen Bank for bringing changes in their socioeconomic conditions.

The Center shall take special care to create a sense of responsibility among the members (and the groups) who are callous and prone to violate rules and regulations of the bank. The Center shall consider as its responsibility ensuring the proper utilization and timely repayment of all loans given by the bank to its members.

11.2 The Center shall take steps to: create new opportunities for training its members, taking new initiatives, helping to increase the skill and efficiency in different trades. These shall be done with the purpose of ensuring the gradual improvement of the members economic condition through financial cooperation with the bank. It shall also take up various programs for marketing transportation of the commodities produced by the members and ensuring a fair price for their product.

11.3 The Center shall build up the capacity to mediate and resolve all disputes and misunderstandings among its members. The Center shall take special care to create and maintain a cordial and cooperative atmosphere among its members.

11.4 The elected officers of the Center shall maintain regular contact with the bank and shall extend all help and cooperation to the bank authorities for the smooth operation of this special credit program.

12.0 Share

12.1 Group members can purchase a share of Grameen Bank in their own name. This share shall be purchased from money which has been deposited in the Group Fund. When the amount in a group's Group Fund reaches 600 taka, the group may purchase shares. In the case of buying a share, section 4.6(b) in the constitution shall not be applicable.

12.2   Shares may not be traded or sold.

12.3   In the case that any share holder leaves the bank, or is expelled, or dies, the group or Center take possession of his share. When a replacement member joins the center, the Center may sell this share to him.

13.0   *Other Funds*

Members of Grameen Bank Centers may open a special savings fund, a children's welfare fund, a disaster fund and individual savings funds. The bank shall extend cooperation in the management of these funds.

14.0   *Interpretation and Amendment of Bye-laws*

14.1   In the case of any ambiguity in the interpretation of these bye-laws, the interpretation of the Managing Director of Grameen Bank shall be final.

14.2   The Managing Director of Grameen Bank shall have the power to change and amend these bye-laws.

14.3   The Managing Director shall have the power to make rulings to cover cases not covered by the bye-laws. These rulings shall have the force of a bye-law.

SOURCE: Gibbons 1992:139–149.

References

Abecassis, David. 1989. *Identity, Islam and Human Development in Rural Bangladesh.* Dhaka: University Press Limited.

Accion International. 1988. *An Operational Guide for Micro Enterprise Projects.* Cambridge, MA: Accion International.

Adamson, W. 1980. *Hegemony and Revolution: Antonio Gramsci's Political and Cultural Theories.* Berkeley: University of California Press.

Afsar, Helen. 1985. *Women, Work and Ideology in the Third World.* London: Tavistock Publication.

Agarwal, Bina. 1994. *A Field of One's Own: Gender and Land Rights in South Asia.* Cambridge, UK: Cambridge University Press.

Agarwal, Bina. 1990. Social Security and the Family in Rural India: Coping with Seasonality and Calamity. *Journal of Peasant Studies* 17 (3):341–412.

Agarwal, Bina, ed. 1988. *Structure of Patriarchy: The State, the Community and the Household in Modernizing Asia.* London: Zed Books.

Ahmed, M. 1985. *Status, Perception, Awareness and Marital Adjustment of Rural Women: The Role of Grameen Bank.* Grameen Bank Paper No. 31. Dhaka: Grameen Bank.

Ahmed, R., and S. Naher 1987. *Brides and the Demand System in Bangladesh: A Study.* Dhaka: Centre for Social Studies.

Ahmed, S. A. B. 1983. *Bizna: A Study of the Power-Structure in Contemporary Rural Bangladesh.* Dhaka: Bangladesh Books International Ltd.

Albee, Alana. 1994. *Support to Women's Productive and Income-Generating Activities.* Evaluation and Research Working Paper Series No. 1. New York: United Nations Children's Fund.

Anderson, Perry. 1975. The Antimonies of Antonio Gramsci. *New Left Review* 100:5–78.

Appadurai, Arjun. 1988. Putting Hierarchy in Place. *Cultural Anthropology* 1 (3):36–49.

Appadurai, Arjun. 1984. How Moral is South Asian Economy? A Review Article. *Journal of Asian Studies* 43 (3):981–997.

Arnes, J., and V. Beurden. 1977. *Jhagrapur: Poor Peasants and Women in a Village in Bangladesh.* Amsterdam: Third World Publication.

Arnold David 1984. Gramsci and Peasant Subalternity in India. *Journal of Peasant Studies* 11 (4):155–177.

Auwal, M. A. 1994. Reaffirming Subaltern Organizational Praxis in Transmodernity: A Study of the Grameen Bank. Ph.D. dissertation, Faculty of the College of Communication, Ohio University, Athens, OH.

Avina, J. 1993. The Evolutionary Life Cycles of Non-Governmental Development Organizations. *Public Administration and Development* 13:453–474.

Aziz, K. M. A. 1979. *Kinship in Bangladesh.* Dhaka: International Centre for Diarrhoeal Disease Research, Bangladesh.

Aziz K. M. A., and C. Maloney. 1985. *Life Stages, Gender and Fertility in Bangladesh.* Dhaka: International Centre for Diarrhoeal Disease Research, Bangladesh.

Balkin, S. 1993. A Grameen Bank Replication: The Full Circle Fund of the Women's Self Employment Project of Chicago. Pages 223–234 in *The Grameen Bank: Poverty Relief in Bangladesh,* A. N. M. Wahid, ed. Boulder: Westview Press.

Bandarage, A. 1984. Women in Development: Liberalism, Marxism and Marxist-Feminism. *Development and Change* 15:495–515.

Bates, Thomas. 1975. Gramsci and the Theory of Hegemony. *Journal of the History of Ideas* 36:351–366.

Beck, Tony. 1991. Review of *Hunger and Public Action* (1989). *Disaster* 15 (4):389–392.

Benería, Lourdes, and Gita Sen. 1982. Class and Gender: Inequalities and Women's Roles in Economic Development—Theoretical and Practical Implications. *Feminist Studies* 8 (1):157–175.

Benería, Lourdes, and Martha Roldán. 1987. *The Crossroads of Class and Gender: Industrial Homework, Subcontracting, and Household Dynamics in Mexico City.* Chicago: University of Chicago Press.

Berger, Marguerite. 1989. Giving Women Credit: The Strengths and Limitations of Credit as a Tool for Alleviating Poverty. *World Development* 17 (7):1017–1032.

Berger, P., and T. Luckmann. 1987. *The Social Construction of Reality: A Treatise in the Sociology of Knowledge.* London: Penguin Books.

Bernasek, Alexandra. 1992. Essays on the Microeconomics of Credit and Households. Ph.D. dissertation, Department of Economics, University of Michigan.

Bertocci, P. J. 1984. Bengalis. Pages 137–143 in *Muslim Peoples: World Ethnographic Survey,* R. W. Weekes, ed. Westport, CT: Greenwood Press.

Besley, T., and S. Coate. 1995. Group Lending, Repayment Incentives and Social Collateral. *Journal of Development Economics* 46:1–18.

Bhatt, Ela. 1989. Toward Empowerment. *World Development* 17 (7):259–265.

Birdwhistell, Ray. 1960. Kinesics and Communication. Pages 54–64 in *Exploration in Communications,* E. Carpenter and M. McLuhan, eds. Boston: Beacon Press.

Blanchet, T. 1984. *Meanings and Rituals in Birth in Rural Bangladesh.* Dhaka: University Press Limited.

Boserup, Ester. 1970. *Women's Role in Economic Development.* New York: St. Martin's Press.

Bourdieu, Pierre. 1996. Passport to Duke. *International Journal of Contemporary Sociology* 33 (2):1 45–150.

Bourdieu, Pierre. 1990. *The Logic of Practice.* Stanford: Stanford University Press.

Bourdieu, Pierre. 1977. *Outline of a Theory of Practice.* Cambridge, UK: Cambridge University Press.

Brow, James. 1990. Notes on Community, Hegemony, and the Uses of the Past. *Anthropological Quarterly* 63 (2):1–5.

Buckland, Jerry. 1994. Nongovernmental Organizations as Intermediaries of Rural Development for the Poor: Different Approaches to Income-Generation in Bangladesh. Ph.D. dissertation, Department of Economics, University of Manitoba, Winnipeg, Canada.

Buvinić, Mayra. 1986. Projects for Women in the Third World: Explaining their Misbehaviour. *World Development* 14 (5):653–64.

Buvinić, Mayra. 1989. Investing in Poor Women: The Psychology of Donor Support. *World Development* 17 (7):1045–1057.

Cain, M. 1978. The Household Life Cycle and Economic Mobility in rural Bangladesh. *Population and Development Review* 4:421–438.

Cain, M., S. R. Khanam, and S. Nahar. 1979. Class, Patriarchy and Women's Work in Bangladesh. *Population and Development Review* 9:405–438.

Calhoun, C. E. 1993. Habitus, Field, and Capital: The Question of Historical Specificity. Pages 61–87 in *Bourdieu: Critical Perspectives*, C. Calhoun, E. LiPuma, and M. Postone, eds. Chicago: University of Chicago Press.

Canadian Broadcasting Corporation. 1991, March 5. The Grameen Bank [interview with Muhammad Yunus]. *CBC-Ideas*. Toronto, Ontario.

Chambers, R. 1986. *Rural Development: Putting the Last First*. Hong Kong: Longman.

Charlton, Sue. 1984. *Women in Third World Development*. Boulder & London: Westview Press.

Chatterjee, P. 1989. Caste and Subaltern Consciousness. Pages 169–209 in *Subaltern Studies: Writings on South Asian History and Society*, vol. 6, Ranjit Guha, ed. Delhi: Oxford University Press.

Chen, Marty. 1989. A Sectoral Approach to Promoting Women's Work: Lessons from India. *World Development* 17 (7):1007–1016.

Chowdhry, A. 1983. *Agrarian Social Relations and Rural Development in Bangladesh*. New Delhi: Oxford & IBH Publishing Co.

Clifford, James. 1986. On Ethnographic Allegory. In *Writing Culture: The Poetics of Ethnography*, J. Clifford and G. Marcus, eds. Berkeley: University of California Press.

Cloud, Kathleen. 1994. Women Households and Development: A Policy Perspective. In *Capturing Complexity: An Interdisciplinary Look at Women Households and Development*, R. Borooah et al., eds. New Delhi and London: Sage Publications.

Counihan, Carole. 1986. Antonio Gramsci and Social Sciences. *Dialectical Anthropology* 11:3–10.

Counts, A. M. 1990. *Training Guide: Grameen Bank 1990*. Dhaka: Grameen Bank.

Das, Veena. 1994. The Anthropological Discourse on India. In *Assessing Cultural Anthropology*, Robert Borofsky, ed. New York: McGraw-Hill, Inc.

Dréze, J., and Amartya Sen. 1989. *Hunger and Public Action*. Oxford, UK: Clarendon Press.

Dwyer, Daisy Hilse. 1978. *Images and Self-images: Male and Female in Morocco*. New York: Columbia University Press.

Ebdon, Rosamund. 1995. NGO Expansion and the Fight to Reach the Poor: Gender Implications of NGO Scaling-Up in Bangladesh. *IDS Bulletin* 26 (3):49–55.

Femia, Joseph. 1981. *Gramsci's Political Thought: Hegemony, Consciousness and the Revolutionary Process*. Oxford, UK: Clarendon Press.

Femia, Joseph. 1975. Hegemony Consciousness in the Thought of Antonio Gramsci. *Political Studies* 23:29–48.

Feldman, S., and F. McCarthy.1983. Purdah and Changing Patterns of Social Control Among Rural Women in Bangladesh. *Journal of Marriage and the Family* 45:949–959.

Fluehr-Lobban, C. 1994. Informed Consent in Anthropological Research: We Are Not Exempt. *Human Organization* 53 (1):1–10.

Foucault, M. 1980. Two Lectures. Pages 78–108 in *Power/Knowledge: Selected Interviews and Other Writings,* Colin Gordon, ed. Brighton, UK: Harvester Press.

Fuglesang, A., and D. Chandler. 1993. *Participation as a Process—Process as Growth—What We Can Learn from Grameen Bank of Bangladesh.* Dhaka: Grameen Trust.

Geertz, Clifford. 1983. *Local Knowledge: Further Essays in Interpretive Anthropology.* New York: Basic Books.

Ghai, Dharam. 1984. *An Evaluation of the Impact of the Grameen Bank Project.* Grameen Bank Paper No. 29. Dhaka: Grameen Bank.

Gibbons, David S., ed. 1992. *The Grameen Reader.* Dhaka: Grameen Bank.

Gledhill, John 1994. *Power and Its Disguises: Anthropological Perspectives on Politics.* London: Pluto Press.

Godelier, Maurice. 1978. Infrastructures, Societies, and History. *Current Anthropology* 19 (4):763–771.

Goetz, Anne Marie. 1996. *Local Heroes: Patterns of Field Worker Discretion in Implementing GAD Policy in Bangladesh.* Discussion Paper No. 358. Institute of Development Studies, University of Sussex.

Goetz, Anne Marie, and R. Sen Gupta. 1996. Who Takes Credit? Gender, Power and Control over Loan Use in Rural Credit Programs in Bangladesh. *World Development* 24 (1):45–63.

Goody, Jack, and S. J. Tambiah. 1973. *Bridewealth and Dowry: Cambridge Papers in Social Anthropology.* Cambridge, UK: Cambridge University Press.

Government of Bangladesh. 1985. *The Third Five-Year Plan 1985–89.* Dhaka: Planning Commission.

Government of Bangladesh. 1980. *The Second Five-Year Plan 1980–85.* Dhaka: Planning Commission.

Government of Bangladesh. 1978. *The Two-Year Plan 1978–80.* Dhaka: Planning Commission.

Government of Bangladesh. 1973. *The First Five-Year Plan 1973–78.* Dhaka: Planning Commission.

Gramsci, Antonio. 1971. *Selections from the Prison Notebooks of Antonio Gramsci.* London: Lawrence and Wishart.

Gramsci, Antonio. 1959. *The Modern Prince and Other Writings.* New York: International Publishers.

Grameen Bank. 1998. Grameen Bank Update: November, 1997. *Grameen Dialogue* 33:14.

Grameen Bank. 1995a. *The Annual Report.* Dhaka: Grameen Bank.

Grameen Bank. 1995b, August 15–18. [Zonal manager conference report]. In Bengali.

Grameen Bank. 1994. *The Annual Report.* Dhaka: Grameen Bank.

Grameen Trust. 1997. Profiles in Poverty—Profiles in Struggle. *Grameen Poverty Research News Letter* 3(2):12.

Greeley, Martin. 1997. Poverty and Well Being: Problems for Poverty Reduction in Role of Microcredit. Pages 83–96 in *Who Needs Credit? Poverty and Finance in Bangladesh*, G. Wood and I. A. Sharif, eds. Dhaka: University Press Limited.

Gregory, James. 1984. The Myth of the Male Ethnographer and Women's World. *American Anthropologist* 86 (2):31–27.

Gugliotta, G. 1993. Microenterprise Is Growing. *Grameen Dialogue* 15:7–9.

Guha, Ranjit. 1996. The Small Voices. In *Subaltern Studies: Writings on South Asian History and Society, vol. 9*, Shahid Amin and D. Chakrabarty, eds. Delhi: Oxford University Press.

Hall, Edward. 1966. *The Hidden Dimension*. New York: Doubleday.

Hammel, E. A., and R. Z. Deuel. 1977. *Five Classy Programs: Computer Procedures for the Classification of Households*. Institute of International Studies Research Series No. 33. Berkeley: University of California.

Hammel, E. A., and P. Laslett. 1974. Comparing Household Structure Over Time and Between Cultures. *Comparative Studies in Society and History* 16:73–109.

Haque, C. E. 1988. Impact of Riverbank Erosion Hazard in the Brahmaputra-Jamuna Floodplain: A Study of Population Displacement and Response Strategies. Ph.D. dissertation, Department of Geography, University of Manitoba, Winnipeg, Canada.

Hartmann, B., and B. James. 1983. *A Quiet Violence: View from a Bangladesh Village*. London: Zed Press.

Hashemi, S., and S. Schuler. 1993. *Operationalising Indicators of Empowerment: A Methodological Note* [draft].

Hashemi, S., S. Schuler, and A. P. Riley. 1996. Rural Credit Programs and Women's Empowerment in Bangladesh. *World Development* 24 (4):635–653.

Hastrup, Kirsten. 1990. The Anthropological Vision—Comments to Niels Einarsson. *Antropologiska Studier*.

Havers, M. 1996. Financial Sustainability in Savings and Credit Programs. *Development in Practice* 6 (2):144–150.

Holcombe, Susan. 1995. *Managing to Empower: The Grameen Bank's Experience of Poverty Alleviation*. London: Zed Books.

Holy, L., and M. Stuchlik. 1983. *Actions, Norms and Representation: Foundation of Anthropological Inquiry*. Cambridge, UK: Cambridge University Press.

Hossain, M. 1988. *Credit for Alleviation of Rural Poverty: The Grameen Bank in Bangladesh*. Research Report No. 65. Washington, DC: International Food Policy Research Institute.

Hulme, D., and P. Mosley. 1997. Finances for the Poor or Poorest? Financial Innovation, Poverty and Vulnerability. Pages 96–130 in *Who Needs Credit? Poverty and Finance in Bangladesh*, G. Wood and I. A. Sharif, eds. Dhaka: University Press Limited.

Indra, D., and N. Buchignani. 1997. Rural Landlessness, Extended Entitlements and Inter-household Relations in South Asia: A Bangladesh Case. *Journal of Peasant Studies* 24 (3):25–64.

Isa, Masud. 1997. Microcredit Summit 1997: In Retrospect, *Grameen Poverty Research* 3 (2):2–3.

Islam, A. K. M. 1974. *A Bangladesh Village: Conflict and Cohesion: An Anthropological Study of Politics*. Cambridge, MA: Schenkman.

Ito, Sanne. 1997. *The Grameen Bank and Poverty Reduction* [draft]. D.Phil. Work in Progress Paper. Institute of Development Studies, University of Sussex.

Jackelen, H., and E. Rhyne. 1991. Towards a More Market-Oriented Approach to Credit and Savings for the Poor. *Small Enterprise Development* 2 (4):4–20.

Jahan, R. 1992. *The Elusive Agenda: Mainstreaming Women in Development*. Dhaka. University Press Limited.

Jahan, R. 1975. Women in Bangladesh. In *Women for Women: Bangladesh*. Dhaka: University Press Limited.

Jansen, Eric G. 1987. *Rural Bangladesh: Competition for Scarce Resources*. Dhaka: University Press Limited.

Jeffery, P. 1979. *Frogs in a Well: Indian Women in Purdah*. London: Zed Books.

Johnson, S., and B. Rogaly. 1997. *Financial Services and Poverty Reduction* [draft]. London: OXFAM & ACTION AID.

Johnston, Jo-Ann. 1995. They Boldly Loan Where No Banker Has Loaned Before. *Business Ethics Magazine. www.condor.depaul.edu/ethics/bizsoc3*

Jones, Delmos J. 1970. Towards a Native Anthropology. *Human Organization* 29 (4):251–259.

Kabeer, Naila. 1997. Editorial: Tactics and Trade-Offs: Revisiting the Links Between Gender and Poverty. *IDS Bulletin* 28 (3):1–13.

Kabeer, Naila. 1995. Targeting Women or Transforming Institutions? Policy Lessons from NGO Anti-Poverty Efforts. *Development Practice* 5(2):108–116.

Kabeer, Naila. 1994. *Reversed Realities: Gender Hierarchies in Development Thought*. London: Verso Press; & Delhi: Kali Publication.

Kabeer, Naila. 1991a. Gender Dimension of Rural Poverty: Analysis from Bangladesh. *Journal of Peasant Studies* 18 (2):241–62.

Kabeer, Naila. 1991b. *Rethinking Development from Gender Perspective: Some Insight from the Decade*. Paper presented at the Conference on Women and Gender in Southern Africa, University of Natal, Durban.

Kabeer Naila. 1988. Subordination and Struggle: Women in Bangladesh. *New Left Review* 168:95–121.

Kearney, Michael. 1986. From the Invisible Hand to Visible Feet: Anthropological Studies of Migration and Development. *Annual Review of Anthropology* 15:331–361.

Keesing, Roger. 1994. Theories of Culture Revisited. In *Assessing Cultural Anthropology*, Robert Borofsky, ed. New York: McGraw-Hill.

Keesing, Roger. 1987. Anthropology as Interpretive Quest. *Current Anthropology* 28:161–176.

Khan, Salma. 1988. *The Fifty Percent: Women Development and Policy in Bangladesh*. Dhaka: University Press Limited.

Khandker, S., B. Khalily, and Z. Khan. 1994. *Grameen Bank Performance and Sustainability*. World Bank Discussion Paper No. 306. Washington, DC: World Bank.

Kiros, Teodros. 1985. *Toward the Construction of a Theory of Political Action: Antonio Gramsci, Consciousness, Participation and Hegemony*. Lanham, MD: University Press of America.

Kleinman, Arthur. 1996. Bourdieu's Impact on the Anthropology of Suffering. *International Journal of Contemporary Sociology* 3 (2):203–210.

Korten, David. 1990. *Getting to the 21st Century: Voluntary Action and the Global Agenda.* London: Kumarian Press.

Korten, David. 1987. Third Generation NGO Strategies: A Key to People-Centred Development. *World Development* 15(Supplement):145–159.

Kotalova, Jitka. 1993 *Belonging to Others: Cultural Construction of Womanhood Among Muslims in a Village in Bangladesh.* Uppsala Studies in Cultural Anthropology No. 19. Uppsala, Sweden: Acta Universitatis Upsaliensis.

Kramsjo, B., and Geoffrey Wood. 1992. *Breaking the Chains.* Dhaka: University Press Limited.

Lear, T. J. 1985. The Concept of Cultural Hegemony: Problems and Possibilities. *American Historical Review* 90 (3):567–593.

Lewis, W. A. 1966. *Development Planning: The Essential Economic Policy.* London: George Allen & Unwin.

LiPuma, E. 1993. Culture and the Concept of Culture in Theory and Practice. Pages 14–34 in *Bourdieu: Critical Perspectives,* C. Calhoun, E. LiPuma, and M. Postone, eds. Chicago: University of Chicago Press.

Lowie, Robert. 1937. *The History of Ethnological Theory.* New York: Holt, Rinehart and Winston.

Luntley, Michael. 1992. Practice Makes Knowledge? *Inquiry* 35:447–461.

MacIsaac, Norm. 1996. *Micro-Enterprise Support: A Critical Review.* Background paper prepared for the Micro-Enterprise Learning Circle. Ottawa: Canadian Council for International Cooperation.

Madhuri, Mathema. 1992. Improving Rural Women's Lives: A Case Study in Nepal. Ph.D. dissertation, Stanford University, Stanford, CA.

Mahar, Cheleen. 1992. An Exercise in Practice: Studying Migrants to Latin American Squatter Settlements. *Urban Anthropology* 21 (3):275–309.

Malinowski, Bronislaw. 1972. *Argonauts of the Western Pacific.* London: Routledge and Kegan Paul. Originally published in 1922.

Maloney, C., and A. B. S. Ahmed. 1988. *Rural Savings and Credit in Bangladesh.* Dhaka: University Press Limited.

Mandelbaum, David. 1988. *Women's Seclusion and Men's Honor: Sex Roles in North India, Bangladesh and Pakistan.* Tucson: University of Arizona Press.

Matin, Imran. 1997. The Renegotiation of Joint Liability: Notes from Madhupur. Pages 261–270 in *Who Needs Credit? Poverty and Finance in Bangladesh,* G. Wood and I. A. Sharif, eds. Dhaka: University Press Limited.

Mauss, Marcel. 1950. The Notion of Body Techniques. Pages 97–119 in *Sociology and Psychology Essays.* London: Routledge.

Mayoux, Linda. 1995. *From Vicious to Virtuous Circles: Gender and Micro-Enterprise Development.* Occasional Paper No. 3. Geneva: United Nations Research Institute for Social Development and United Nations Development Programme.

McKee, Katharine. 1989. Microlevel Strategies for Supporting Livelihoods, Employment, and Income Generation of Poor Women in the Third World: The Challenge of Significance. *World Development* 17 (7):993–1006.

Mead, Margaret. 1977. *Letters from the Field.* New York: Harper Colophon Books.

Microcredit Summit. 1998a. *Draft Declaration.* Washington, DC: Result Educational Fund.

Microcredit Summit. 1998b. *Councils of Private Commercial Banks. www. microcreditsummit.org/campaign/banks.htm*

Mies, Maria. 1986. *Patriarchy and Accumulation on World Scale: Women in the International Division of Labour.* London: Zed Press.

Mitchel, T. 1990. Everyday Metaphors of Power. *Theory and Society* 19 (5):545–577.

Mizan, Ainun Nahar. 1994. *In Quest of Empowerment: The Grameen Bank Impact on Women's Power and Status.* Dhaka: University Press Limited.

Montgomery, Richard. 1995, March 27–28. *Disciplining or Protecting the Poor? Avoiding the Social Costs of Peer Pressure in Solidarity Group Microcredit Schemes.* Paper presented to the Conference on Finance Against Poverty, University of Reading.

Morduch, J. 1997. *The Microfinance Revolution* [draft]. Department of Economics, Harvard University, Cambridge, MA.

Mouffe, Chantal. 1979. Hegemony and Ideology in Gramsci. Pages 168–204 in *Gramsci and Marxist Theory,* Chantal Mouffe, ed. London: Routledge and Kegan Paul.

Naiman, Joanne. 1995. Beyond Oppression, Beyond Diversity: Class Analysis and Gender Inequality. *Socialist Studies Bulletin* 41:11–29.

North-South Institute. 1990. *Rural Poverty in Bangladesh: A Report to Like-Minded Group.* Dhaka: University Press Limited.

Omvedt, G. 1990. *Violence Against Women: New Movements and New Theories in India.* New Delhi: Kali Primaries.

Otero, M., and E. Rhyne, eds. 1994. *The New World of Microenterprise Finance.* London: Intermediate Technology Publications.

Palsson Gisli. 1993. Household Words: Attention, Agency and the Ethnography of Fishing. In *Beyond Boundaries: Understanding, Transition and Anthropological Discourse,* G. Palsson, ed. Oxford, UK: BERG.

Papanek, Hanna. 1964. The Women Field Worker in Purdah Society. *Human Organization* 23 (2):126–166.

Parpart, J., and M. Marchand. 1995. Exploding the Canon: An Introduction/Conclusion. Pages 1–22 in *Feminism, Postmodernism, Development,* M. Marchand and Jane Parpart, eds. New York Routledge.

Patton, M. Q. 1990. *Qualitative Evaluation Methods.* London: Sage Publications.

Pischke, V. 1995, March 27–28. *Managing the Trade-off Between Outreach and Sustainability by Measuring the Financial Performance of Microenterprise Lenders.* Paper presented at the Conference on Finance Against Poverty, University of Reading.

Pitt, M., and S. R. Khandaker. 1995. *The Impact of Group-Based Credit Programs on Poor Households in Bangladesh: Does the Gender of Participants Matter?* [draft]. Brown University and World Bank.

Postone, M., E. LiPuma, and C. Calhoun. 1993. Introduction: Bourdieu and Social Theory. Pages 1–13 in *Bourdieu: Critical Perspectives.* C. Calhoun, E. LiPuma, and M. Postone, eds. Chicago: University of Chicago Press.

Rahman, Aminur. 1996. Micro-Credit for Women in Rural Bangladesh: Retrenchment of Patriarchal Hegemony as a Consequence. *Chicago Anthropology Exchange* 23 (Spring):6–22.

Rahman, Aminur. 1994. Gender Relations and Empowerment for Women: A Study of Hegemony, Counterhegemony and Change in Rural Bangladesh. Dissertation Research Proposal funded through the International Fellowships Competition of the Social Science Research Council, New York.

Rahman, Aminur. 1992. Notions of Children, Fertility, and Contraception in the Domestic Domain: An Anthropological Study in a Bangladesh Village. M.Phil. thesis, University of Oslo, Norway.

Rahman, Atiur. 1986a. *Impact of Grameen Bank Intervention on Rural Power Structure*. Working Paper No. 2. Dhaka: Bangladesh Institute of Development Studies.

Rahman, Atiur. 1986b. *Consciousness Raising Efforts of Grameen Bank*. Working Paper No. 3. Dhaka: Bangladesh Institute of Development Studies.

Rahman, H. Z. 1996. Crisis and Insecurity: The "Other" Face of Poverty. Pages 113–131 in *Rethinking Rural Poverty: Bangladesh as a Case Study*, H. Z. Rahman and M. Hossain, eds. Dhaka: University Press Limited.

Rahman, H. Z., and M. Hossain, eds. 1996. *Rethinking Rural Poverty: Bangladesh as a Case Study*. Dhaka: University Press Limited.

Rahman, Matiur. 1992. Peasants' Adjustment to Natural Hazards in Bangladesh: A Case Study of Two Upazillas in the Brahmaputra Floodplain. Ph.D. dissertation, Department of Geography, University of Manitoba, Winnipeg, Canada.

Rahman, R. I. 1997. Poverty, Profitability of Micro Enterprises and the Role of Credit. Pages 271–287 in *Who Needs Credit? Poverty and Finance in Bangladesh*, G. Wood and I. A. Sharif, eds. Dhaka: University Press Limited.

Rahman, R. I. 1986. *Impact of the Grameen Bank on the Situation of Poor Rural Women*. Grameen Bank Evaluation Project Working Paper No. 1. Dhaka: Bangladesh Institute of Development Studies.

Rappaport, Roy. 1993. Distinguished Lecture in General Anthropology: The Anthropology of Trouble. *American Anthropologist* 95 (2):295–303.

Rathgeber, E. M. 1990. Trends in Research and Practice. *Journal of Developing Areas* 24 (4):489–502.

Ray, J. K. 1988. *To Chase a Miracle: A Study of the Grameen Bank of Bangladesh*. Dhaka: University Press Limited.

Rodman, Hyman. 1970. *Marital Power and the Theory of Resources in Cultural Context*. Detroit: Merill Palmar Institute.

Rogers, E. M. 1976. Communication and Development: The Passing of the Dominant Paradigm. In *Communication and Development: Critical Perspective*, E. M. Rogers, ed. Beverly Hills, CA: Sage Publications.

Rosenberg, R. 1996. Micro-Credit Interest Rates. Consultative Group to Assist the Poorest Occasional Paper No. 1. *www.worldbank.org/html/cgap/occ1.htm*

Rostow, W. W. 1960. *The Stages of Economic Growth*. Cambridge, UK: Cambridge University Press.

Salamani, L. 1974. Gramsci and Marxist Sociology of Knowledge: An Analysis of Hegemony-Ideology-Knowledge. *Sociological Quarterly* 15:359–380.

Schatzki, T. R. 1987. Overdue Analysis of Bourdieu's Theory of Practice. *Inquiry* 3:113–135.

Scheper-Hughes, N. 1992. *Death Without Weeping: The Violence of Everyday Life in Brazil*. Berkeley: University of California Press.

Schuler, S., and S. Hashemi. 1995. Family Planning Outreach and Credit Programs in Rural Bangladesh. *Human Organization* 54 (4):455–461.

Schuler, S., and S. Hashemi. 1994. Credit Programs, Women's Empowerment, and Contraceptive Use in Rural Bangladesh. *Studies in Family Planning* 25 (4):65–76.

Schuler, S., S. Hashemi, and A. P. Riley. 1997a. The Influence of Women's Changing Roles and Status in Bangladesh's Fertility Transition: Evidence from a Study of Credit Programs and Contraceptive Use. *World Development* 25 (4):563–575.

Schuler, S., S. Hashemi, and A. P. Riley. 1997b, March. *Men's Violence Against Women in Rural Bangladesh: Undermined or Exacerbated by Micro-Credit Programs?* Paper presented at the 1997 Population Association of America Annual Meetings, Washington, DC.

Schuler, S., S. Hashemi, A. P. Riley, and S. Akhter. 1996. Credit Programs, Patriarchy and Men's Violence Against Women in Rural Bangladesh. *Social Science Medicine* 43 (12):1729–1742.

Scott, James. 1990. *Domination and the Art of Resistance: Hidden Transcripts.* New Haven: Yale University Press.

Scott, James. 1985. *Weapons of the Weak: Everyday Forms of Peasant Resistance.* New Haven: Yale University Press.

Scully, N. D., and D. Wysham. 1996. *The World Bank's Consultative Group to Assist Poorest: Opportunity or Liability for the World's Poorest Women?* Washington, DC: Institute for Policy Studies.

Sen, Amartya. 1990. Gender and Cooperative Conflicts. Pages 123–149 in *Persistent Inequalities: Women and World Development,* Irene Tinker, ed. Oxford, UK: Oxford University Press.

Sen, Amartya. 1988. Family and Food: Sex Bias in Poverty. Pages 453–472 in *Rural Poverty in South Asia,* T. N. Srinivasan and P. K. Bardhan, eds. New York: Columbia University Press.

Sen, Amartya. 1983. Economics and the Family. *Asian Development Review* 1 (2):14–21.

Sen, Amartya. 1981. *Poverty and Famines: As Essay on Entitlement and Deprivation.* Oxford, UK: Oxford University Press.

Sen, Amartya. 1977. Starvation and Exchange Entitlement: A General Approach and Its Application to the Great Bengal Famine. *Cambridge Journal of Economics* 1:33–59.

Sen, G., and C. Grown. 1987. *Development, Crises, and Alternative Visions: Third World Women's Perspectives.* New York: Monthly Review Press.

Sharma, Ursula. 1993. Dowry in North India. In *Family, Kinship and Marriage in India,* Patricia Uberoi, ed. Delhi: Oxford University Press.

Shehabuddin, R. 1992. *Empowering Rural Women: The Impact of Grameen Bank in Bangladesh.* Dhaka: Grameen Bank.

Siddiqui, Kamal. 1982. *The Political Economy of Rural Poverty in Bangladesh.* Dhaka: National Institute of Local Government.

Sobhan, Rehman. 1992. *Planning and Public Action for Asian Women.* Dhaka: University Press Limited.

Spivak, G. C. 1985. Subaltern Studies: Deconstruction of Historiography. In *Subaltern Studies: Writings on South Asian History and Society, vol. 5,* Ranjit Guha, ed. Delhi: Oxford University Press.

Statistical Yearbook of Bangladesh. 1994. Dhaka: Bureau of Statistics.

Stiglits, Joseph. 1990. Peer Monitoring and Credit Markets. *World Bank Economic Reviews* 4 (3):351–366.

Subrahmanian, Ramya. 1997. If You Build It, Will They Come? Educational Decision-Making in the Context of Economic Uncertainty and Social Risk. *IDS Bulletin* 28 (3): 112–121.

Tinker, Irene, ed. 1990. *Persistent Inequalities: Women in World Development.* Oxford, UK: Oxford University Press.

Todd, Helen. 1997. *Women at the Center: Grameen Bank Borrowers After One Decade.* Dhaka: University Press Limited.

Todd, Helen. 1995. *Women at the Center: Grameen Bank Borrowers Ten Years On* [mimeo].

Udayagiri, Mridula. 1995. Challenging Modernization: Gender and Development: Postmodern Feminism and Activism. Pages 159–177 in *Feminism, Postmodernism, Development*, M. Marchand and Jane Parpart, eds. New York: Routledge.

United Nations Development Programme. 1997, June 8–13. *Emerging Issues on Gender and Microfinance.* Report of the International Workshop on Microfinance Schemes: Models for the Empowerment of Women and Poverty Reduction, Rajendrapur, Dhaka.

Van Mannen, M. 1988.*Tales of the Field: On Writing Ethnography.* Chicago: Chicago University Press.

Varian, Hall. 1990. Monitoring Agents with Other Agents. *Journal of Institutional and Theoretical Economics* 146 (1):153–174.

Wahid, Abu N. M., ed. 1993. *The Grameen Bank: Poverty Relief in Bangladesh.* Boulder: Westview Press.

Wax, Rosalie. 1971. *Doing Fieldwork: Warning and Advice.* Chicago: Chicago University Press.

Williams, Raymond. 1977. *Marxism and Literature.* Oxford, UK: Oxford University Press.

Wilson-Moore, M. 1989. Women's Work in Homestead Gardens: Subsistence, Patriarchy, and Status in Northwest Bangladesh. *Urban Anthropology* 18 (3–4):281–297.

White, Sarah. 1992. *Arguing with the Crocodile: Gender and Class in Bangladesh.* Dhaka: University Press Limited.

Wiest, Raymond. 1998. A Comparative Perspective on Household, Gender, and Kinship in Relation to Disaster. In *The Gendered Terrain of Disasters: Through Women's Eyes*, Elaine Enarson and Betty Hearn Morrow, eds. Westport, CT: Praeger.

Wiest, Raymond. 1991. Domestic Group Dynamics in the Resettlement Process Related to Riverbank Erosion in Bangladesh. Page 246–271 in *Riverbank Erosion, Flood and Population Displacement in Bangladesh*, K. M. Elahi, K. S. Ahmed, and M. Mafizuddin, eds. Riverbank Erosion Impact Study, Jahangirnagar University, Dhaka.

Wiest, Raymond. 1984. External Dependency and the Perpetuation of Temporary Migration to the United States. Pages 110–135 in *Patterns of Undocumented Migration: Mexico and the United States*, R. C. Jones, ed. Totowa, NJ: Rowman & Allanheld.

Wiest, Raymond. 1973. Wage-Labour Migration and the Household in a Mexican Town. *Journal of Anthropological Research* 29:180–209.

Wood, G., and I. Sharif. 1997. Introduction. Pages 28–58 in *Who Needs Credit? Poverty and Finance in Bangladesh*, G. Wood and I. A. Sharif, eds. Dhaka: University Press Limited.

World Bank. 1990. *Bangladesh: Strategies for Enhancing the Role of Women in Economic Development*. A World Bank Country Study. Washington, DC: World Bank.

Yunus, Muhammad.1997. The Grameen Bank Story: Rural Credit in Bangladesh. Pages 9–24 in *Reasons for Hope: Instructive Experiences on Rural Development*, A. Krishna, N. Uphoff, and M. J. Esman, eds. London: Kumarian Press.

Yunus, Muhammad. 1995. *New Development Options Towards the 21st Century*. Dhaka: Grameen Bank.

Yunus, Muhammad. 1994a. *Banking on the Poor*. Dhaka: Grameen Bank.

Yunus, Muhammad. 1994b. *Grameen Bank As I See It*. Dhaka: Grameen Bank.

Yunus, Muhammad. 1994c, June 12–15. *Does the Capitalist System Have to Be the Handmaiden of the Rich?* Keynote address at the 85th Rotary International, Taipei, Taiwan. *www.soc.titch/icm/icm-documents.htm*

Yunus, Muhammad. 1993. *The Poor As Engine of Development* [reprint]. Dhaka: Grameen Bank. Originally published 1987 in *The Washington Quarterly* 10 (4).

Yunus, Muhammad. 1992. Grameen Bank—The First Decade: 1976–86. Pages 21–40 in *The Grameen Reader*, David Gibbons, ed. Dhaka: Grameen Bank.

Yunus, Muhammad, ed. 1988. *Jorimon and Others: Faces of Poverty*. Dhaka: University Press Limited.

Yunus, Muhammad. 1987. *Credit for Self-Employment of the Poor* [Transcript of telephone conference held with Muhammad Yunus in Washington, DC].

Zaman, Habiba. 1998. *Patriarchy and Purdah: Structural and Systemic Violence Against Women in Bangladesh*. Research report. Uppsala, Sweden: Life and Peace Institute.

Zaman, Habiba. 1996. *Women and Work in a Bangladesh Village*. Dhaka: Narigrantha Prabartana Bangladesh.

Zaman, M. Q. 1991. Social Structure and Process in Char Land Settlement in the Brahmaputra-Jamuna Floodplain. *Man* 26 (4):549–566.

Index

Printed in the United States
56499LVS00005B/40-48